Studies of the Americas

Series Editor
Maxine Molyneux
Institute of the Americas
University College London
London, UK

The Studies of the Americas Series includes country specific, cross-disciplinary and comparative research on the United States, Latin America, the Caribbean, and Canada, particularly in the areas of Politics, Economics, History, Anthropology, Sociology, Anthropology, Development, Gender, Social Policy and the Environment. The series publishes monographs, readers on specific themes and also welcomes proposals for edited collections, that allow exploration of a topic from several different disciplinary angles.

This series is published in conjunction with University College London's Institute of the Americas under the editorship of Professor Maxine Molyneux.

More information about this series at
http://www.palgrave.com/gp/series/14462

Ainhoa Montoya

The Violence of Democracy

Political Life in Postwar El Salvador

Ainhoa Montoya
Institute of Latin American Studies
University of London
London, UK

Studies of the Americas
ISBN 978-3-030-09467-6   ISBN 978-3-319-76330-9   (eBook)
https://doi.org/10.1007/978-3-319-76330-9

Cover image © Ainhoa Montoya
Cover design by Fatima Jamadar

Printed on acid-free paper

This Palgrave Macmillan imprint is published by the registered company Springer International Publishing AG part of Springer Nature.
The registered company address is: Gewerbestrasse 11, 6330 Cham, Switzerland

To my two families

ACKNOWLEDGMENTS

The research on which this book is based would not have been possible without the love and support of the close friends in El Salvador whom I consider a second family. Since my first trip to Santiago Nonualco in 2001, they provided for me a place that feels like home, where I have been welcomed, cared for, and treated as one of their own. During that first visit and several subsequent ones, they did their utmost to ensure that I stayed out of harm's way as I pursued my research. Moreover, by sharing their stories, exchanging ideas, and challenging my views, they enriched my understanding of postwar El Salvador and nurtured this book's development in a myriad of ways. I hope they see it as an attempt to contribute to a conversation about the roots of El Salvador's grim contemporary political life and where the possibilities for more hopeful prospects might lie. This book is largely thanks to them and for them!

There are, of course, many other Salvadorans who have contributed to the research for this book as well as its ideas and discussions. It would be impossible to acknowledge them all. However, I would like to extend my fondest gratitude to the members of the Father Cosme Spesotto Committee, La Paz's grassroots organization of war victims. I learned immensely from attending their meetings, participating in their activities, listening to their recollections of wartime and postwar stories, and exchanging views on issues relating to memory work and contemporary Salvadoran politics. They and their work comprise an important part of the book's ethnography and arguments and have shaped it in interesting and initially unexpected ways. I consider myself fortunate to have had the opportunity to participate in their organization and write about their memory work, and I feel deeply indebted to them.

The book's research was supported financially by doctoral funding from the University of Manchester and the Caja Madrid Foundation. The actual writing of the book manuscript was done largely during an Alliance 4 Universities postdoctoral fellowship at the Department of Social and Cultural Anthropology at Universidad Autónoma de Madrid, for which I am extremely grateful. The Institute of Latin American Studies at the University of London provided the financial support for the design of the book's maps as well as the supportive institutional base for the book's final revisions.

I cannot adequately express my gratitude to my PhD supervisors, John Gledhill and Stef Jansen, who were extremely supportive and generous, as well as a source of inspiration, throughout the writing of the doctoral dissertation that served as the foundation for this book. Leigh Binford and Madeleine Reeves, my PhD examiners, also provided extensive and thoughtful feedback that was invaluable in the preparation of the book manuscript. I have also benefited greatly from the critical feedback I received at the Department of Anthropology at Manchester University, the Department of Social and Cultural Anthropology at Universidad Autónoma de Madrid, and the Institute of Latin American Studies at the University of London. These intellectually stimulating environments played an important role in helping me refine the book's arguments. Special thanks go to the colleagues whose reading of my drafts and sharing of ideas have made a great difference to the book's arguments. Among others, I am particularly grateful to Ellen Moodie, David Pretel, Amy Penfield, Ernesto García López, Marta Pérez, Víctor del Arco, Adrian Bergmann, Susanne Hoffman, Ralph Sprenkels, Dennis Rodgers, Camilo José Melara, Laura Jordan, Čarna Brković, Rachel Wilde, Jonathan Mair, Martha-Cecilia Dietrich, and Rafa Gude. Deep appreciation goes also to Suzanne Smith, who helped edit the book manuscript and bring clarity to my Spanish-influenced writing style.

The love and generous friendship of Ernesto García López, Alba Arteaga Leiras, Marta Pérez, Elisabeth Schimpfoessl, Mira Mattar, Julia Calver, Inga Tejedor López, and Merryn and Dave Cooke has unquestionably helped this book come to life. Finally, my heartfelt thanks go to my parents and sister. They have encouraged and nurtured my interest in many of the issues at the heart of this book and are a source of continual love and support.

*   *   *

Portions of this book and the arguments in it have appeared in the following prior publications:

2013. 'The Violence of Cold War Polarities and the Fostering of Hope: The 2009 Elections in Post-War El Salvador.' In Jennifer L. Burrel and Ellen Moodie (eds.). *Central America in the New Millennium: Living Transition and Reimagining Democracy.* New York: Berghahn Books, pp. 49–63.

2015. 'The Turn of the Offended: Clientelism in the Wake of El Salvador's 2009 Elections.' *Social Analysis* 59(4): 101–118. Reprinted in: Mateusz Laszczkowski and Madeleine Reeves (eds.). 2017. *Affective States: Entanglements, Suspensions, Suspicions.* New York: Berghahn Books.

CONTENTS

LIST OF ABBREVIATIONS

18th Street	La 18, Calle 18 or Barrio 18
ADESCO	Communal Development Association (Asociación de Desarrollo Comunal)
AISAPANM	Intercommunal Administrator of Los Nonualcos and Masahuat Drinkable Water and Sewage Systems (Administradora Intermunicipal de los Servicios de Agua Potable y Alcantarillados Los Nonualcos y Masahuat)
ANDA	National Administration of Aqueducts and Drains (Administración Nacional de Acueductos y Alcantarillados)
ANEP	National Association of Private Enterprise (Asociación Nacional de la Empresa Privada)
ARENA	Nationalist Republican Alliance (Alianza Republicana Nacionalista)
ASVEM	El Salvador's Veterans Association 'General Manuel José Arce' (Asociación de Veteranos Militares de El Salvador 'General Manuel José Arce')
CAFTA-DR	Dominican Republic-Central America Free Trade Agreement
CEBs	Ecclesial Base Communities (Comunidades Eclesiales de Base)
CEJIL	Center for Justice and International Law (Centro por la Justicia y el Derecho Internacional)

CO-MADRES	Committee of Mothers and Relatives of the Political Prisoners, Disappeared and Assassinated of El Salvador 'Monseñor Óscar Arnulfo Romero' (Comité de Madres y Familiares de Detenidos, Desaparecidos y Asesinados Políticos 'Monseñor Óscar Arnulfo Romero')
CPDH	Centro para la Promoción de los Derechos Humanos 'Madeleine Lagadec' (Center for the Promotion of Human Rights 'Madeleine Lagadec')
DPLF	Due Process of Law Foundation (Fundación para el Debido Proceso)
DUI	Unique Identity Document (Documento Único de Identidad)
ERP	People's Revolutionary Army (Ejército Revolucionario del Pueblo)
FAL	Armed Liberation Forces (Fuerzas Armadas de Liberación)
FDR	Revolutionary Democratic Front (Frente Democrático Revolucionario)
FESPAD	Foundation for Studies on the Application of Law (Fundación de Estudios para la Aplicación del Derecho)
FMLN	Farabundo Martí National Liberation Front (Frente Farabundo Martí para la Liberación Nacional)
FPL	Popular Liberation Forces Farabundo Martí (Fuerzas Populares de Liberación Farabundo Martí)
FUSADES	Salvadoran Foundation for Economic and Social Development (Fundación Salvadoreña para el Desarrollo Económico y Social)
GANA	Great Alliance for National Unity (Gran Alianza por la Unidad Nacional)
IACHR	Inter-American Commission on Human Rights (Comisión Interamericana de Derechos Humanos)
IDB	Inter-American Development Bank
IDHUCA	UCA Institute of Human Rights (Instituto de Derechos Humanos de la UCA).
IMF	International Monetary Fund
IML	Institute of Forensic Medicine (Instituto de Medicina Legal)
MS or MS 13	Mara Salvatrucha

ONUSAL	United Nations Observer Mission in El Salvador (Misión de Observadores de las Naciones Unidas en El Salvador)
ORDEN	Nationalist Democratic Organization (Organización Democrática Nacionalista)
PCN	National Conciliation Party (Partido de Conciliación Nacional)
PCS	Salvadoran Communist Party (Partido Comunista Salvadoreño)
PDC	Christian Democratic Party (Partido Demócrata Cristiano)
PDDH	Office of the Human Rights Ombudsperson (Procuraduría para la Defensa de los Derechos Humanos)
PNC	National Civilian Police (Policía Nacional Civil)
PRD	Democratic Revolutionary Party (Partido Democrático Revolucionario)
PRI	Institutional Revolutionary Party (Partido Institucional Revolucionario)
PT	Workers' Party (Partido dos Trabalhadores)
SATRC	South African Truth and Reconciliation Commission
TPS	Temporary Protected Status
UCA	Central American University 'José Simeón Cañas' (Universidad Centroamericana 'José Simeón Cañas')
UN	United Nations
USAID	United States Agency for International Development
WB	World Bank

LIST OF FIGURES

CHAPTER 1

Introduction

Almost a hundred people congregated in the central plaza of Santiago Nonualco, between the municipality's council building and the local market, to celebrate the leftwing Farabundo Martí National Liberation Front's (FMLN) victory in El Salvador's presidential elections. It was the evening of 15 March 2009. The results had already been announced even before the local FMLN members had finished their electoral work at the polling station. Excitement among FMLN members had initially arisen when they saw their party leading in Santiago. Phone calls from cells by FMLN leaders in San Salvador and other neighboring municipalities, and from relatives watching TV, confirmed what would later be described in the national and international press as 'an historic victory': with a tight 51.3 percent share of the electoral vote, the former guerrilla organization-turned leftwing party, headed by presidential candidate Mauricio Funes, an independent journalist, had triumphed over the rightwing Nationalist Republican Alliance (ARENA). When the results had been officially released, Funes described this electoral victory as 'a new peace accord'.[1] At the close of election day, once the counted votes had been placed under lock and key and were being guarded by local police officers, FMLN loyalists converged in Santiago's central plaza despite the late hour. Since I had finished my duties as a volunteer international observer with the Office of the Human Rights Ombudsperson (PDDH), I decided to join the celebrants to check out the municipality's postelection atmosphere.

[1] 'Victoria histórica de la ex guerrilla izquierdista en El Salvador', *El País*, 16 March 2009.

© The Author(s) 2018
A. Montoya, *The Violence of Democracy*, Studies of the Americas, https://doi.org/10.1007/978-3-319-76330-9_1

1

In the plaza, men and women of all ages shouted or wept for joy and embraced each other, still stunned by the election results, which concluded 20 years of ARENA rule and were unprecedented given the country's long history of authoritarian, military, and conservative governments. They toasted the FMLN victory with sodas[2] bought at the market's lone open stall. Some FMLN loyalists danced the *merengue, bachata,* and *cumbia* to music drifting from speakers rented by the local FMLN leadership for the occasion. The dance music alternated with songs from the FMLN campaign whose choruses were familiar to all those congregated in the plaza: 'nace la esperanza, viene el cambio' (hope is born, change is coming), sung in euphoric unison by the merrymaking crowd. Children played and ran around, oblivious to the momentousness of the events, yet clearly sharing the contagious animation and joy of the adults. The plaza, which just two months earlier had been saturated with the blue and white colors of the country's rightwing National Conciliation Party (PCN) to celebrate that party's fourth successive victory in the municipal election, was now drenched in FMLN red. Red flags and T-shirts competed with the blue and white with which Santiago's mayor had had the plaza painted as well as the tricolor ARENA flag that flew over the small FMLN-aligned crowd that night. After the municipal contest, the ARENA flag had symbolized the publicly undeclared support of the mayor, herself a PCN member, for ARENA in the presidential campaign.[3]

In the capital city of San Salvador, in contrast to Santiago, the event was celebrated on a massive scale, with a large, red-colored jubilant crowd pouring into the streets and converging in the city center in a gathering that recalled the post-Peace Accords celebrations in 1992. The celebration in Santiago was comparatively low key, even accounting for the municipality's smaller size. Indeed, aside from the plaza, Santiago's streets were deserted and the doors and windows of the municipality's houses closed as on any other evening. The population from the *cantones* (rural areas of the municipality) had had to leave early via the transport that the FMLN, like other parties, had arranged to bring voters from the areas where the party enjoyed widespread support to Santiago's polling station. Yet another

---

[2] The Salvadoran electoral code (Art. 342) prohibits the sale, distribution, and consumption of alcoholic beverages on Election Day as well as on the days immediately preceding and following it.

[3] Only FMLN and ARENA competed in the 2009 presidential election. For more details about this election, see Chap. 5.

important reason for the low turnout in Santiago's celebration that night was fear—a fear that still suffused postwar political practices and relations at the time. This was especially so during the 2009 presidential election given the wartime polarities and imageries that had been resurrected by ARENA and the media, and the hostilities that had pervaded the country's political life.

Throughout the electoral campaign, I had listened to the many conversations of the family that had embraced me as one of their own, as well as those of their neighbors, friends, and relatives, that spoke to the ongoing relevance of the wartime past. Friends would often advise members of the family not to express their political preference in public. On one occasion, sitting at the entrance of the family's house, above which a large poster of Mauricio Funes hung prominently, an old friend of Marta,[4] the family's 70-year-old matriarch, lowered her voice to suggest that Marta not show such overt support for the FMLN: 'If Ávila[5] wins the election, you may regret it. You should be careful.'[6] Although Marta seemed to disregard this kind of advice herself, she would repeatedly insist, in the intimacy of her home, that I should leave El Salvador if Rodrigo Ávila were to win, because atrocities had been perpetrated even against foreigners during the country's war in the 1980s. 'If this man wins, there is going to be *matazón* (a blood-bath)', she would insist when I suggested that the situation seemed to have changed significantly since the war. In idle moments, she would sometimes recount stories of wartime atrocities perpetrated by the various police forces in Santiago so as to offer me evidence of the brutality of which the country's rightwing was capable, given the precedent of the war.

Crucially, accounts of wartime violence often shifted abruptly to anecdotes of postwar violence. This may not come as a surprise given that homicides spiked in 2009—a 37 percent increase relative to the previous

[4] My policy throughout the book has been to anonymize friends and acquaintances, research participants, and places inasmuch as possible. However, I have maintained the names of prominent political actors and municipalities and towns. Where anonymity did not suffice to conceal the identity of research participants, I have also distorted details to better achieve that goal while making sure to preserve the integrity of the evidence.

[5] Rodrigo Ávila was the ARENA presidential candidate in the 2009 elections and the former National Civilian Police (PNC) director in 1994–1999 and 2006–2008, thereby evoking the alliances between economic elites and the country's institutions of order that characterized previous eras (see Stanley 1996). During the campaign, rumor had it that he had belonged to paramilitary groups in the past.

[6] All translations of research participants and extracts from Spanish texts throughout the book are my own.

year.[7] Yet, the abrupt shifts from wartime recollections to the postwar era and back were also symptomatic of the continuities that Salvadorans have traced between the two. Allusions to a possible connection between postwar homicides and the country's political life, as had existed during the war, were never missing in conversations about present-day violence. As we watched news of daily homicides in the evenings, the adults in the family I lived with would often remark how unlikely it was that these homicides were all gang related, as the media consistently reported. Family members would suggest, as did many friends, relatives, and neighbors in the context of informal conversations, that something else must be going on, possibly a political link. Often they insinuated the persistence of 'political violence' against leftwing Salvadorans, during but also beyond electoral seasons.

This book examines Salvadorans' interpretations of postwar violence and offers an explanation for how these relate to their citizenship practices and political subjectivities. As an ethnographic project, it seeks to capture El Salvador's ongoing problem of endemic violence at a particular point in time: the period surrounding the 2009 elections, about 17 years after the end of the country's civil war. During the 2009 electoral season—when 'change' was revised, conjured, denied, or pursued—questions about what had changed and what had continued since the end of the war became relevant anew. It was also a point in time at which a tremendous sense of possibility emerged—one at which hopes for a different political project took shape. The expectations engendered by the FMLN's electoral victory that year highlighted the pertinence of scrutinizing political life, especially at a juncture in which violence seemed to have become routine. Most importantly, ordinary Salvadorans often described the postwar moment as one of 'neither war nor peace' or one even 'worse than the war' (Montoya 2007; Moodie 2010: 84). In invoking the war as a constant point of reference against which the present was assessed, such statements called into question the country's transition to democracy. While hardly suggesting that the country's ongoing violence implies a continuation of the war, ordinary Salvadorans across the political spectrum have shared the view that the end of the war has not brought peace and that democracy does not, by definition, imply an absence of violence. Their interpretations were confirmed by my observations of the country's postwar political life.

---

[7] '2009 el año más violento desde 1992', *El Faro*, 3 January 2010.

BEYOND THE GANG TROPE

Gangs have come to constitute the dominant and recurrent trope with which to explain postwar El Salvador's problem of endemic violence, thereby justifying a spate of writing on them.[8] Without clear future prospects or employment opportunities in a country wrecked by war, and with abundant war weapons available, many marginalized youth have turned to the support and opportunities offered by gangs in various territories of El Salvador. The main gangs, the infamous *Mara Salvatrucha* (MS or MS 13) and *La 18* or *Barrio 18* (18th Street),[9] originated in Los Angeles but expanded throughout Central America as the United States stepped up its mass deportation of those accused of criminal offenses, including gang members, to their countries of origin—in this case, a country that many had never even set foot in, born as they were into migrants' and exiles' families based in the United States (Cruz 2007a; Zilberg 2004, 2011).[10] In El Salvador, where gangs already existed, deportations of gang members from the United States resulted in an escalation of gang membership, the spread of the United States gangs' organizational model and cultural codes, and the gradual expansion of gang-controlled territories in numerous towns and municipalities, as well as increased gang involvement in homicidal violence, extortion, kidnapping, and small-scale drug distribution. In the early 2000s, estimates indicated that there were already between 75,000 and 250,000 active gang members in Central America, 10,000 to 30,000 of them in El Salvador (Hume 2007b: 480–481). A decade later, estimates of El Salvador's gang members had doubled, with unsubstantiated figures of up to 60,000 depending on the source (see UNHCR 2016: 10).

While not aiming to minimize the violence or criminal activities perpetrated by these gangs, I suggest in this book that the very hyper-visibility of gang members—especially of their tattooed bodies, hand language, and

---

[8] Although much of the writing on gangs is journalistic in nature, there is also abundant scholarly work. See, for instance, Smutt and Miranda (1998), Santacruz Giralt and Concha-Eastman (2001), Cruz (2007b), Savenije (2009), Bruneau et al. (2011), Wolf (2012d), Ward (2013), and Martínez D'Aubuisson (2015).

[9] It should be noted that *Calle Dieciocho* split after 2005 into two factions, *Sureños* and *Revolucionarios*, which have fought each other ever since while continuing to fight their arch-rival *Salvatrucha*. To read about the events that led to this split, see Amaya and Martínez (2015).

[10] From the mid-1990s to the mid-2000s, between 200 and 600 Salvadorans were deported monthly (Zilberg 2011: 129).

style of dress,[11] as well as their daily presence in the media—has partly contributed to concealing other dimensions of El Salvador's postwar violence. Throughout my research I have thus been careful not to take the perspective offered by the gang trope at face value and to explore instead the extent to which the trope has actually accounted for Salvadorans' experiences of postwar violence. In short, I have sought to find out what I could apprehend about postwar violence if my research was not gang centered but focused instead on the myriad and more complex explanations that emerged from Salvadorans' own narratives and practices. Needless to say, gangs have frequently populated the conversations and rumors about violence of the Salvadorans I have engaged with; yet gangs have not always been their only or even their main source of concern. What, then, can our gaze capture when we leave the gangs out of focus?

In staying with a Salvadoran family and meeting their neighbors, extended family, and friends over the course of numerous trips to El Salvador from 2001, I learned about El Salvador's contemporary political history through their narrations of war stories and confidences about atrocities perpetrated in the country by military-controlled police forces and death squads during the war. While listening to these accounts in the intimacy of people's homes, I often relived conversations and stories about the Spanish Civil War and its aftermath that I had grown up hearing from my own family in Spain. I found parallels in the extraordinary grief and frequent silences with which many of these stories were recounted in both contexts, and it was these parallels that sparked my interest in El Salvador's political history. Eventually, I conducted research on issues related to this country's war and its aftermath, especially on how ordinary people remembered the war and what reconciliation might mean for them in the absence of redress.[12]

On my 2007 trip to El Salvador, three years after my prior visit, I noticed that while Salvadorans were continuing to narrate war stories, their concern had shifted to the new forms of violence that were afflicting the country. Unresolved war memories were still invoked but more often

[11] It should be noted, however, that in recent years, gang members have begun to avoid any outward signs that might facilitate police identification and detention.

[12] Chapter 6 discusses local appropriations of the global discourse of reconciliation that has accompanied peacebuilding operations. For critical approaches to the discourse of reconciliation, see, for instance, Wilson (2001), the edited volume of Focaal (Eastmond and Stefansson 2010), and the dialogue in Public Culture (Borneman 2002, and the responses to him in the same issue).

than not for the purpose of drawing comparisons to the postwar violence. In hindsight, I realized that this shift in concern from wartime to postwar violence occurred during the years following the Salvadoran governments' adoption of a tougher approach on the country's gangs—an approach that reportedly resulted in a greater sophistication in gang organization and a concomitant escalation of homicide rates and police corruption (see, for instance, Aguilar Villamariona 2006; Hume 2007a; Wolf 2017). From the early 2000s, the government as well as the media had focused on gangs as the country's sole reason for violence, ignoring the structural roots of gang violence, gangs' links to other actors, or alternative sources of violence. I thus undertook the research on which this book is based by asking how and why ordinary Salvadorans have experienced and made sense of ongoing routine violence throughout the democratization process and in the context of a violent peace. By qualifying my interlocutors as 'ordinary', I have sought to underline my focus on Salvadorans who are not part of elites, whether economic or political. This book's focus on ordinary people is partly a response to the need for an approach to peacebuilding and democratization that goes beyond the elite- and institution-centered studies yielded by comparative politics.

During the late 2000s in El Salvador—whose population is just 5.74 million, with an additional 2.66 million Salvadorans residing in the United States and other countries[13]—an average of over ten people were killed daily and more than 3000 annually, bringing the annual homicide rate to over 50 per 100,000 inhabitants and making El Salvador one of the most violent countries in Latin America.[14] Quite strikingly, while El Salvador attracted wide international attention during the Cold War era for levels of violence similar to, or actually lower than, contemporary ones, postwar El Salvador has to some degree fallen under the radar of the international community (cf. Burrell and Moodie 2013). For that matter, many members of the international community have considered El Salvador's transition a success (Orr 2001: 153; Call 2003: 829; Paris 2004: 113, 124), implicitly normalizing this country's dramatically high postwar homicide

[13] These figures are estimates since there is no consensus on the global count of Salvadoran migrants (PNUD 2005b: 40).

[14] Indeed, since the signing of the Peace Accords, the homicide rate went down only slightly, to under 40 per 100,000 inhabitants, in the early 2000s (PNUD 2010: 275). Following the enactment of *mano dura* (iron fist) policies from 2003, homicide rates dropped under that level only after the 2012 gang truce. For the evolution of homicide rates between 2009 and 2014, see FUNDAUNGO (2014).

rates. My research, however, elicited expressions of confoundment vis-à-vis postwar violence from Salvadorans themselves, who were wont to ask me, 'Is it as violent in your country? Are people killed every day in Spain?'—even as they seemed accustomed to the routine of daily homicides. Prompted by Salvadorans' simultaneous familiarity and distance vis-à-vis the country's problem of violence, I set out to explore the continuities and discontinuities of violence that have characterized El Salvador's transition to democracy.

THE MULTIVALENT NOTION OF DEMOCRACY

This book's title, *The Violence of Democracy*, has a dual meaning: it denotes both a temporal and a substantive dimension of contemporary El Salvador. In one sense, 'democracy' serves to denote a historical stage. Assumed as the end result of the peacebuilding and democratization processes undergone by El Salvador since the signing of Peace Accords at the Castle of Chapultepec, Mexico, in 1992, the term democracy has taken on an equivalency with the postwar era. In another sense, 'democracy' denotes the political regime that has resulted from the aforementioned processes set off by the Accords. Since 1989, with the end of the Cold War era, a belief prevailed that political liberalization and parallel marketization—in other words, a 'liberal market democracy'—would foster the conditions necessary for a durable and sustainable peace (Paris 2004). This book, then, explores Salvadorans' experiences of violence at a temporal juncture in which democracy is considered to have been consolidated and against the background of a liberal market regime that was pursued through internationally monitored reform and has been construed as antagonistic to the previous decades of authoritarian and repressive regimes.

The end of the Cold War set the stage for liberal market democracy to triumph and become the dominant political model—one that would be replicated worldwide. In war-torn societies that underwent peace negotiations and subsequent peacebuilding during the 1990s, the United Nations (UN) as well as other participating organizations, such as key financial institutions, led efforts to transform these countries' political institutions and to marketize their economies (Paris 2004; Guilhot 2005). Former combatants were demobilized and reintegrated into society, insurgent organizations were legalized as political parties, the institutions of order were reformed and trained in human rights, and civil and political rights such as individual free speech, an uncensored mass media, freedom of association, and public participation in competitive multiparty elections were promoted. Parallel to these transformations, structural adjustment programs were requested by international financial institutions in exchange for the funds that the governments needed for postwar reconstruction. These structural adjustments included the lifting or lowering of barriers to the movement of capital and goods, the drafting of legislation and enactment of policies to promote private investment or to attract foreign direct investment, and an overall reduction in state intervention. At least in El Salvador, these economic reforms were never part of the peace settlement.

Anthropologists have shed light on the cultural and historical rootedness of this understanding of democracy in Western liberalism (see, for instance, Nugent 2008; Paley 2008b). This is a thin notion of democracy, conceived as a political regime or mode of governance based on the consolidation of formal institutions in which the procedures and mechanisms of elections are central. Yet the transition paradigm that underlies democratization studies has largely rested on Dahl's notion of polyarchal democracy, which is in turn premised on the assumption that elections are necessary but not sufficient (1971: 5; 2005: 195). Dahl (2005) further includes freedom of expression and access to information as well as associational rights as equally essential to the establishment of a large-scale polyarchal democracy. Scholars of democratization, building upon the notion of polyarchy, have defined liberal democracy as predicated upon free and fair electoral competition, accountability, and entitlement to political and civil rights (Diamond 1999; see also O'Donnell et al. 1986; Przeworski 1991). This notion of democracy has worked as an organizing principle that has overshadowed alternative political forms and against which democratizing polities have been measured, thus revealing itself as highly ideological in defining divergent regimes as failed or weak (Arias and Goldstein 2010b: 2–5).

Furthermore, as mentioned earlier, in El Salvador as well as in other countries, the political developments advanced through transitions to democracy occurring from the late 1980s and throughout the 1990s have served to legitimize parallel neoliberal transformations that have allowed capitalism to persist and adjust to the new historical circumstances (Cammack 1997; Robinson 2003; Paris 2004; Paley 2008b: 14). Indeed, peacebuilding in Central America engendered the conditions for neoliberal restructuring while enabling the elite class to reconstitute its power (Robinson 2003; Paris 2004: 112–134). In these regimes, democracy and the market have become deeply entangled and shaped one another, thereby justifying adjectives for democracy such as 'liberal market', 'free-market', or 'neoliberal' (Paris 2004; Paley 2008b: 13; Moodie 2013). Such political regimes, peacebuilding practitioners assumed, would inevitably evolve into peaceful ones that consolidated the rule of law and provided substantive citizenship. From this vantage point, ongoing violence after a conflict has been neglected or conceived as external or antithetical to democracy.

Nevertheless, democracy, as Paley (2008b) observes, can denote different political forms and be bestowed with variegated meanings or become attached to radically different referents. This is clear in the various ways that Salvadorans have envisioned their country's political life. As the postwar era has unfolded, different developments have contributed to imbuing the notion of democracy with new meanings. Democracy as both a historical stage and a political form has been linked to violence in Salvadorans' imaginaries and citizenship practices—a link that has also become apparent in my analysis of how El Salvador's democracy works. In this book, I thus shed light on the concrete ways in which violence and democracy have become entangled. Their entanglement emerges through my examination of on-the-ground practices, processes, and relations concerning political subjectivities, citizenship, and statecraft, and how these invoke, employ, or contest aspects of the normative notion of democracy promoted by the international community. As the book chapters will demonstrate, violence has not posed a threat to the country's postwar political regime but has instead become constitutive of its practices, relations, and processes.

In the face of the consistent lawlessness and violations of civil rights in Latin American democracies, O'Donnell (1998: 27) has proposed a distinction between democracy as a 'political regime' and democracy as a 'mode of relationship'. This distinction, I suggest, can be helpful in exploring how democratic institutions might coexist with pervasive violence in postwar El Salvador. Indeed, I conceive of democratization as the process through which Salvadorans define, negotiate, and materialize their relationship to a state polity rather than simply as the process that resulted in the UN-monitored reformed regime after the end of the war (cf. Nugent 2008: 22–24). O'Donnell's distinction thus enables an understanding of why ordinary Salvadorans are concerned about issues of equality, justice, and state-citizenry relations even as they do not challenge the idea that a democratic regime has been consolidated in El Salvador.

It may well be that the postwar disillusionment and disaffection of ordinary Salvadorans is linked to an aspiration to a substantive democracy that includes the socioeconomic as much as the political and civil components of citizenship (see also Moodie 2010: 139–168; 2013). In other words, the distinction between democracy as a political regime and as a mode of relationship might explain how it is that Salvadorans, especially those on the Left who lived through the war, while critical of their country's democracy, have not renounced the idea of democracy. Their notion of democracy was once rooted in the socialist-oriented projects underpinning the struggles in Central America in the 1980s—a notion that included elements of popular sovereignty, development, and welfare (Grandin 2004). While in the postwar era a new common sense of increasing individualization of the self and society has become widely extended, these Salvadorans' socialization in a more participatory and solidary form of politics has inevitably continued to shape their views of democracy and their political practices (Binford 2013; Moodie 2013).

This book shows that narratives, citizenship practices, and state-citizenry relations all indicate that violence has become part and parcel of El Salvador's democratic life, thereby calling into question the international community's positive assessments of the country's democratization and peacebuilding. This does not imply that violence pervades all aspects of El Salvador's political life but rather that violence is built into how various aspects of political life under democracy operate, are imagined, or are performed. In other words, my ethnography suggests that in postwar El Salvador, violence and democracy 'must be understood in tandem, rather than as two distinct points on a single evolutionary trajectory or as contradictory elements of an ongoing teleology' (Arias and Goldstein 2010b: 25). In this vein, the 'neither-war-nor-peace' and 'worse-than-the-war' statements are direct challenges to the teleology of a transition that has brought about something other than peace: a violent democracy in which the persistence of public and economic insecurity bespeaks constant violations of the civil and socio-economic components of citizenship even as democratic processes and procedures are staged and performed.

The relationship between violence and democracy has been illuminated by critical views on the ontology of the law (see Agamben 1998; Derrida 2002; Benjamin 2007). In their efforts to deconstruct the law, these authors have defined it as neither intrinsically different from nor independent of violence. The 'enforcement of the law', suggests Derrida, itself constitutes a form of violence (2002: 233). In exposing the inherent violence of an archetypal element of democracy such as the rule of law, these authors dissolve the detachment between violence and democracy that characterizes the transition paradigm underpinning peacebuilding operations. While I do not intend to portray the mechanisms of democracy as violent per se, they have in the case of El Salvador accommodated and become deeply entangled with various forms of violence, as in the enactment of *mano dura* (iron fist) policies and the practices and discourses thereof.

The plausibility of this entanglement is elucidated by Schirmer (1998: 2) in her study of the military in postwar Guatemala. She suggests that 'Rather than naked military rule based on emergency measures, juntas, and coups—instruments of power that have lost their legitimacy internationally—it is the appropriation of the imagery of the rule of law, of the mechanisms and procedures of electoral democracy, that is perilous to the human rights of Guatemalans'. Similarly, postwar El Salvador differs from previous authoritarian regimes in having been authorized and sanitized by the transition to democracy, at least in the eyes of the international community, which has lauded this process despite routine violence that, while different from wartime violence in its forms and actors, has continued to yield a high annual death toll. Even more significantly, Arias and Goldstein (2010a) have posited violence as a defining feature of Latin American democracies. Political regimes throughout Latin America, they affirm, are 'violently plural', not just because a plurality of actors resort to violence but because violence has been critical to the foundation, maintenance, and contestation of many of the region's democratic regimes rather than a symptom of their failure. It is from this vantage point that we can comprehend Salvadorans' imageries of democracy as deeply entangled with various forms of violence. Throughout the book, I elucidate the roots and shape of those entanglements—as they emerge in ordinary people's views but not only—and their implications for political subjectivities and citizenship practices in the postwar era, specifically in the context of the 2009 electoral competition and subsequent political handover.

Democratization and democracy have long been the purview of political science. As Paley observes, 'By and large, these studies of democracy were conducted by political scientists whose concerns with political institutions, formal regime shifts, and comparative country studies shaped the questions and set the agendas for debate' (2002: 469). Anthropologists, however, have gradually gained an interest in democracy, even though their references to it have often been embedded in the discussion of other related issues (Paley 2002: 470). This increasing interest notwithstanding, there exists an epistemological and methodological gulf between political science and anthropology that cannot easily be bridged given the different focus and understandings of disciplinary rigor underpinning the two disciplines. Not only do political scientists focus on formal institutions and elite actors, policy and macro-perspectives, and large-scale comparisons, but they also seek to establish disciplinary rigor through typological models and clear-cut definitions, broad arguments, and a sense that objectivity is both desirable and possible. An anthropology of democracy, however, is instead interested in understanding how the notion of democracy is conferred meaning by differently positioned actors and how normative notions of democracy are formed, maintained, reproduced, and contested (Paley 2002, 2008a).

Despite the disciplinary gulf, this book seeks to shed light on how an ethnographic lens can contribute to understanding peacebuilding and democratization. Given that scholarship within comparative politics has underpinned the work of democratization practitioners (Paris 2004), I avow the need to complement it with research that draws on the lived experiences of transition and peace- and democracy-making—beyond the elites involved in negotiation and institution building—and that investigates how the changes galvanized by peacebuilding and democratization unfold in everyday life. Anthropology's appreciation of rich description and detail, messiness, and the ordinary, its lack of aspiration to objectivity, and its ethical protocol of anonymizing details are only a few of the issues that make ethnographies an easy target for criticisms revolving around lack of reliability and inconsistency. Yet these distinctive traits of ethnography allow for a focus on neglected domains as well as a level of complexity, nuance, and contradiction that rarely emerge with other research methodologies.

THE EPISTEMOLOGICAL VALUE OF RUMOR

I began this research asking whether one could *see* everything about El Salvador's postwar violence or whether the preeminence of the gang trope in explanations of postwar violence was not rather the result of a pervasive assumption about the notion of violence: the prevalence of its physical and visible qualities. The stress on visibility is indeed predicated upon a deep-rooted notion of 'violence', evidenced in its firstly listed definition in the Oxford English Dictionary as 'the deliberate exercise of physical force against a person, property, etc.' (OED 2016). This definition is evidence of the commonplace reduction of violence to a physical expression that underlies our insistence on *seeing* violence and our dismissal of its less visible expressions. Not only is the focus on visible violence limiting given the elusiveness and cultural rootedness of the notion of violence, but also, as I argue throughout this book, violent democracies like El Salvador's manage to manufacture a certain degree of legitimacy precisely because not everything about their violence can be seen or is made publicly visible. Several questions then arise concerning the ethnographic study of violence. How do we study violence in a violent democracy? How do we identify that which is scarcely visible, whether intrinsically or as a result of efforts to render it as invisible as possible? How do we study that which is there yet not there? How might the not-so-visible and more elusive dimensions of violence be rendered manifest ethnographically?

To begin with, there is a need to downplay the preeminence of visible qualities of violence and instead acknowledge that violence can be visible and invisible, physical and psychological, destructive and creative, irrational and rational, good and bad, senseless and useful, legitimate and illegitimate. The elusiveness of violence implies that it may or may not become visible to the eyes or be recognized as such. While I did *see* violence in several instances during my fieldwork—for instance, when I arrived at a location where someone had just been killed and when I witnessed physical aggression and death threats during the 2009 electoral campaign—much of my ethnographic material on violence consists of narratives in the form of rumors and other forms of speech as well as the observations and media material that allowed me to contextualize them. It was chiefly through rumor that I learned about homicides, extortion, drug trafficking, death threats, and fears. Of course, far from settling the problem of how to study violence, rumors only raise new concerns. As a form of 'anonymously authored speech', rumors are per se anecdotal, unverifiable, and hence open to contestation (Ghosh 2008).[15] Yet rumors are often the primary means through which ordinary Salvadorans put forth reasoning and theories about postwar violence that contest official depictions, perhaps because of the protection conferred by the anonymous quality of rumors—'*se dice*' (it is said) or '*la gente dice*' (people say) are some of the

---

[15] Ghosh (2008) focuses mainly on the role of rumor as a historical source. In anthropology, extensive research has focused on gossip and scandal, rather than rumor, as a means of morality and community making (Gluckman 1963).

ways that rumors restate their own anonymity. I thus argue that rumor—whether transmitted through word of mouth, or through conventional or social media—is often the limited means through which one can perceive the grayness and clandestinity of violence in a democracy that renders some forms of violence, some violent actors and their interconnections relatively illegible.

Rumors and crime stories have served as the ethnographic evidence for previous studies of Latin America's violent democracies. These works have examined the performative role of the talk of crime, crime stories, and rumor. Caldeira's (2000) ethnography on the rise of private security in São Paulo, Brazil, in the 1980s and 1990s, explores how 'the talk of crime' operated by stimulating fear, stereotyped reorderings of the world, and exclusionary practices such as the spatial segregation resulting from the increasing resort to private protection. Likewise, Moodie's (2010) research in San Salvador during the post-Accords decade examines how 'crime stories' by ordinary people are a means of knowledge production that reproduces official and mass media representations of violence while also critiquing the democracy yielded by the country's peace negotiations. In chronicling his two-week stay in a Colombian town in 2001, when paramilitary violence had reached a peak, Taussig (2003) relied instead on rumor. He observed that because rumors allow for a chronological ordering of violent events but fail to shed light on the threads that connect them, they act as a trigger of confusion and fear. As these ethnographic works have suggested, narratives of violence—whether in the form of stories or rumor—constitute an important heuristic device that allows us to understand how ordinary people experience and make sense of violence.

In this book I am interested in what rumors *hint at* as much as what they *do*. Whether or not every detail of the rumors circulating among ordinary people in Santiago is credible, rumors are interesting in and of themselves insofar as they hint at the existence of clandestine relations that have also been elicited through other means, whether interviews, media scandal, or investigative journalism. As an object of inquiry, rumors can be a means by which to access fragments and details of what is seemingly illegible or invisible in a violent democracy. In El Salvador, I found that rumors, perhaps due to their very anonymity, dared to identify forms of violence and violent actors that have a manifest presence despite their clandestine nature, as well as their connections with the country's political life. As Comaroff and Comaroff (2006: 9) have observed of post-colonial countries rife with violence, '"dark circuits" of rumor and popular media alike flash signs of inchoate danger lurking beneath the banal surface of things, danger made real by sudden, graphic assaults on persons and property.' The anecdotal nature of the information obtained through rumor is to be taken seriously since it points to the mesh of violent actors and activities that are otherwise kept out of view. Ethnography is well positioned to contextualize rumors and shed light on the cracks through which we can learn about what lies beneath the surface. Yet the value of rumors as ethnographic evidence does not simply lie in their attempt to unravel the tangle of violent actors and activities in a violent democracy. The 'dark circuit' of rumor also bespeaks ordinary people's concern with a problem of violence about which they feel they have a modicum of awareness yet cannot fully comprehend; it points to the very illegibility of violence and Salvadorans' attempts and struggles to make sense of it. In this sense, rumors constitute a valuable means to access ordinary people's modes of reasoning about postwar violence.

THE TRANSITION FROM WAR TO PEACE

A civil war was waged in El Salvador in the 1980s. Five political-military groups joined under the umbrella of the FMLN[16] launched the so-called final offensive on 10 January 1981, seeking to emulate the 1979 Sandinista uprising. Ironically, the 1981 FMLN uprising at the national level turned out to be the beginning of a 12-year civil war between the guerrillas, on the one hand, and El Salvador's military-controlled government on the other. The description of this war as a 'civil' strife has been subject to contention given that El Salvador, like other Central American countries, was turned into a Cold War battleground during the 1980s (see, for instance, Arnson 1982; Americas Watch 1991; Binford 1996). The United States government provided military and financial backing to the Salvadoran government with the goal of promoting counterinsurgency operations. Meanwhile, the Marxist–Leninist-oriented FMLN guerrilla organization obtained logistical and military support from the Soviet-aligned Cuban and Nicaraguan governments. The involvement of other countries in the war was often

---

[16] The FMLN was born in October 1980 as an agglutination of five political-military organizations founded in the 1970s (except for the Salvadoran Communist Party, PCS, which had been founded in 1930). The Revolutionary Democratic Front (FDR) was the political arm of the FMLN during the war and peace negotiations. For comprehensive accounts of the structure of the FMLN, see Martín Álvarez (2006, 2010) and Sprenkels (2014: 75–138).

invoked in my interviews with ex-combatants, whether they had partici-pated with El Salvador's armed forces or with guerrilla organizations. The importance of foreign intervention notwithstanding, it is necessary to acknowledge that the war was the culmination of historically rooted prob-lems of structural inequality and repression by the military regimes that had ruled the country since 1931 (Baloyra 1982: 2; Dunkerley 1982: 3; Montgomery 1982: 2; Byrne 1996: 17; Paige 1997: 3, 14). Against this background, El Salvador's war in the 1980s did not come as a surprise but was the intensification of a preexisting conflict between the Salvadoran gov-ernment and ordinary Salvadorans participating in various kinds of political and military organizations. The collapse of the reformist 1979 military coup due to opposition from within the conservative wing of the military and the country's elite, as well as the organizations that would later com-prise the FMLN, contributed to precipitating the outbreak of El Salvador's civil war.

After the 1981 offensive proved insufficient to destabilize the Salvadoran state, the FMLN guerrillas retreated to rural areas, where they could hide more easily while relying on the support of the local populations.[17] From 1981 until another FMLN offensive in 1989, a great part of the war was fought in the country's rural areas. Politically motivated assassinations by police forces were commonplace in both San Salvador and rural areas. In the case of the latter, during the early 1980s, sweeping military operations were carried out and legitimized as critical to the fight against the guerril-las despite the fact that they often consisted of massacres and the summary executions of civilians (United Nations 1993: 155–171; Binford 1996, 2016). The largest numbers of wartime casualties were registered in the earlier stages of the war, yet high figures continued to be tallied through-out the conflict.[18] Following the FMLN 1989 offensive[19] launched in San Salvador, negotiations monitored by the UN began between

---

[17]Wood (2003) has provided a thorough study of popular support in various rural areas of El Salvador's Usulután Department during the war.

[18]Socorro Jurídico, a human rights organization within the San Salvador Archbishopric, registered 11,903 civilian victims in 1980 and 16,266 in 1981 (United Nations 1993: 24). From then onward, the annual figure of victims—both civilian and military—oscillated between 1000 and 6000.

[19]The 1989 offensive, which lasted from 11 November to 12 December, left behind 2000 victims; according to the Commission on the Truth for El Salvador, it was one of the most violent events of the war (United Nations 1993: 49).

representatives of the ARENA government and the FMLN.[20] The war had come to a standstill, with both sides aware that neither of them was in a position to defeat the other (Karl 1992: 148–151). Meanwhile, the business elite that came to control ARENA,[21] which had replaced the Christian Democratic Party (PDC) in the country's presidency after the 1989 elections, harbored the pragmatic view that an end to the conflict would positively impact the country's investment opportunities (Paige 1997: 37; Robinson 2003: 98–99)—a view reinforced by the ongoing reality of undefeated insurgent activity (see Wood 2000). International pressure on the military and Salvadoran government for a peaceful settlement increased after the assassination of six Jesuit Fathers, and their housekeeper and her daughter, by members of the United States-trained Atlacatl Battallion of the Salvadoran army on the campus of El Salvador's Central American University (UCA) in 1989. The UN-brokered negotiations advanced but risked collapse when the discussion turned to military reforms, partly because of the ongoing reluctance of the military to agree to a negotiated end to the conflict (Karl 1992: 152, 155). Finally, after two years of negotiations, an agreement was reached, and the Peace Accords were signed by the two opposing sides in 1992.

The most conservative estimates indicate that at least 75,000 people were killed, 7000 disappeared, and another 500,000 displaced in El Salvador's war (Wood 2003: 8). In all, 85 percent of the wartime human rights violations investigated by the Commission on the Truth for El Salvador were attributed, by those testifying, to the army and police forces, state-sponsored paramilitary groups, and death squads (United Nations 1993: 58). The peace negotiations therefore concentrated on the reform of the country's institutions of order (i.e. the military, the military-controlled police forces and the judicial system) and the electoral system. While the dissolution of military rule may be considered a success, the same cannot be said of the practical functioning of other institutions of order. The independence of the judiciary and the efficacy

---

[20] Although peace negotiations among the five Central American presidents, led by the Costa Rican President Óscar Arias, had already begun in 1987 as a joint effort to pacify the region, the UN-brokered negotiations between El Salvador's opposing sides did not begin until 1989 (Karl 1992: 154; United Nations 1992a: i–ii; Montgomery 1995: 141).

[21] As I explain later, although initially led by the most reactionary sector of the elite, by the end of the 1980s, a shift in the balance of power within the party fostered a new leadership more open to negotiation.

of the rule of law, for instance, have yet to be achieved (Popkin 2000). Partly as a result, the prewar and wartime human rights violations that have traumatized and fragmented the Salvadoran population remain unaddressed (Gaborit 2006).

Likewise, the problem of structural inequality underlying the country's war was only secondarily addressed in the Peace Accords. During the 1990s, El Salvador experienced economic growth and a reduction in poverty, largely due to an increased flow of remittances from the United States and other countries[22] (see Gammage 2006). However, this reduction in poverty was not distributed evenly: poverty in the rural areas, especially among families involved in agriculture and headed by men, rose dramatically following the collapse of the country's agricultural economy in the 1990s (Segovia 2002: 185). In 1999, a total of 47.3 percent of Salvadorans remained poor, and the percentage increased to 61.8 in the country's rural areas (Segovia 2002: 182). While poverty and extreme poverty rates have improved over the years, the gap between urban and rural areas as well as overall inequality have persisted (Hammill 2007). El Salvador's transition from an agrarian to a manufacturing and service-based economy—which was concurrent to the peacebuilding process—was made possible to a great extent by the privatization and deregulation introduced by the ARENA governments from 1989. Against this background, the limited programs included in the Peace Accords that aimed at tackling poverty, such as land transfers, were rather ineffective.[23] Public and economic insecurity have thus continued to characterize ordinary Salvadorans' everyday lives in the postwar era, transforming the immense hope they invested in the Peace Accords and the democratization process into a sense of profound disillusionment (see Moodie 2010: 145; Silber 2011: 2). There is thus a need to examine how legacies of the past have operated in tandem with emergent processes of neoliberalization as the transition to democracy has unfolded.

---

[22] In the postwar era, migration has become Salvadorans' main way to escape increasing economic insecurity, to the extent that the flow of remittances sent by Salvadoran migrants has amounted to an average of more than 16 percent of El Salvador's GDP (Gammage 2006).

[23] The land transfer program was negotiated mainly for demobilized guerrillas and communities already occupying the land in regions or areas that had been FMLN strongholds during the war (Sprenkels 2014: 174).

LEGACIES OF THE PAST

As the opening ethnographic vignette shows, the wartime past pervades contemporary El Salvador in a myriad of ways, including the memories of wartime violence, the persistence of wartime political cleavages, the fears of a revival of generalized state-sponsored repression, and the rumors about the persistence of political violence. In addition, as a by-product of ongoing political cleavages, rightwing Salvadorans have recurrently depicted the FMLN as a threat during elections as well as expressed angst, at least until 2009, about a possible repetition of an FMLN-led uprising or the enactment of a communist regime (see Chap. 5). I thus trace in this book the great degree of continuity that has characterized El Salvador's transition to democracy, even as the country has undergone important transformations. As Humphrey (2002a: 12) has argued about former socialist countries after the demise of the Soviet Union, 'there never can be a sudden and total emptying out of all social phenomena and their replacement by other ways of life'. To acknowledge continuities between the prewar and wartime eras is essentially to recognize that postwar El Salvador cannot be under-stood without considering how its political and economic structures were founded, how they have transformed over time, and how aspects of these structures have endured even in the face of contemporary transformations.

In this book I use the term 'legacies' to refer to prevailing prewar and wartime processes, structures, and dispositions. Since there are a number of aspects of the past to which I refer by legacies, I find it necessary to unravel why the term is useful to describe the continuities between war-time and postwar El Salvador and exactly what continuities it denotes in this book. Burawoy and Verdery (1999: 7) have argued that metaphors such as legacies do not adequately evoke the creativity with which transi-tions to postsocialism have occurred. Nevertheless, my use of 'legacies' to account for El Salvador's transformations throughout its transition to democracy lies precisely in my attempt to convey the relationship between this country's contemporary problems, including the persistence of vio-lence, and inherited elements of statecraft and citizenship. By using the metaphor of 'legacies' I seek to evoke how certain aspects of past pro-cesses, structures, and dispositions—both material and ideational—remain salient despite their refashioning and do not facilitate further transformations. By prewar and war legacies I refer fundamentally to El Salvador's processes of statecraft and citizenship but also to elements such as haunting war memories.

To understand the processes of state and class formation underlying the outbreak of El Salvador's civil war, as well as how the country's political and economic structures are resistant to deep change, it is necessary to revise the country's history. Explanations for the genesis of contemporary El Salvador's unequal social structure have generally focused on the expansion of the nineteenth-century agro-export economy and on coffee as the key product that triggered land accumulation by the small elite controlling the post-colonial state (see Browning 1971; Lindo-Fuentes 1990; Paige 1997). The liberal reforms of 1881 and 1882 that abolished the ejidos and communal lands (the latter belonging to the Indian population) are considered by these studies to have contributed to the consolidation of the country's landed elite, the proletarianization of the landless population, and the socio-economic inequality that has persisted through the present day. Lauria-Santiago's (1999: 2–6) critique of these elite-centered analyses, however, suggests a rather different origin of El Salvador's twentieth-century social structure. His study of El Salvador's peasant economy downplays the role of international trade, coffee, and the liberal state in the process of land accumulation. He suggests that while it was in the nineteenth century that the conditions of possibility for the formation of the elite were laid, it was not until the 1920s that El Salvador saw the consolidation of, on one hand, the economic and political elite that dominated the country throughout the twentieth century and, on the other, the increasing landless population (1999: 155, 157–162). Indeed, Lauria-Santiago (1999: 132–133) argues that until then, El Salvador's landholding pattern had been characterized by the coexistence of large farms and small properties, all participating in coffee production. It was indeed through the concentration of processing, export, and finance activities, rather than simply land, that the country's elite formed.

Despite these discrepancies within the country's historiography, what seems clear is that the foundations of the elite and the class structure and inequality that characterize contemporary El Salvador must be traced back to at least the beginning of the twentieth century. This is not to suggest that the elite class has remained unchanged or that it can be considered a monolithic group. Two relatively distinct factions have conformed El Salvador's elite throughout much of the twentieth century: the 'agrarian' and the 'agro-industrial' (Paige 1993, 1997; see also Baloyra 1982:

22–32). While the wealth of the agrarian elite was distinctively attached to land and coffee production, the members of the agro-industrial elite diminished their reliance on agriculture by making incursions into other economic sectors throughout the twentieth century, while still participating in coffee growing as well as in the associated processing and export activities. Familial and entrepreneurial links between members of the country's two elite factions allowed them to consolidate their power vis-à-vis reforms affecting their mutual interests. It was precisely through inter-marriage and entrepreneurial alliances that the Salvadoran elites reproduced their power over time (Paniagua Serrano 2002), thereby following dynastic patterns similar to those of other Central American elites (see Casáus Arzú 1992; Paige 1997: 15–22).

The relatively distinct nature of the wealth of El Salvador's two elite factions did not preclude them from closing ranks when it came to political decisions (Paige 1993: 7–8; Paniagua Serrano 2002: 688–689). Both factions coalesced with the military after 1931, thereby maintaining a symbiotic relationship in which the military resorted to coercion and repression to maintain a status quo that benefited the military governments and the economic elite alike. The resort to coercion and repression by the state is epitomized by the army's violent crushing of the 1932 peasant rebellion that originated in western El Salvador against General Martínez's dictatorship and was officially claimed to have been organized by the then-recently founded Salvadoran Communist Party (PCS) (Anderson 1971; López Bernal 2007; Gould and Lauria-Santiago 2008). From that point until the war, the army's recurrent pattern of repression against alleged insurgents for the purpose of legitimizing its political power vis-à-vis the elite led Stanley (1996) to deploy the analogy of El Salvador's military state as a 'protection racket'. Indeed, the military-controlled police forces, particularly the National Guard, provided security to hacienda and business owners and enforced labor discipline throughout the twentieth century (Alvarenga 1996: 85, 145–146; Stanley 1996: 48–49, 72). Yet, within the military-elite alliance, the former wielded enough power that tensions sometimes erupted between the two (Stanley 1996: 58–59; Paige 1997: 29; Williams and Walter 1997: 9–10).

The political liberalization of the 1960s that ended El Salvador's one-party rule and introduced competitive elections alongside the country's increasing urbanization, industrial growth, and rise in public spending allowed for the proliferation of opposition political parties and reform-minded popular mobilization (Almeida 2008: 70–102). Popular mobilization decayed, however, in the early 1970s, after electoral fraud and a reversal of political liberalization—partly influenced by the support of United States military and intelligence for El Salvador's government—demonstrated the futility of reform-minded strategies (Stanley 1996: 80–83). The trade unions, student organizations, and church-related movements—including peasant organizations, cooperatives, and Ecclesial Base Communities (CEBs)[24] that developed mainly in the rural areas—of the 1960s persisted nonetheless and constituted the basis of subsequent radicalized political activity (Almeida 2008: 97–98). The activity and protests by this constellation of organizations increasingly gained momentum during the 1970s, partly due to the increase in state repression that culminated in the outbreak of civil war in 1980. As explained earlier, the war was essentially a popular uprising against a status quo of concentration and exploitation by elites and increasing repression by the military government.

The 1979 reformist coup by junior military officers, in alliance with a coalition of political progressive sectors led by the PDC, sought to avoid a conflict that seemed imminent and to implement political and economic reforms (Baloyra 1982: 86–96; Segovia 2002: 10–18). Even though the coup failed to avert war, it was successful at deposing the government of General Romero, as well as displacing from power the PCN, the military party that had ruled for 18 years, and the traditional landed elite. A military junta was formed after the coup and subsequently dissolved when its civilian members abandoned it; a second junta was created out of an alliance between the military and the PDC. With support from the United States, this junta enacted a policy of 'reform and repression' consisting of the nationalization of the banking sector and coffee and sugar exports, land reform,[25] and the heavy repression of the Salvadoran population. The reforms were

[24] Ecclesial Base Communities were formed in El Salvador's rural areas as well as in other Latin American countries from the late 1960s, linked to parishes led by priests who embraced liberation theology, in order to promote critical and progressive religious practice. The activity of CEBs contributed in turn to increased political participation in rural areas.

[25] The land reform promoted by the United States and implemented by the PDC from the early 1980s consisted of three stages, of which only the first (expropriation of large estates and their transformation into cooperatives) and third (the legal titling of individually owned plots) phases were implemented. Phase two, which would have had the largest impact in terms of the amount of land expropriated and redistributed, was never enacted (Byrne 1996: 73). Since the land initially managed by cooperatives was divided into small parcels and redistributed in the late 1980s, both implemented phases ultimately sought to generate a land market while weakening the landed elite and diminishing support for guerrillas among the rural population (Robinson 2003: 92).

insufficient to solve the country's structural problems, but they did negatively impact the interests of the traditional landed elite and marked a decisive shift in the balance of power that had existed between the two elite factions (Robinson 2003: 88). In 1981, the agrarian elite contributed to founding the ARENA party in order to recover the power lost after the 1979 reformist coup.

Founded as an anti-communist and nationalist party by the most conservative sector of the Salvadoran elite, which had traditionally supported hardline measures, ARENA initially advocated counterinsurgency actions against the FMLN and its allies among the Salvadoran population. Although ARENA lost the 1984 presidential election to the PDC, its victory in the 1989 presidential election, three years before the signing of the Peace Accords, marked the return of the economic elite to power (Segovia 2002: 30). Yet the faction of the elite that gained power in 1989 was radically different, both on the basis of its wealth and ideologically, from the one that had preceded it (Paige 1997: 23–24, 36–37; Font Fàbregas 1998; Robinson 2003: 95). After the Second World War, the diversification of El Salvador's export economy had allowed for the emergence of a new class of industrialists; later, the 1979 coup and the reforms that followed contributed to a further reconfiguration of the elite by weakening the agrarian faction and ultimately benefiting the more progressive agro-industrial faction (Paige 1997: 29; Robinson 2003: 87–102). ARENA was elected when its leadership shifted to the agro-industrial faction of the elite that advocated an end to the war so as to stimulate business through participation in an increasingly globalized economy.

The perpetuation of El Salvador's elite has represented a degree of continuity that manifests not just materially—that is, in the ongoing concentration of political and economic capital—but also as a haunting presence in ordinary Salvadorans' memories. I invoke here the notion of 'haunting' employed by Gordon (1997). Gordon considers 'haunting' to describe a 'ghostly presence' that is invisible yet manifests through certain symptoms. This kind of invisible presence is particularly clear with regard to memories concerning wartime violence and the wartime state (see Chap. 3). ARENA, having governed the country from 1989 to 2009, has represented a troubling presence for a large number of the ordinary Salvadorans who lived through the war. Although founded after the war had already begun, ARENA originated in an alliance between the military and the faction of the elite that advocated repression. One of ARENA's main founders, Major Roberto D'Aubuisson, is widely reputed to have orchestrated

Archbishop Romero's[26] assassination and instigated the country's death squads (United Nations 1993: 180, 185). Given that ARENA ruled the country for 17 years after the war ended, and given that wartime human rights violations have not been addressed as recommended by the Commission on the Truth, continuity has come to manifest itself through the recurrence of haunting memories.

It is thus not surprising that postwar ethnographies have highlighted the need to recognize the great degree of continuity between wartime and postwar El Salvador (see Binford 1996; Lauria-Santiago and Binford 2004; Silber 2011). This book further seeks to show how the war and postwar eras are related through inherited problems. Yet, as Burawoy and Verdery (1999: 14) have suggested, 'we cannot conceive of the transition as either rooted in the past or tied to an imagined future. Transition is a process suspended between the two'. Although they are referring to transitions from socialism to postsocialism, I would argue the same claim of ambiguity holds for El Salvador's transition to democracy. Likewise, nor can the present be understood as a complete rupture with the past. Yet, notwithstanding the prevalence of prewar and war legacies in contemporary El Salvador, there are also emergent processes, such as the country's neoliberalization, that have contributed to shaping the country's democratization process.

Neoliberalization

In the 1990s, El Salvador's agro-export model of accumulation collapsed, partly as a result of the agrarian reform of the 1980s, and was gradually replaced by a new economic model that allowed for a substantial breadth of participation by traditional elite families as well as a degree of elite recomposition. A think-tank, the Salvadoran Foundation for Economic and Social Development (FUSADES), had been founded in 1983 by members of the country's elite, with funding from the United States Agency for International Development (USAID) and training from economists from the Chicago School that promoted free-market economics (Segovia 2002: 27). FUSADES's technocrats represented the financial, manufacturing, and transnationalized rather than agrarian-based coffee

---

[26] Romero was the archbishop of San Salvador from 1977 to 1980, when he was killed. Although initially pro-elite, Romero radically changed his attitude due to El Salvador's increasingly violent conjuncture and the influence of liberation theology (see Chap. 6).

elite (Paige 1997: 37; Robinson 2003: 95–97). In 1989, ARENA won El Salvador's presidential elections, giving FUSADES a more direct impact on policy. Indeed, FUSADES's board of directors was composed of members of the notorious elite families that had controlled and modernized ARENA from 1988 (Paige 1997: 36–37; Robinson 2003: 95). FUSADES's 1989 report, entitled Hacia una Economía de Mercado en El Salvador [Towards a Market Economy in El Salvador] (see DEES 1989), designed an economic liberalization proposal for El Salvador—a sort of 'shock therapy' that would jolt the country into recovering from the economic impasse caused by the war and the crisis of the agricultural sector.

After coming to power in 1989, ARENA followed a trend in the Global South and implemented a program of rapid economic liberalization in order to gain support from international financial organizations (Segovia 2002: 32). While USAID had supervised the country's economic policy in the 1980s, the International Monetary Fund (IMF), World Bank (WB), and Inter-American Development Bank (IDB) did so from the 1990s (Segovia 2002: 33).[27] The government deregulated interest rates and the prices of a large number of products, suppressed the state monopoly on the external commerce of coffee and sugar, and reversed the nationalization of the banking system (Segovia 2002: 37). Although the first ARENA government had designed the restructuring of the public sector as well as tariff barriers and fiscal reforms, it was not until Calderón Sol's administration, from 1994, that a large program of privatization (telecommunications, ports and airports, electric energy, and social security) and reform (tariff barriers and taxes) was undertaken (Segovia 2002: 44). These measures sought to attract foreign investment and integrate the Salvadoran and United States economies with the final aim of 'turning El Salvador into an offshore zone of maquila,[28] financial and market services' (Segovia 2002: 44). The dollarization implemented in 2001 by the ARENA government headed by Francisco Flores and the ratification of the Dominican Republic-Central America Free Trade Agreement (CAFTA-DR) in 2004 by the next ARENA administration would come to consolidate El Salvador's economic liberalization and increasing integration with the United States economy. The

---

[27]From the 1980s, both the IMF and WB attached policy conditionalities, specifically structural adjustment programs, to their loans (Paris 2004: 29). Yet the adoption of these programs was not simply a response to the pressure of international organizations; neoliberal policies were enthusiastically embraced by the ARENA governments (Paige 1997: 51; Robinson 2003: 87–102).

[28]A maquila is a factory in which products are assembled by a low-cost labor force.

transformations implemented by ARENA since 1989, alongside the collapse of traditional agricultural exports and the increasing role of remittances, gave way to a new model of accumulation in the country (Segovia 2002: 222; Robinson 2003: 87–102). These transformations necessarily had an impact on the composition of the country's elite.

Interestingly, the composition of the boards of directors of El Salvador's main privatized companies revealed the inter-linkages, both matrimonial and entrepreneurial, among those companies controlled by the handful of elite families belonging to the modernized agro-industrial faction (Paniagua Serrano 2002; Robinson 2003: 98). This process of concentration has led to the designation of the elite as 'the hegemonic entrepreneurial block' (Paniagua Serrano 2002). Even as divisions and tensions remained between the faction of the elite rooted in coffee growing and the agro-industrial faction that benefited from neoliberal policies, the two have politically converged in ARENA.[29] In El Salvador, it is thus clear that neoliberalization has been a project by which the country's elite has restored its power and consolidated itself; indeed, some would argue that this is the essence of neoliberalism worldwide (see Duménil and Lévy 2004; Harvey 2005: 16–19). Arguably, neoliberalization has involved processes of statecraft that have not simply destroyed the basis of previous economic and political structures but have created others or consolidated existing ones anew. The Marxist concept of 'creative destruction' (Harvey 2006), along with the delineation of the initial dismantling of the state (*roll-back*) and the subsequent redefinition and retasking of the state (*roll-out*) (Peck and Tickell 2002), captures the contradictory processes involved in neoliberalization.

The reconfiguration and parallel consolidation of the country's elite points to the limitations of the 1992 Peace Accords that put an end to El Salvador's civil war. During the peace negotiations leading up to the Accords, the FMLN emphasized demilitarization and the reform of the

[29] However, the elite divisions have sparked constant intraparty tensions, and the loss of votes and affiliates to the PCN in the late 1990s and to the Great Alliance for National Unity (GANA) after 2009. Following the electoral defeat of ARENA in 2009, former president Elías Antonio Saca was expelled in an attempt by the Cristiani-led faction of ARENA to regain control of the party from a new generation of politicians relatively independent of the traditional elite (Réserve 2016: 180–183). As a reaction, Saca and the faction of the party that supported him founded GANA. This party, which competed in the 2012 municipal and legislative elections for the first time, has contributed to dividing the rightwing share of vote and weakening ARENA.

country's institutions of order, with the result that the neoliberal economic reforms already underway went largely uncontested during the 1990s. Paradoxically, while demilitarization was the central reform pursued by the Accords, ongoing public insecurity has legitimized increasing remilitarization by the ARENA governments during the postwar era, especially during the early 2000s. This increase defied certain aspects of the Peace Accords mandate; for example, Salvadoran military forces have been used to enforce public security in the streets and prisons even though the Peace Accords had stipulated that the military be relegated to external security functions. The initial *roll-back* of the social components of the state has, in other words, been coupled with a *roll-out* of its military and punitive components. This situation is not unique to El Salvador but indeed mimics United States statecraft (see Wacquant 2009a, b; Zilberg 2007, 2011). Paige (1997: 50) argues that in contrast to Central American nineteenth-century liberalism, which avowed economic liberalization but advocated important state intervention, neoliberalism has facilitated a wholesale reduction of the state. Yet a primary role of the neoliberal state has remained to create and maintain the conditions in which business can develop and flourish (Harvey 2005: 79).

Neoliberalization, which as we shall see persisted after the FMLN took office in 2009, has necessarily impacted El Salvador's democratization process. Yet neoliberalization is not just the elite-led enactment of an economic doctrine; it is also a process that produces new modes of governing, regulatory relationships, and social life itself (Gledhill 2004b: 240; Ong 2006: 3). In this process, political rights and values that are assumed to strengthen 'civil society' within a democracy—including freedom, equality, empowerment, and participation—are held up as virtues and yet at the same time stripped of their meaning by being put to the service of market-driven economies (Gledhill 2004b: 342; Harvey 2005: 36–38). Neoliberalization was achieved in El Salvador through techniques promoted by internationally funded postwar development projects that molded and regulated political subjects' actions and aspirations even as these projects simultaneously served, at least in former FMLN strongholds or repopulated areas, to promote oppositional politics (see Silber 2011: 118–134). In this sense, the deep transformations that ordinary people hoped would occur throughout El Salvador's transition to democracy have been limited and largely turned to the advantage of a parallel process of economic liberalization (Robinson 2003: 101).

Moodie (2010) has described how neoliberalization shaped political subjectivities in the aftermath of El Salvador's war. The crime stories that circulated during this period not only produced a resignification of violence but also impacted how ordinary people strategized within this new context. In contrast to the collective strategizing that characterized the wartime era, San Salvadorans managed postwar risks and insecurities privately, thus accommodating themselves to the self-responsible citizenship promoted by El Salvador's liberal market democracy (Moodie 2010: 110). El Salvador's liberal market democracy likewise affected value regimes concerning death: in the aftermath of war, death was divested of the public value it had had during wartime in the eyes of the international community, and became increasingly individualized (Moodie 2006). It is thus clear that even as the transition from war to peace has been influenced by inherited legacies, it has also taken new directions, opened new opportunities, and deepened certain problems. Throughout this book I examine El Salvador's violent democracy with attention to its correlations with the country's process of neoliberalization, as revealed by ordinary people's modes of reasoning and citizenship practices.

LOCATING FIELDWORK

This research is based on a one-year stretch of ethnographic fieldwork undertaken from early August 2008, as well as on follow-up one-month trips in December 2010 and February 2014. Santiago Nonualco, the second largest municipality in the south-central La Paz Department,[30] with fewer than 40,000 inhabitants, was my home base and the main site of my research (see Fig. 1.1). A predominantly rural municipality, Santiago consists of 6 *barrios* (urban neighborhoods) and the 22 *cantones* (rural areas) that surround the urban nucleus and are populated by two-thirds of Santiago's population (Bonilla Alvarado 1995: 3–4; DIGESTYC 2007). The population's main economic pursuits in the postwar era have been sugarcane agriculture and cattle raising, commerce, and small-scale manufacturing (see FUNDE 2013). A number of professionals and service-sector employees who live in central Santiago commute daily to Zacatecoluca (La Paz's departmental capital) or San Salvador, the latter over an hour's bus trip away. Since Santiago has no industries, and both agriculture and cattle

---

[30] A department is an administrative regional division equivalent to a province.

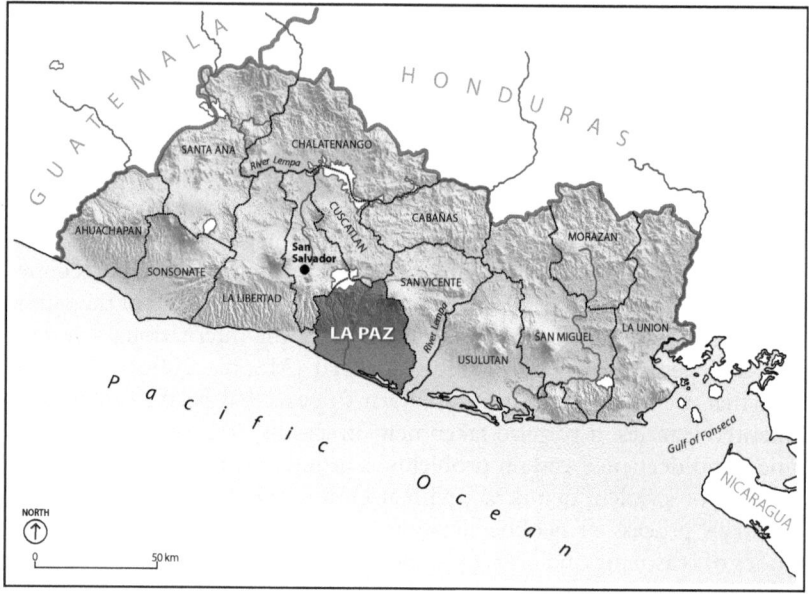

Fig. 1.1   Map of El Salvador

raising have steadily declined, an increasing number of Santiagueñas[31] started working in the maquilas of the offshore zone El Pedregal—located within the department and a half-hour bus trip from Santiago—or have migrated to San Salvador or the United States.

During my fieldwork research in 2008/2009 I stayed with a female-headed, three-generation family who lives in a central neighborhood of Santiago and with whom I had developed close ties since meeting them in 2001. Although it was my previous knowledge of the municipality and personal connection with this family that defined the location of my research, there were a number of reasons why Santiago and its neighboring towns and municipalities prompted interesting research questions and issues. To begin with, being predominantly rural, Santiago allowed me to explore postwar violence in a different context than previous ethnographic

---

[31] Throughout the book, I use the Spanish demonym as a short form for 'residents of Santiago'. Because the Spanish language lacks a gender-neutral form, I use both the feminine (Santiagueñas) and masculine (Santiagueños) interchangeably to refer to both men and women unless I specify otherwise.

research that has focused on similar issues yet was largely urban-based. This is relevant since in 2009, aside from the San Salvador and San Miguel departments, the majority of homicides occurred in El Salvador's rural areas (see IML 2009: 579–580). Meanwhile, Santiago afforded me the opportunity to explore questions about wartime and postwar geographies of violence and what contributed to their delineation. The municipality's geographic characteristics (i.e. the flatter condition of the southern lands in which Santiago is located and which made it difficult for the guerrillas to hide during the war, in contrast to the country's mountainous north), as well as its hacienda-centered past, most likely had an important impact on political participation and patterns of violence in the area during the war.

Given that most research in El Salvador has been conducted in former war zones (see, for instance, Pearce 1986; Binford 1996; Wood 2003; Silber 2011; Sprenkels 2014) or in the capital (see Hume 2009a; Moodie 2010), my research offers a contrasting view of the country's wartime and postwar experiences. The south-central La Paz region is not considered a former war zone, nor has Santiago been one of the country's most violent municipalities in the postwar era.[32] In this sense, Santiago provides a context for interesting questions about memory-building processes within population groups that can be presumed to be much more variegated than those of former war zones. Not only does Santiago's population support various parties across the political spectrum, but a large part of its population was displaced from former war zones in the 1980s, when violence had abated in Santiago itself. Interestingly enough, Santiago's relatively low rates of postwar homicidal violence—at least compared to neighboring Zacatecoluca and San Juan Nonualco—also allowed me to investigate how fear operates via a conjuring of the violence that occurs elsewhere in the country.

In addition, Santiago makes an interesting location for a study of the country's political life and the extent to which wartime political cleavages between ARENA and FMLN persist, due to local support for both these parties as well as the significant presence of a third party, the PCN. Santiago

[32] According to the Institute of Forensic Medicine (IML), 1134 homicides occurred in La Paz between 2001 and 2008, making this department the sixth most violent of the 14 into which El Salvador is divided (IML 2009: 56). However, this was largely due to the high number of homicides occurring in Zacatecoluca, which by the end of the decade was considered to be among the ten municipalities with the highest risk of homicide (see IML 2009: 127, 129).

was governed by the PCN from 2000 to 2012 and had previously been governed by the PDC and ARENA. Since the 18 January 2009 municipal and legislative elections and the 15 March 2009 presidential election were held during the main period of research on which this book is based, the possibility of studying the country's ongoing political cleavages arose as a relevant issue through the fieldwork period. The overlapping of my fieldwork with all three elections—which coincided for only the second time since the end of the war—shaped my research in ways I had only partially anticipated. Indeed, two-thirds of my fieldwork was defined largely by the electoral agendas of the political parties in Santiago and beyond, as well as by the milieu of menace and distrust that existed during the campaign (for more details about how the hostile milieu of the elections interfered with my research, see Chap. 5).

When I arrived in El Salvador in August 2008, all political parties were already deeply enmeshed in election-related activities, even though the electoral season had not officially begun. As some of my friends and acquaintances were involved in the campaigns, and given the overwhelming sway of these campaigns in the country's social and political life, I ended up dividing my time among meetings of all the contending parties. Much of my research, both during and after the elections, has drawn on informal conversations with Santiagueños and other Salvadorans about political as well as mundane issues. At the end of my year's research and during follow-up trips, I conducted formal interviews that allowed me to delve more deeply into certain aspects of what I had learned in my more informal conversations. I also followed media coverage of election-related matters and ongoing violence—mostly via printed media and occasionally via television and radio.

The people among whom I did research came from across the political spectrum, from both urban and rural areas, various age and gender groups, and different religious sensibilities. My ability to obtain the views and perspectives of a variegated range of people was partly due to my attending, and at times participating in, the activities of different political parties, popular organizations and religious groups, along with my frequent visits with relatives and friends of the family I lived with. However, the majority of the people with whom I developed close ties, because of shared political views and experiences, were left-leaning and had lived through the war. Considering the spatialized Left–Right metaphor that is typically employed to describe Latin America's political spectrum, I consider 'left-leaning' to denote a range of positions within the Left, from outright FMLN loyalists to those who position themselves as ideologically affine to the Left but do not clearly identify with the FMLN, the country's only leftwing party,[33] or feel largely disappointed by it. I thus include in this category, but do not limit it to, Salvadorans who have developed a 'post-insurgent individuality', that is, former rebels or populations supportive of the FMLN guerrillas whose insurgent socialization has inevitably shaped their postwar maneuvering (see Binford 2013; Sprenkels 2014).[34] My close relationships with left-leaning Salvadorans have undeniably colored my arguments and given shape to much of this book, as participant observation inevitably yields coproduced knowledge.

One of the main organizations with which I worked closely was the Father Cosme Spessotto Committee, a liberation theology-minded group composed of relatives of war victims devoted to writing the history of the war in La Paz and honoring war victims. Given the crucial role of religion in El Salvador's everyday life and public opinion, in addition to participating in religion-centered commemorative events organized by the committee, I joined friends when they attended mass at one of the two Catholic parishes in central Santiago. Although a significant portion of the municipality's population is Catholic, a diverse array of Evangelical and Pentecostal churches with roots in the United States have increasingly attracted many. Interestingly, in Santiago, most Evangelical and Pentecostal Christian churches, in contrast to Catholic ones, demonstrably cut across social divides such as political affiliation and social class. On at least a few occasions I also attended the religious services (*cultos*) of some of these churches.

While my fieldwork was grounded in Santiago, it also took me throughout La Paz and beyond. I traveled frequently to neighboring Zacatecoluca, San Juan Nonualco, and San Rafael Obrajuelo, all of them municipalities a short bus trip away from Santiago via the Coastal Road that runs parallel to the coast (see Fig. 1.2), as well as to San Salvador. I attended countless FMLN meetings and rallies throughout the department because, as a close friend of FMLN loyalists, I could easily participate in this party's electoral events and travel safely with party members—a level of access I did not enjoy with other political parties. Participation in the activities of a few grassroots organizations, especially the Father Cosme Spessotto Committee's mourning activities held at different sites in La Paz, also took me throughout the

---

[33] Although in the past there have been other leftwing or Center–Left alternatives, these have never obtained any significant support and eventually dissolved.

[34] Although both Binford and Sprenkels refer to Salvadorans from former war zones, some of Santiago's residents migrated from those regions and had socialized as insurgents or joined popular organizations linked with the FMLN.

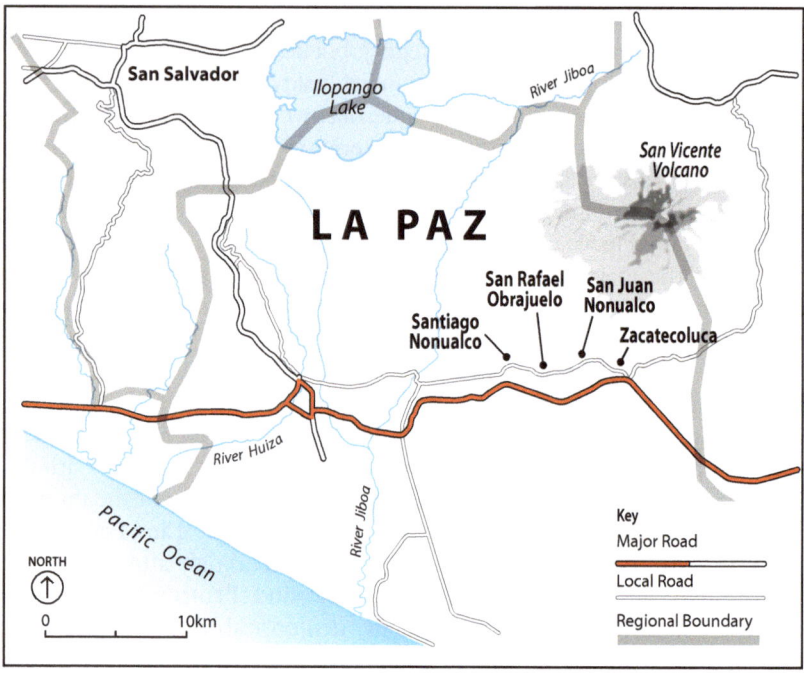

Fig. 1.2   Map of La Paz

department and to the capital. Finally, sharing time with friends meant that I also traveled to other regions of El Salvador. These trips were motivated not just by the aims of my research but also by the occasional need to escape the stresses of conducting research on violence and political division, especially during the highly polarized 2009 electoral campaign. My return for follow-up research in 2010 and again in 2014, and subsequent trips for other research purposes, have allowed me to keep up with the reverberations of the FMLN victory in the 2009 presidential election.

A Map of the Book

I argue in this book that violence has become intrinsic to how Salvadorans imagine and perform democracy as well as to how El Salvador's democracy works. El Salvador's postwar violence is not merely a wartime residue. Nor is it a transient phenomenon or one unleashed by the transition to democracy. In postwar El Salvador, violence is part and parcel of its democratic regime rather than a feature of an unfinished or failed democratization process that diverges from a democratic ideal type. Crucially, democracy can take on different meanings and denote myriad political forms. El Salvador's is a liberal market democracy that has incorporated both public and economic insecurity. It is a democracy very different from the one that many ordinary Salvadorans had hoped for at the end of the war—one that has accommodated forms of violence whose roots reach back to the country's pre-war and wartime eras. I thus examine ethnographically the kinds of violence that ordinary Salvadorans have experienced in the postwar era and how they relate this violence to various political events and processes, both contemporary and historical. Rather than pinpointing a single explanation, I surmise that ordinary people's difficulty in explaining El Salvador's postwar violence lies in its layered nature, that is, not only the multiplicity of violent actors but also the myriad connections among these actors and various political and economic processes. I also suggest that a politics of (in)visibility is at work that further complicates efforts at understanding a violent democracy like El Salvador's.

The book is divided into two parts. The chapters that make up Part I, A Violent Democracy, explore how violence is built into the country's political life and the relationship that ordinary people perceive between El Salvador's problem of violence and processes of statecraft. Chapter 2 introduces Santiago Nonualco and describes the forms of violence and the violent actors that have characterized both the wartime and postwar eras in this municipality as well as much of El Salvador. In so doing, the chapter unpacks the notion of violence and explores the continuities that have become evident between wartime and peacetime forms of violence. In light of the persistence of violence in the postwar era, this chapter problematizes El Salvador's much-lauded democratization process and the transition paradigm that underpins it, avowing the need for more research that engages ethnographically with aspects of democratization and peacebuilding. Each of the subsequent chapters analyzes one aspect of the entanglement between violence and democracy in postwar El Salvador.

Chapter 3 explores how ordinary people make sense of postwar violence. A multiplicity of actors, criminal activities, and connections among them is at work, but these have been partly eclipsed by the government's as well as the Salvadoran media's portrayal of gangs as the country's main problem of public insecurity. This chapter shows how the official representation of violence, along with the grayness of political life, has contributed to making violence largely unintelligible in the eyes of ordinary people. Against this background, I explore how interpretations of violence are shaped by political subjectivities. Chapter 4 examines the relationship between the country's seemingly unintelligible violence and the neoliberalization that began in 1989. Public militarization has been promoted as one of the state's main tasks—even though the Peace Accords had aimed at limiting the *mano dura* of the state—and this public militarization coexists with a burgeoning private security industry. In this chapter I examine how the privatization of protection is perceived by ordinary people to have reconfigured anew the relationship between statecraft and violence. In juxtaposing licit and illicit economies of violence, the chapter also suggests that a mutual resemblance seems to have developed between postwar criminals and political actors. Chapter 5 focuses on electoral participation, an archetypal democratic citizenship practice. El Salvador's 2009 electoral campaign was characterized by heightened hostilities and fears, which in turn arose out of wartime divisions that had acquired wide currency among active political opponents as well as among neighbors and acquaintances. Observation of this campaign yielded insights into how violence pervades El Salvador's political culture, which is deeply rooted in wartime, even as wartime political cleavages have become increasingly diffused.

Part II, Toward Substantive Democracy, shifts attention to two processes that carried the promise of deepening democracy and were therefore able to foster hopeful envisioning: first, the memory work performed by ordinary Salvadorans, and, second, the 2009 FMLN victory. Chapter 6 examines postwar memory work through the praxis of the residents of La Paz who participate in the Father Cosme Spessotto Committee. The chapter shows how memory-building practices have engaged with human rights discourses as the language that has dominated democratization processes since the 1990s. It explores the outcomes of the committee's endeavors to transform El Salvador's current violent democracy via a reassessment of the wartime past. Chapter 7 explores the political imaginaries attached to the FMLN victory in the 2009 presidential election and how this party's victory affected the citizenship practices of ordinary people in the aftermath of the election—especially as large numbers of Santiagueños took action to resolve their pressing economic and social problems. It examines how Santiagueños' sudden attempts to address these problems impacted postwar citizenship practices and what this revealed about Salvadorans' postwar political subjectivities.

The conclusion, and the book as a whole, demonstrate the concrete ways in which various forms of violence and democracy have become entangled, and how these entanglements have in turn impacted citizenship practices and political subjectivities. A corollary of the book's argument is that violence may typify democracy as much as it does explicitly illiberal regimes. The postwar violence and insecurity experienced by ordinary Salvadorans highlight the correlations between the persistence of violence and contemporary processes such as the pervasiveness of war legacies and the country's neoliberalization. Meanwhile, El Salvador's democratic governments, in contrast to earlier regimes, have overtly employed certain forms of legitimate violence (e.g. *mano dura* policies) while contributing to concealing more patently illegitimate forms of violence or connections between violent actors and political actors. A politics of (in)visibility, which plays out through a combination of hyper-visibility and shadows, has thus contributed to the sanitizing of El Salvador's violent democracy. This selective representation of postwar violence has foregrounded violent actors such as gangs and eclipsed their connections with political actors and the country's political life as well as other sources of insecurity and violence. The public face of El Salvador's democracy thus conceals a complex dynamic between onstage and backstage political domains, with roots in earlier authoritarian regimes. This book has relevance for the analysis of other countries that, having transitioned from authoritarianism to violent democracy, combine transparency and murk to manufacture the legitimacy of their new regime.

Lastly, the Epilogue returns to the question of whether the party shift, on the one hand, and memory work, on the other, may have worked to imbue democracy with new meanings and ultimately to transform the country's violent democracy—an idea embraced by various segments of Salvadoran society in 2009. While yearnings for change did surround both these processes, I suggest here—in light of events that have transpired in recent years—that the 2009 party shift was not the historic turning point that it initially seemed to be, nor has memory work progressed enough to substantially enable the justice-based future envisioned by those leading it.

PART I

A Violent Democracy

CHAPTER 2

The Fallacy of the Telos of Transition

Violence and fear, far from being confined to El Salvador's wartime past, have become commingled with and incorporated into the country's democracy. Their postwar manifestations have both resembled and differed from those of wartime, thus evidencing El Salvador's contradictory transformations since the signing of Peace Accords in 1992. In this chapter, I describe the various forms of violence and violent actors that have typified the war and postwar eras in Santiago Nonualco. Santiago is not reputed for its degree of violence, either during the war or during the decades that followed. However, there are specific ways in which wartime and postwar violence have impacted this municipality that resonate with those in the rest of the country. In describing this violence, I introduce Santiago as well as some of the events and actors that will appear throughout the book. I begin this chapter with a brief retrospective reconstruction of the wartime violence that occurred in Las Ánimas—one of the sectors of Santiago most harshly impacted by the war. This reconstruction, which briefly describes how the war unfolded in a rural area of Santiago, is conveyed through the memories of some of this area's inhabitants, in part due to the absence of any written account of how the war affected La Paz. The historical period of the war is documented through my research on, and attendance of, the mourning activities of the Father Cosme Spessotto Committee, a grassroots organization active in La Paz. I continue with a description of the various forms of violence and violent actors—documented

© The Author(s) 2018
A. Montoya, *The Violence of Democracy*, Studies of the Americas,
https://doi.org/10.1007/978-3-319-76330-9_2

through conversations, rumors, and media accounts—that appeared relevant during my fieldwork in Santiago in 2008 and 2009. These two sections unpack the notion of violence, which would otherwise remain highly elusive and abstract. In so doing, they expose the ambiguity lurking in distinctions typically drawn among various categories of violence, as well as between violence and cognate notions such as war, crime, and fear.

This chapter's synoptic representation of the war and postwar eras in Santiago follows mainstream representations of El Salvador's violence—representations that have depicted a transition from political to depoliticized forms of violence, from death squads and guerrillas to gangs, and from rural to urban areas. These mainstream representations will be challenged in the remaining chapters. In addition, the apparent distinctions between wartime and postwar violence notwithstanding, the postwar era's continuity of violence as an everyday phenomenon and its entrenchment in the country's democracy provide a platform on which to critique the tenets of the transition paradigm. In the last section, I suggest that the persistence of everyday violence and in turn personal insecurity—a persistence that betrays the contradictory nature of El Salvador's transition to democracy—has been downplayed by those members of the international community and Salvadoran governments who have persistently lauded the country's democratization process. In problematizing the telos of transition, this chapter sheds light on the nature of the democracy that has resulted. An emphasis on proceduralism and the introduction of neoliberal engineering characterized the transformation of the country's political and economic institutions from wartime to the postwar era. The procedural, rather than substantive, nature of the transformation largely explains the pessimism that I encountered among Salvadorans during my fieldwork, even after the 'historic' 2009 FMLN victory, which succeeded in instilling only a short-lived hope in the Salvadoran population (see Montoya 2015).

Remembering Wartime Violence

During my fieldwork I was able to document an endeavor to write 'history from below'[1] through my participation in the activities of the Father Cosme Spessotto Committee, a non-funded grassroots organization

---

[1] 'History from below' seeks to convey the perspective and experience of ordinary people often neglected by mainstream historical paradigms, which have focused on national scale, great events, and great men (Sharpe 1991). Interestingly, the history from below that the

composed of relatives of war victims and born out of a desire to redress wartime offenses. Founded in 2005, this organization, based in Zacatecoluca, set as its main goals the research of wartime human rights violations in the municipalities of La Paz and the writing of the history of the war as it occurred in this department. In addition to this endeavor, committee members have held mourning events at the sites of some of the wartime massacres and assassinations that occurred in La Paz. The goal of these events has been twofold: first, to deal collectively with and alleviate the grief of families who lost relatives during the war, and, second, to forestall an oblivion about the war and its victims that has appeared ineluctable given the public silence[2] that has prevailed since the war with regard to wartime human rights violations. Through my participation in the monthly meetings and mourning events of the Father Cosme Spessotto Committee, as well as through collaboration in their research, I learned about the unorthodox and neglected history of the war in La Paz. Since it was the civil war that attracted international attention to El Salvador, this region's location outside the country's former war zones—generally identified as the northern and eastern regions, where guerrillas could find relatively easy refuge in the mountainous landscape along with support from local peasant populations—is at the root of its exclusion from research.[3]

Research by committee members has shown that the war significantly impacted the municipalities of La Paz, especially those like Santiago with rural areas in the foothills of the Chichontepec Volcano (also known as the San Vicente Volcano).[4] This volcano, which delineates the border between the La Paz and San Vicente departments, was itself the site of numerous armed skirmishes between the army and guerrillas as well as a hideout (along with San Salvador) for many refugees from La Paz who were displaced during the war. The narratives collected through my research

Father Cosme Spessotto Committee members have intended to write has been documented by the ordinary people themselves.

[2] Here I should note that there is some question as to how silent 'public silence' actually is. In El Salvador, silence prevails even in the face of a recurrent, and formulaic, invocation of the past during electoral periods as well as the relatively abundant postwar testimonial literature. I will specifically address the clamorous silence of formulaic war accounts in Chap. 5.

[3] Studies on Santiago Nonualco are limited to historical narratives, some with a legend-like quality, on the rebellion led by the Indian Anastasio Aquino against El Salvador's rulers in 1832 (see Barraza Ibarra 2001; Domínguez Sosa 2007; López Bernal 2008).

[4] To learn more about the results yielded by the research conducted by Father Cosme Spessotto Committee members, see Chap. 6.

collaboration with the committee on the violence that occurred in the region during the 1970s and early 1980s have revealed certain discrepancies vis-à-vis the country's relatively scant historiography on the war. The temporal landmarks and categories of violence cited in national-scaled historical accounts of the war are inconsistent with those mentioned in oral accounts of the war in La Paz. I will illustrate this through a description of the history of the war in the Cantón Las Ánimas, in whose reconstruction I participated along with members of the Father Cosme Spessotto Committee.[5] Las Ánimas, a highland covered by tropical forest, is located in northern Santiago Nonualco and is about an hour's walk away from its central neighborhoods. Before, during, and after the war, Las Ánimas was and remains a site where residents—especially, though not exclusively, males—have been actively involved in collective action and politics. Indeed, in the aftermath of war and until the 2009 presidential elections, it was one of the few FMLN strongholds in Santiago. Its mountainous terrain and dense vegetation as well as its relative remoteness from central Santiago facilitated political activity with the PCS from the late 1960s and made it a convenient hiding place for Armed Liberation Forces (FAL) guerrillas—the military arm of the PCS—from the late 1970s through the early 1980s. However, relative to FMLN strongholds in the country's northern and northeastern departments such as Chalatenango and Morazán, armed combat in Las Ánimas as well as other mountainous areas of La Paz was intermittent and did not play a major role in the evolution of the war on a national scale.

The collection by the Father Cosme Spessotto Committee of testimonies and evidence of wartime massacres and assassinations in Las Ánimas had no public reverberations among the population of this rural area until a mourning event was held by committee members on 25 July 2009. As in other areas of La Paz, the event consisted of a commemoration ceremony, including a Catholic mass, to honor and remember the Las Ánimas war victims.[6] Prior to the mourning event, the committee members visited Las Ánimas and met with residents of the area on several occasions to agree on logistics. One of the major decisions involved the site where the

---

[5] Along with committee members, I conducted interviews with, and collected testimonies from, residents of Las Ánimas. The interviews on which I base this section were recorded and shared with committee members, who aimed to use them to write the history of the war in La Paz as narrated by the victims and relatives of the victims themselves.

[6] For more details on the mourning events held by the Father Cosme Spessotto Committee, see Chap. 6.

mourning event would be held. The one finally chosen by committee members, which appears on the book cover, was the former site of the old Las Ánimas chapel and the current site of five graves. The mourning event was perceived by many Las Ánimas residents as a welcome opportunity to share publicly the war experiences about which they had hitherto remained silent; this was evident in their active participation in both the lead-up organizational meetings and the commemoration itself. During the weeks preceding the mourning event, discussions about logistics intermingled with emotive stories of personal wartime experiences, many of which had scarcely been shared.

One of the stories recounted by several elderly residents of Las Ánimas dealt with one of the five people buried in the plot where the event was to be celebrated. I was told by relatives and neighbors that on 28 May 1980, Gaudencio Galán Hueso[7] left his house and rode his horse along the dusty path leading to central Santiago to meet with the person who would sell him the fertilizer he needed for the corn crop he was cultivating on a small self-owned plot. When Gaudencio was riding past the entrance of the Las Ánimas School, he encountered a military vehicle. Without warning or any interaction with those in the vehicle, he and his horse were shot and their bodies left on the path. According to his wife Rosa, this was not an isolated incident; Gaudencio had suffered persecution by the National Guard and a two-year imprisonment without trial during the 1970s. She suspected that he had become involved in political activity through his participation in a local agricultural cooperative. However, she could not confirm this given that the men of the area who participated in political organizations during this time kept quiet about it and made no mention of it even to their relatives. His body was found by a local resident who buried it in the plot where it now lies. That same year, 1980, one of Gaudencio's daughters was abducted, as his two sons who had joined the guerrillas would be in 1981 and 1983. In 1980, Rosa and her five remaining daughters fled Las Ánimas, continually relocating throughout the following decade to different parts of the country due to ongoing persecution. One of the daughters eventually went into exile in the United States,

---

[7] As explained in the Introduction, I have anonymized research participants as a general rule. However, in the description of this section in particular, as well as in Chap. 6, I have maintained the names of many participants since it was their wish that I do so. Indeed, they have themselves endeavored to publicly disseminate their wartime stories so as to reverse their omission from existing war accounts and imageries.

where she has remained ever since. It was not until 2004 that Rosa resettled in Las Ánimas. Since no reparation program[8] to benefit war victims had been implemented by the postwar Salvadoran governments, she was able to rebuild her house only, thanks to international relief aid invested in the area in 2001 in the wake of two devastating earthquakes.

According to various Las Ánimas residents, the four bodies buried alongside Gaudencio's were those of his extended kin, who were killed shortly after he was. As close relatives of these other victims had not been located by committee members, the details of their deaths were unknown and the dates unconfirmed. Unmarked graves of other residents killed before the war are scattered throughout the *cantón* (rural area), their locations known only by resident elders. Although armed combat did occur in Las Ánimas between guerrillas and the army or military-controlled police forces, wartime violence manifested primarily in the form of harassment, looting, repression, incarceration without trial, and selective as well as seemingly arbitrary assassination. Between the late 1970s and early 1980s, more than 100 people were killed in Las Ánimas alone, most of them members of the same families.[9] The Galáns, the Garcías, the Crespíns, and the Gonzálezs are some of the families wiped out or displaced from Las Ánimas. As of 2009, committee members, along with residents of Las Ánimas, had managed to document the assassinations of 124 people and the abductions of eight others in the early 1980s. More Las Ánimas residents were killed in other sectors of Santiago after they fled their homes. As the violence escalated, most of the population abandoned their property and belongings in Las Ánimas just as Gaudencio's family did. They either took refuge in the homes of relatives who lived in the center of Santiago or in neighboring *cantones* such as San Sebastián Abajo and San Sebastián Arriba, or they left the area altogether and relocated in the peripheral municipalities of San Salvador. Many joined the guerrillas encamped on the slopes of the Chichontepec Volcano. To hear firsthand accounts of Las Ánimas residents who had been involved in political

---

[8] Reparation, both moral and material, has been one of the main demands of professional organizations and grassroots movements involved in postwar memory work. These organizations met several times with representatives of the two successive FMLN administrations, finally seeing a program approved in 2013 (Decreto Ejecutivo 204, *Diario Oficial*, 23 October 2013). The program was, however, meager partly due to El Salvador's public budget's shortfall and has been criticized by victims' organizations and human rights NGOs for its neglect of the justice component.

[9] Families in the area were at the time fairly large due to widespread endogamic practices.

activity during the war, members of the committee and I had to interview people who had fled Las Ánimas during the 1970s and early 1980s and had been living for years in the periphery of San Salvador.

A 70-year-old member of the Crespín family, known in the area for its political involvement, was our source of substantial information on the political history of Las Ánimas. Committee members and I visited Andrés at his current home in Apopa, a municipality in the periphery of San Salvador. His age and deafness notwithstanding, Andrés spent long hours vividly describing to us how political activity, and the repression that ensued, had begun in Las Ánimas. In the mid-1960s, Andrés spent a year in San Salvador living in the same house as Salvador Cayetano Carpio, then the leader of the PCS and the founder, in 1970, of the Popular Liberation Forces Farabundo Martí (FPL), a political-military organization that would subsequently become part of the FMLN.[10] Conversations with Cayetano led Andrés to read classical Marxist texts and engage in further political discussions. A year later, when Andrés returned to Las Ánimas after finishing his job in San Salvador, he disseminated Marxist ideas among his brothers and friends. Soon afterward, they formed the first communist cell in Santiago with the support of the PCS delegate in La Paz, thereby consolidating political discussion and organized activity in Las Ánimas. While largely absent in Santiago's southern lowlands and the remaining northern sectors, political activity flourished in Las Ánimas partly due to Andrés's fortuitous experience in San Salvador. However, it could also be argued that the small-scale land tenure pattern that predominated in Las Ánimas was propitious for the emergence of peasant support and organization as a means of overcoming deprivation—just as Lauria-Santiago (1999: 8) has posited was the case for the massive peasant support enjoyed by the FMLN in El Salvador's northern and eastern regions. Because of the area's geographical remoteness and difficult terrain, haciendas[11] were never established

---

[10] The FPL formed after a split in the PCS and became the largest guerrilla group throughout the 1980s. During the war, the organizations that made up the FMLN were differently distributed across the country. The FPL had more leverage in San Salvador, Santa Ana, and north-central El Salvador, whereas the People's Revolutionary Army (ERP)—the other main organization in the FMLN—enjoyed a greater presence in eastern El Salvador.

[11] Haciendas are a colonial legacy consisting of particular land tenures and work patterns (Browning 1971; Lindo-Fuentes 1990: 88–89). While initially stimulated by the expansion of indigo production, El Salvador's haciendas harbored a diversified production throughout the nineteenth century that included cattle raising. Work was carried out by peasants hired

in Las Ánimas.[12] The majority of Las Ánimas residents, being small land-owners who cultivated foodstuffs, were thus relatively unsupervised in comparison to those who lived and worked in the haciendas of Santiago's southern lowlands, where discipline could be more easily enforced.[13] In cases where political activity did emerge in the lowlands in the 1970s, it was led by progressive priests who had embraced liberation theology.

Like Andrés, other local residents recalled that police forces had initiated repression in the late 1960s against residents who were collectively organizing public works projects such as the construction of a new path in Las Ánimas. Several of them recounted that in the 1970s, in the face of increasing repression, Las Ánimas residents founded cooperatives to collectivize agricultural work and provide a front for outlawed political meetings and initiatives. Had they assembled as members of the PCS or simply as neighbors, their actions would have been judged 'subversive' by the National Guard that occasionally policed the area, making them vulnerable to arrest. Yet, even as members of cooperatives, residents of Las Ánimas like Andrés or Gaudencio suffered frequent persecution during the 1970s—most often in the form of arrest and assassination at the hands of the National Guard or local paramilitary groups. Andrés recalled that the population of Las Ánimas had been regarded as 'communists' by Santiago residents beginning in the late 1960s and relabeled 'guerrillas' or 'collaborators' in the 1970s, when insurgent armed groups were founded in El Salvador. Residents of Las Ánimas explained that while prewar and wartime assassinations were generally reserved for those deemed 'subversive', they were sometimes carried out against male and female residents who were not involved in political activity at all, followed by the seizing of victims' cattle or belongings. I was told similar stories that had transpired in

by the owner on a temporary basis. In decline or abandoned by the mid-nineteenth century, El Salvador's haciendas eventually benefited from the 1881 and 1882 liberal reforms that privatized communal lands and ejidos (Lindo-Fuentes 1990: 89; Lauria-Santiago 1999: 194). Many haciendas were expropriated and turned into cooperatives, or their land was redistributed among the Salvadoran rural population by the agrarian reform program implemented by the PDC in the early 1980s.

[12] It should be noted, however, that Wood (2003) studied a case of insurgent action among peasants who used to work at a hacienda in the Usulután Department and had heretofore exhibited a quiescent attitude.

[13] Control of the population working in the haciendas was likely facilitated by the haciendas' spatial structure. In Santiago, at least, workers' dwellings surrounded the hacienda infrastructure that housed the machines, an arrangement that remains in place today even after the demise of the haciendas.

central Santiago, where familial and personal enmities led some residents to report relatives and neighbors to police as alleged guerrilla collaborators, resulting in their subsequent assassination. The ambiguity of the motives underlying many of the assassinations perpetrated during this era speaks to the problem of defining wartime violence as indisputably 'political'; sheer rapacity and personal disputes apparently motivated many wartime human rights violations.[14]

Andrés and his wife left Las Ánimas in the early 1970s and moved first to central Santiago and then, due to the increasing repression, to Apopa. By 1982, Las Ánimas was empty, its inhabitants' belongings having been looted and its houses and plots burned by the local *defensas civiles* (civil defenses) that were so active in northern Santiago during the late 1970s and early 1980s.[15] Only in 1985, after guerrillas had attacked and crushed local civil defenses in neighboring Cantón Santa Cruz Loma, did the violence decline and the former residents of Las Ánimas begin to return to their land. Fear prevented most from returning until the Peace Accords were signed in 1992, and some, like Andrés, never returned. Many former residents could not afford to rebuild their burned dwellings. There was no postwar reconstruction program in the area—most likely because, as mentioned earlier, it lies outside what are considered the country's former war zones[16]—and running water, electricity, and other basic utilities have yet to be introduced in Las Ánimas. Moreover, in the wake of the 1990s' agrarian crisis, Las Ánimas residents' small properties

---

[14] Bourgois (2001: 19, 21–22) has already addressed the ambiguity of wartime assassinations by guerrillas, although he attributes this ambiguity to the normalization of violence that had occurred in El Salvador and ordinary Salvadorans' mimicry of state-sponsored violence due to their prolonged exposure to wartime brutality.

[15] Civil defenses were the paramilitary structures created in El Salvador's rural areas during the war with local populations who obtained military training and weapons. They originated in the Servicio Territorial (Territorial Service), which amounted to a reserve military force (Von Santos 2016). In Santiago, they played a prominent role in the northern *cantones* that neighbored Las Ánimas: Santa Cruz Loma, San Antonio Arriba, San Antonio Abajo, and San Sebastián Arriba. In these areas, civil defenses were locally known as Comandos Chencho Beltrán, named after a leader infamous for the atrocities he perpetrated.

[16] International funds for reconstruction were channeled mainly through newly created or already existent NGOs, most of which were linked to the political-military organizations that made up the FMLN. Under these circumstances, reconstruction programs and initiatives were largely parochial, targeting mainly the constituencies of these organizations, whether living in areas that had been these organizations' strongholds during the war or that they had repopulated thereafter (Sprenkels 2014: 171–179).

were no longer sufficient for subsistence, forcing many former residents to seek jobs in San Salvador (e.g. in the maquilas or as private security guards) after the war.

Despite assertions by rightwing residents of the Santiago lowlands that the civil war did not reach the municipality, it is clear that the population of Las Ánimas did experience the war, albeit within a timespan that differs from that generally accepted as the wartime era.[17] Political activity and harassment by local police forces commenced in the late 1960s in Las Ánimas, with an upsurge in violence and unrest occurring in the late 1970s and early 1980s. By 1985, the war had ended in Las Ánimas, partly because the whole *cantón* had been deserted, but also because the guerrillas had defeated the paramilitary groups of the surrounding northern *cantones*. This was the case not just in Las Ánimas; repression enforced by terror had been practiced since the 1970s in other rural areas of La Paz, such as the Zacatecoluca *cantones*, where scorched-earth military operations and massacres in the early 1980s displaced the entire population. Although the war had not yet been officially declared in El Salvador before 1980 and an uprising at the national level did not occur until 1981, the violence Salvadorans experienced in areas of La Paz during the prewar years was, for some, more than an uneasy peace. This chronology and pattern of violence match those in other departments where the climax of repression occurred during the 1970s and mass scorched-earth operations were launched in 1981 and 1982.

Just as periodization[18] conceals specific war histories, so do conventionally accepted notions of war. Conventional notions of war are resonant with Clausewitz's (1993) classic definition: a relatively structured and organized event in which opposing sides that pursue the same political object can be neatly identified (see also Kalyvas 2006: 17 for 'civil war'). Violent events that differ from this definition, such as routine selective repression or assassination, are overlooked or trivialized. The mourning event organized by

---

[17]The war is generally understood to have begun in 1980. Yet there are divergences regarding the specific temporal landmarks that signal its outbreak, ranging from the 1979 coup to Archbishop Romero's assassination in 1980 to the 1981 FMLN offensive (see Baloyra 1982: 105; Dunkerley 1982: 132, 162; Montgomery 1982: xi; Byrne 1996: 73–74). More agreement exists that the war ended with the signing of the Peace Accords on 16 January 1992.

[18] 'Periodization' refers to the division of the past into stages or temporal units not just to make historical narration manageable, but also to put forth narratives that are crucial to processes of national identity formation (Wilson 2001: 16).

the Father Cosme Spessotto Committee underscored the oblivion to which La Paz has been relegated in a history-writing that has favored a conventional notion of war as well as national-scaled and sensational instances of violence, such as guerrilla exploits or large massacres by the army. In aiming to shed light on the extensive suffering of the population of La Paz during the war, committee members have focused their research efforts on episodes of mass assassinations that qualify as 'massacres'—a term employed by NGOs and grassroots organizations performing memory work in El Salvador and other Latin American countries (e.g. the Guatemalan Human Rights Commission), all of them agreeing on its definition as the extrajudicial execution of at least three to six defenseless people (the number varying from one organization to another) in a single violent episode. A member of the human rights NGO Tutela Legal[19] explained that the term 'massacre', unlike 'genocide', is not employed in international human rights law but is nonetheless frequently invoked by NGOs performing memory work to denote mass assassinations with a genocidal pattern, whether grounded in ideological, political, racial, or other motives. Committee members explained they have deployed the term extensively to refer to the army and police forces' tendency to kill entire families and wipe out communities during the war, whether in a single military operation or consistently over a few years, as in Las Ánimas.

Yet in El Salvador, during the 1970s and 1980s, violent wartime episodes conforming to such a definition occurred alongside numerous other forms of repression, including selective assassinations and summary executions, abduction, and torture. It was largely in these latter forms that the war manifested in Santiago, mainly in mountainous areas like Las Ánimas, but also in central neighborhoods. Since historical accounts of other Salvadoran regions during the 1970s have likewise reported selective repression and assassination, committee members have not argued for the exceptionalism of La Paz; rather, they have sought to draw attention to their region's absence from historical accounts of the war and the consequent neglect of the region's war victims. Crucially, the committee has drawn on a language that evokes the high magnitude and collective nature

---

[19] Oficina de Tutela Legal (Legal Guardianship Office) was a human rights organization overseen by the Archbishopric of San Salvador. It was founded by Archbishop Arturo Rivera Damas in 1982 with the aim of dealing with allegations of human rights violations during the war. In the aftermath of war and until its closure in 2013, not only did Tutela Legal continue investigating cases of wartime human rights violations (see Chap. 6), but it also conducted research on postwar human rights violations.

of wartime violence most likely to draw attention to La Paz's neglected war impact but also to the shared experience of mourning.

Finally, the wartime experiences of Las Ánimas residents reveal the political foundation and contested nature of both the term 'civil war' and the prevailing categories of wartime violence (cf. Kalyvas 2006: 17). The FMLN defined the conflict as rooted in a struggle over El Salvador's very sovereignty, thus underscoring the appropriateness of the label 'civil'. The Salvadoran government, by contrast, portrayed the insurgency as part of an international 'communist threat', thus denying the intrastate nature of the war. In addition, as Kalyvas has pointed out (2006: 20), the motivations and nature of wartime violence cannot be subsumed into the causes of a civil war. In other words, rapacity, vandalism, displacement, and other essentially non-ideological reasons motivated a great deal of wartime violence, as evidenced by the experiences of many Las Ánimas residents. In this sense, retrospective assertions by Salvadorans that 'there was no crime during the war' or that 'one could be safe while not collaborating with either side' likely speak more of the speakers' contempt for the postwar era than they do of any wholesale political motivations that may have been behind wartime violence.[20] Not only is it important to make a distinction between the causes of the war itself and the causes of wartime violence in order to understand what occurred during wartime that might have been silenced and neglected, but we should likewise undertake an extrication of the notions of 'peace' and 'crime', the latter generally conceived as a depoliticized form of violence.

POSTWAR SCRIPTS OF VIOLENCE

While Santiago has not stood out as a particularly violent Salvadoran municipality in the postwar era relative to others, the information I collected on its forms of violence and violent actors is representative of those of El Salvador as a whole. In Santiago, the number of homicides was low during the electoral campaigns of 2008 and 2009. From June 2009, after the FMLN had taken office, however, homicides in this municipality increased, following that trend in the country as a whole. Most often, ordinary people could not pinpoint the motive behind a given homicide,

---

[20] As Moodie (2010: 67) has noted, 'common crime' may have existed during the war, but it was most likely underreported or categorized as 'political violence', thus giving the impression that there was little or no wartime criminality.

generally of a male; perpetrators and their motives remained unknown and became a matter of constant conjecture, making violence an unintelligible and seemingly arbitrary phenomenon. Some homicide victims in the municipality remained anonymous; they may even have been killed in another municipality, with their bodies subsequently abandoned in Santiago. Other victims were known by Santiago residents, and their deaths remained a source of deep concern for weeks thereafter. Such was the case for the 15- and 16-year-old cousins gunned down in a central neighborhood in the late afternoon of 13 August 2009 as they were heading home. At a crossroads in the Anastasio Aquino Avenue, near the municipality's House of Culture,[21] a car slowly approached the two boys; a few young men inside the car then fired shots at the boys through the car window. As the car drove off, one of the boys, still alive, tried to sit up. The car backed up, allowing one of the gunmen to finish him off, then sped toward the Coastal Road and out of Santiago.

On the evening of this episode, I had planned to go to Zacatecoluca with a group of friends to eat *pupusas*[22]; it was one of my final days in Santiago, and I had arranged various farewell dinners before my departure. Just as I was leaving for Zacatecoluca, I received a phone call from a member of the family I lived with; she nervously told me about the assassination of the two boys and implored me to return home early that evening. The consternation caused by the assassination of the two cousins soon gave way to anxiety among neighbors and residents throughout central Santiago. The assassination brought close to home the threat of the seemingly arbitrary violence that has been so pervasive nationwide in the postwar era and that makes its way into Salvadorans' homes via the media on a daily basis. Two teenage boys, well regarded by friends, neighbors, and teachers, had been assassinated for no apparent reason while walking home in broad daylight. Their assassination had occurred in one of the municipality's most central and well-traveled avenues, one crossed everyday by Santiagueñas, whether to go to work, school, or the market. The motive underlying the assassination seemed largely arbitrary, although the fact that the gunmen had bothered to put the car into reverse to finish off

---

[21] The House of Culture is the state cultural institution that exists in Salvadoran municipalities and whose building generally harbors an underresourced library and recreational space.

[22] Typically, Salvadoran corn-flour or rice-flour tortillas stuffed with cheese, beans, meat, or vegetables.

the boy who had initially survived seemed to indicate a certain purposefulness.

The incident conjured in the minds of Santiagueños the perpetual threat of violence as 'a possibility' that could manifest at any moment. Although Santiago has not been one of the most violent municipalities in El Salvador, news on TV, radio, and newspapers have served as constant reminders of the everyday possibility of homicidal violence. The lack of details and explanations has seemed to imply that homicides could occur when and where one least expected it. This ubiquitous 'possibility of violence', while not quite a constant state of alarm, has informed a wide range of bodily dispositions and practices. For instance, I was sometimes reminded by Marta, the head of the family with whom I lived, how to sit on a bus, especially when traveling alone:

> You should never sit at the back of the bus. They would easily rob you there. Nor should you sit next to a window. Robbers can sit next to you and point at you with a gun and nobody will notice. And the front has not been safe either lately. When they kill the driver and the collector because of unpaid extortions, they sometimes kill a passenger sitting in the front too. Of course, give everything you have if you are robbed; today they don't even hesitate to kill people!

Interestingly, these detailed instructions were proffered by someone who had never been robbed or even witnessed a bus assassination herself. Even in locations like Santiago, where homicide rates are comparatively low, the everyday nature of homicidal violence throughout the country, along with the circulation of rumors and crime stories, have worked as a form of knowledge production (Moodie 2010: 97, 101) and fear-fueling (Caldeira 2000: 19, 35).

The anxieties stemming from the assassination of the two young boys led friends and neighbors to maximize precautions—shutting themselves in their homes in the early evening or avoiding public spaces—for some time. A couple of days after the episode, I paid a visit to Jesús, a 40-year-old man with whom I used to chat for hours whenever we ran into each other in the central Santiago streets. I had not seen him for a while. Jesús, a state-employed social worker, lives with his family just a few meters from the crossroads where the two boys were assassinated. The metal windows and the two front doors of his house were closed. After knocking on the door, I was initially greeted by two fierce dogs. Once Jesús heard my voice, he tethered the dogs, unlocked the main door, and invited me in. He explained that after the assassinations, he and his family had decided to limit their movements in public spaces and cloister themselves at home. This was not the first time they had felt compelled to do so. Just a month before the assassination of the two cousins, Jesús's family had received a death threat via an anonymous letter slid under their front door, leading them to believe that extortion would ensue. This had happened to several of their neighbors as well.

'I have to pay university tuition for my two sons, the price of water and electricity keeps going up, and so does the price of beans and rice. How am I going to pay a monthly extortion?' Jesús had remarked bitterly when telling me about the death threat a month earlier, explaining that his five-person family lives on two monthly salaries hovering around US$400 each. The family's response to the death threat had been to stay at home as much as possible, leaving only to go to work or when strictly necessary. Jesús never reported the threat to the police because he had heard rumors that a local police officer was himself involved in extortion. Jesús explained to me, 'When the death threat arrived I had a meeting with all my brothers. We decided that, for the sake of the family, it would be better not to report. My brothers are all Evangelical, and they suggested that we should instead pray; that is what we have done so far.' He gave up his weekly participation in a local association dedicated to the development of a water system, as well as the FMLN meetings that he had begun attending after that party's victory in the 2009 presidential elections. Although he and his family had relaxed their precautions a few weeks after receiving the death threat, the assassination of the two boys, whom the family knew well, reminded them once again just how immediate the threat of homicidal violence remained.

Jesús's case exemplifies the fear of 'the possibility' of extortion and homicidal violence that has often followed death threats. Extortion has affected Santiago's business owners since the mid-2000s and extended to the municipality's broader population, regardless of social class or purchasing power, since 2009. Extortion is an emerging form of crime to which many residents of Santiago's central neighborhoods are or have been subject since the late 2000s (see Chap. 4). Women owning or renting a stall in the market, families running small stores or diners, men and women employed in the maquilas of El Pedregal—an offshore zone in La Paz—or the periphery of San Salvador, low-paid professionals, and even unemployed Santiagueños have all been subject to extortion since 2009.

Given that there are precedents in Santiago, as well as nationwide, of individuals being assassinated or kidnapped when extortionists' demands are unmet, the few Santiagueños who can afford it have resorted to private security. In 2006, the daughter of a wealthy family was kidnapped and released only after the family paid a large ransom. Since then, this family, which owns a business of basic grain distribution in central Santiago, has maximized security measures, including hiring a security guard to invigilate the family business and protecting the property with barbed wire. I was also told of several Santiago residents who had relocated their homes or even migrated to the United States after receiving extortion-related death threats; the numbers of those fleeing Santiago and neighboring towns have only increased over the years.

Local precedents of extortion-related assassinations, as well as daily reports of homicides by the Salvadoran media, have led Santiago residents facing death threats, many of them extortion-related, to change their lifestyles when they find themselves unable to afford private security or relocate. In 2009, several friends and neighbors changed their telephone numbers immediately after receiving death threats. A number of them told me that they no longer replied to phone calls from numbers they did not recognize and had prohibited their children from answering the phone. At least temporarily, most of them had restricted their outdoor activities to work and the procurement of essential goods. In referring to these impromptu and 'self-imposed' temporary states of exception, Santiagueñas sometimes drew parallels with the prewar era and even wartime: 'Before the war you could walk until 8 or 9 pm in the streets of Santiago. Today we lock ourselves up at home around 6 pm'. Given prewar and wartime stories of violence, such nostalgia-inflected remarks should be taken as an idealization, rather than a literal depiction, of the past as it compares to the postwar era. What is clear is that these remarks are largely suffused by fear. In her research with Guatemalan women widowed by the war, Green (1999: 60) has suggested that the routinization of fear allows a semblance of normalcy that is only occasionally punctuated by the overt expression of this fear. Whether or not we can surmise from Salvadorans' 'self-imposed' temporary states of exception that they live in a state of chronic fear, it is clear that postwar violence has become an everyday experience, arising in both material and ideational forms.

If the homicide of the two cousins on 13 August 2009 had occurred in San Salvador, Santiagueños would have readily assumed that the cousins were members of one of the country's main rival gangs, MS 13 or 18th

Street, most likely killed by members of the other gang. This is how homicides, most often affecting young men, have been reported by the country's mainstream media—sometimes accompanied by a sensational headline stressing the number of homicides in the past month or invoking a term like 'massacre' when several victims have been killed in a single incident. However, since Santiagueñas in the central neighborhoods knew the family and the two cousins well, the initial consternation was followed by a rash of rumors trying to make sense of the killings and suggesting that they had likely been a mistake. Youth from a local gang tended to gather near the site of the homicides, so it was assumed that members of this gang, and not the cousins, had been the actual targets of the gunmen. The assassination a month later of two teenage members of this gang would come to reinforce those rumors—as I learned in phone conversations with friends after leaving El Salvador.

The local gang, which rumors suggested might have been the actual target of the cousins' assassins, had frequently been boosted by Santiago's PCN mayor, with whom the gang collaborated during municipal elections (see Chaps. 3 and 5). Members of this gang, often loitering in central Santiago, had accompanied the mayor on her visits to the various urban and rural areas of Santiago during the 2008 electoral campaign, and previous campaigns as well, as I was told by several Santiagueños, thus suggesting that this gang was part of the mayor's large political clientele that had enabled the PCN to win four successive municipal elections. Further evidence pointing to an alliance with the mayor was the fact that the gang members seem not to have encountered obstacles to their incipient participation in the local, small-scale distribution of drugs even though the gang was based right next to Santiago's police subdelegation and its drug-related activities were known by everyone in the neighborhood. I myself could easily spot this gang's drug-dealing activity when, in 2010, approximately 20 of its members rented a property just three houses away from where I was living. Although initially distinct from the MS 13 and 18th Street gangs and, according to neighbors, named *La Cinco* after the local football team in which some of its members used to play,[23] by 2014, Santiago residents recognized the local gang as having become part of the 18th Street. Its members sported the same kind of baggy clothing, shaved heads, and gothic tattoos, and

---

[23] See Moser and Winton's (2002: x) arguments against the ubiquitous conflation of different sorts of gangs.

neighbors drew links between this gang and gang members in Soyapango, a municipality in the periphery of San Salvador that was popularly known to be gang-controlled, speculating that some had migrated from there to escape police control.[24] Yet the gang continued to be supportive of the mayor during municipal elections. Its role in the municipality's political life, I argue, is evidence of the need to recenter the analysis of postwar violence on political links, relations, and practices.

While the MS 13 and 18th Street gangs were also invoked by Santiagueñas in contradictory rumors attempting to explain the homicides and criminal activities, such as extortion and armed assaults, that were occurring throughout Santiago, more consensus existed when it came to these gangs' territorial control of specific sectors of the municipality. According to Santiago residents, 18th Street gang members used to assemble in Colonia Alvarado and MS 13 members in Colonia Santa Inés, both central neighborhoods, in the early 2000s. Those in Colonia Alvarado later moved on to rural areas of Santiago, namely, Concepción Jalponga in southern Santiago, where their activity was subject to less police control. In the late 2000s, Santa Inés and Concepción Jalponga became 'no-go zones' in the words of residents of central Santiago, who identified them as meeting places for gang members, and hence areas to be avoided. A local police officer confirmed that the majority of the gang members who assembled in Colonia Santa Inés did not live in Santiago, but rather in the neighboring municipalities of Zacatecoluca, San Juan Nonualco, San Rafael Obrajuelo, and El Rosario. Assembling outside their own neighborhoods allowed them to remain relatively anonymous. The gangs managed to conceal their activities, including drug trafficking, and avoid the interference of rival gangs by imposing dusk-to-dawn curfews on residents. Gang members let it be known that residents of the Colonia Santa Inés should not leave their homes between 6 pm and 6 am, regardless of whether this interfered with their work schedule. The same police officer explained that only during periods in which gang leaders had been arrested did the Colonia Santa Inés become calmer. This pattern of territorial control has been reportedly common throughout El Salvador.[25]

[24] Aguilar Villamariona (2006) has explained that the repressive *mano dura* approaches enacted from 2003 have resulted in the transformation of local gangs into professional crime structures and in an expansion of the territorial control of the main gangs. These gangs increasingly felt compelled to leave their own communities, where they were easily found, and move into new areas.

[25] See 'La violencia trastorna estilo de vida de jóvenes en Centroamérica', *Prensa Libre*, 30 October 2015.

Postwar forms of violence and violent actors differ greatly from those of wartime, as evidenced by the narrations by Santiagueños from Las Ánimas. Drawing from my ethnographic research, I will show throughout the book that this chapter's description of postwar Santiago as significantly different from wartime speaks to the subtle nature of past legacies. My move from Las Ánimas—which as a rural sector is an exemplary space with which to illustrate wartime violence—to the urban municipality center mirrors the manner in which postwar violence has become depicted as an urban phenomenon. This move is nonetheless not fully descriptive of the postwar problem of violence. As I will show in the following chapters, postwar violence has also affected the country's rural areas. The apparent discontinuities between wartime and postwar violence—both in terms of forms and actors—have legitimized what Moodie (2010: 55–58) has labeled the 'critical code-switching' of violence: a transition in the taxonomies of violence promoted by the ARENA governments and the rightwing media in postwar El Salvador. No longer was the violence occurring in the aftermath of war deemed 'political'. Nor was it 'critical', as publicly expressed by President Cristiani after the assassination in 1993 of ex-guerrilla and FMLN legislative candidate Francisco Velis as he was walking his one-year-old child to the nursery in a middle-class San Salvador neighborhood (Moodie 2010: 53–54). In being relabeled 'crime' or, later, 'social violence', 'criminal violence', or 'delinquency', postwar violence was resignified and depoliticized. An implicit suggestion of this resignification was that, unlike during the war, violence no longer led to states of exception. As Moodie has shown in her work, the crime stories circulating in the 1990s among San Salvadorans themselves contributed to reproducing and performing this code-switching.

By the late 2000s, I could recognize the extent to which this transition in taxonomies had consolidated, with terms like 'social violence' /'crime' /'criminal violence' /'delinquency' being widely deployed by state institutions as well as social scientists (see, for instance, Bourgois 2004; Cruz 2003: 31), and gangs deemed the primary violent actors in both official and popular representations of El Salvador's postwar violence. Nevertheless, as the link between PCN and the local gang shows, the postwar gang problem is not the depoliticized phenomenon that the ARENA governments and the rightwing media have suggested. Additionally, I noticed that the very same Santiagueñas who invoked the category of 'social violence' in conversation and made ready associations between daily homicides and gangs also articulated critical views on mainstream depictions of postwar violence. Even as they embraced the gang trope, many left-leaning and disaffected Santiagueños also suggested that political links might plausibly be at play. Their comments, suggestive of the shadowy aspects of postwar violence, were corroborated by evidence revealed through anecdotal media scandals and information gathered in confidence from police officers (see Chap. 3). Years later, police reports and investigative journalism have shed further light on political links that had previously been largely invisible.

This book thus underscores the need to repoliticize the analyses of post-Cold War violence. This is not to suggest that the Cold War era term 'political violence'—generally defined as 'targeted physical violence and terror administered by official authorities and those opposing it' (Bourgois 2004: 426)—is a useful descriptive or analytical category of violence here. Yet I would not want to completely underestimate it. The disaffected and left-leaning Salvadorans with whom I worked have actually employed it themselves to make sense of part of the physical violence of the postwar era. Rather, I seek to draw attention to the social life of this term, that is, how it has been employed or discarded by Salvadorans and scholars alike, as well as to the complexity of the relationship between violence and the country's political life.

Reaching Liberal Market Democracy

On 16 January 1992, representatives of the Salvadoran government—including members of the ruling party ARENA and high-ranking military officials—and FMLN commanders signed the Chapultepec Peace Accords. The Accords constituted the culmination of a two-year negotiation process between the war's opposing sides and marked the consensual cessation of armed struggle. As stated in the opening of the Peace Accords document, with the UN-brokered peace negotiations initiated by the end of 1989, the two sides sought 'to end the armed conflict by political means as speedily as possible, promote the democratization of the country, guarantee unrestricted respect for human rights and reunify Salvadorian society' (United Nations 1992b: 2). The Accords stipulated a number of institutional reforms that the Salvadoran government would have to observe in order to attain peace and democracy and that would be verified by the UN. These reforms pertained mainly to the country's institutions of order as well as to the enactment of a more inclusive liberal democracy. Core reforms included the purification, reduction, reorganization, and retasking of the armed forces; the abolition of the existing police forces, which were military-controlled, and the foundation of a new civilian police force independent of the armed forces; the promotion of the independence of the judiciary and the creation of the Office of the National Counsel for the Defence of Human Rights (the future PDDH); a commitment to reform the electoral system; and the legalization of the FMLN as a political party (United Nations 1992b).

In addition, the Accords addressed issues such as the reintegration of ex-combatants, both military and guerrillas, into civilian life; land transfers and agricultural loans to the peasant population; the establishment of a Forum for Economic and Social Consultation by which the government, labor organizations, and the business community could negotiate a social pact on equal footing; and the design of a national governmental reconstruction plan. However, these and other mandates aimed at mitigating the social and economic problems at the root of the outbreak of civil war in 1980—mandates essential for effectively leaving the war behind—were only secondarily and partially addressed by the negotiating parties (Martín Álvarez 2006: 116–117). For instance, the land transfer program was limited in scope, benefiting almost exclusively FMLN constituencies and having little lasting impact because of the collapse of agriculture that occurred in the 1990s. Moreover, the national reconstruction plan devised to rebuild infrastructure and address the most immediate needs of the Salvadoran population instead became a means of promoting the private sector and foreign direct investment, among other things, thereby limiting the scope of the Forum envisaged in the Peace Accords for a negotiated discussion of economic and social policy (Robinson 2003: 101). Revealingly, the Peace Accords explicitly mentioned that 'the general philosophy or orientation of the Government's economic policy, which FMLN does not necessarily share, is not covered by this Agreement' (United Nations 1992b: 31)—a statement that expressly admitted that the essence of El Salvador's economic problem was being sidelined in favor of demilitarization and the end of armed conflict. In the text that resulted from the negotiations, the emphasis was placed on the dissolution of military rule, thereby implicitly defining democracy in rather narrow terms.

Throughout the negotiation process, it was agreed that El Salvador, like other countries undergoing peacebuilding and democratization from the mid-1980s, would establish a postwar truth commission (United Nations 1993: 55, 260–262). The commission was entrusted with the investigation of serious high-profile unresolved cases of human rights violations perpetrated from 1980 and the publication of a final report that included conclusions and binding recommendations resulting from the investigation. Within a global context that has increasingly adopted a therapeutic approach—underpinned by transitional justice mechanisms—to peacebuilding and democratization, truth commissions have acquired legitimacy 'as one of the main mechanisms for announcing a new democratic order' (Wilson 2001: xviii).[26] As quasi-judicial institutions, truth commissions have an ambiguous role—they have no jurisdictional functions, that is, they cannot prosecute nor can their findings be used to prosecute, yet they can name human rights offenders in their public reports (Wilson 2001: 19). El Salvador's truth commission, the peace settlement established, would not serve as a replacement for judicialization through Salvadoran courts. However, in 1993, just five days after the publication of the commission report, ARENA's government passed an amnesty law effectively granting immunity to wartime human rights offenders, thereby crushing any possibility that Salvadorans might pursue restorative and retributive justice and eluding guarantees of non-repetition.[27]

El Salvador's transition to democracy was lauded by its architects—including members of the international community and the country's government—and social scientists alike. In 1995, Boutros Boutros-Ghali, then-secretary-general of the United Nations, stated in a report on the ONUSAL's[28] performance of its verification duty that 'there is much reason for satisfaction at what has been accomplished by the Salvadorians during this time. ONUSAL can take credit for having helped the Salvadorians to take giant strides away from a violent and closed society towards a democratic order where institutions for the protection of human rights and free discourse are being consolidated' (Boutros-Ghali

---

[26] Truth commissions are considered key mechanisms in transitions from war to peace due to their report of human rights violations and encouragement of postconflict reparations and human rights guarantees. For a critical view of the work performed by truth commissions, see Laplante and Theidon (2007) and Wilson (2001).

[27] Salvadorans had to wait until 13 July 2016 to see the amnesty law declared unconstitutional and repealed by El Salvador's Supreme Court. See Chap. 6 for further discussion of this issue.

[28] The United Nations Observer Mission in El Salvador (ONUSAL) was founded in 1991 as an external commission that would verify the implementation of the Peace Accords (United Nations 1992a: iii).

1995: 15). The UN secretary-general's declaration did not acknowledge the levels of violence that persisted in the aftermath of war; the homicide rate in 1995 paralleled and even surpassed that of certain wartime years (Cruz et al. 1998: 6; Ramos 2000: 9). In addition, its implied definition of democracy—as the absence of large-scale armed conflict and access to previously denied political entitlements such as free speech—was rather thin. The triumphalism underpinning the assertion by the UN secretary-general was bolstered by post-Accord assessments of the UN's role and the transition itself (see Montgomery 1995; Hampson 1996: 11, 129–170; López Pintor 1999: 61; Burgerman 2000). Even though they admitted certain shortcomings, these assessments downgraded the persistence of homicidal and structural violence, and relied on minimalist definitions of democracy that highlighted its procedural aspects, such as regular multiparty elections.

Celebrations by ordinary Salvadorans on 16 January 1992 in San Salvador, as well as in some municipalities, reflected how thrilled they were, at least initially, by the promise of the Peace Accords. In San Salvador, a multitude crowded the Gerardo Barrios central square, where armed forces had once repressed rallies in front of the Metropolitan Cathedral during the 1970s and 1980s (Murray 1997: 2–3). At this celebration, red flags with the white FMLN logo overlaid the façade of buildings in the square, including the National Palace and the cathedral, their public display indicative of the popular perception that a political opening was underway. The initial hopes placed on both the Peace Accords and their implementation were, however, followed by 'disillusionment' (Silber 2011: 2) and 'democratic disenchantment' (Moodie 2010: 145). Insofar as public insecurity has remained a source of anxiety in the postwar era, Salvadorans' postwar pessimism does not seem surprising. As the two preceding sections have shown, daily homicides and death threats, along with concomitant feelings of insecurity, have characterized the postwar era just as they did the wartime era. Yet the wartime and the postwar eras cannot be said to be alike, and the postwar problem of violence cannot be reduced to a mere prolongation of wartime violence.

In postwar El Salvador, the phenomenon of gangs is not simply a media product, and organized crime, such as extortion, has indeed consolidated. These seemingly depoliticized violent actors and forms of violence have justified the 'code-switching' from 'political violence' to 'social violence' noted in the previous section. However, a degree of continuity exists that has been overlooked by triumphalist assessments of El Salvador's democratization process and representations of El Salvador's postwar era, both of which ignore the country's ongoing violence and Salvadorans' feelings of insecurity or overstate the gang phenomenon and the alleged depoliticization of postwar violence. Postwar homicidal violence has coexisted with the unaddressed problems of wartime: the wartime memories not dealt with; the lack of research on, and restorative justice with regards to, wartime human rights violations; the ongoing material deprivation in rural areas aggravated by the looting and destruction of dwellings during the war and the collapse of the agricultural economy in the 1990s; the neglected problems of displaced populations, which have both national and transnational dimensions; and the absence of a comprehensive program for the reparation of war victims.

El Salvador's indices of poverty and extreme poverty based strictly on income levels and the price of the family shopping basket registered a reduction from 65 to 38 percent and from 31.5 to 12.6 percent, respectively, between 1992 and 2006 (PNUD 2010: 193). Inequality has, however, persisted (Hammill 2007: 25), and a more multidimensional approach to the assessment of poverty has revealed severe deficiencies as well as significant underfunding of education, healthcare, housing, and other pressing problems, especially in the rural areas (PNUD 2010: 189–205). Indeed, although public expenditures have increased in El Salvador since the 1990s (mostly due to international donations and loans), their percentage of the GDP has consistently been one of the lowest in Central America and Latin America at large (see PNUD 2003: 65; Hammill 2007: 51–53; Agosin et al. 2008). Moreover, due to high levels of inflation affecting international food prices from 2007 and to the global financial crisis of 2008, El Salvador's levels of poverty and extreme poverty reverted back to the levels of a decade earlier (PNUD 2010: 193; 2013: 105). It is thus clear that the socio-economic problems at the root of the conflict have not been resolved.

As I will show throughout this book, a continuity between the war and postwar eras can also be discerned from ordinary Salvadorans' attempts to make sense of postwar violence and the country's political life. On the basis of my ethnographic research, I will show that ordinary people draw more parallels between wartime and the postwar era than might appear to exist in the official analysis of transition or in the descriptions of the previous pages of this chapter. These parallels, which manifest both discursively and materially, and the unresolved problems laid out earlier, call into question the transition paradigm as well as the ostensible success of postwar transformations. Transformations have undeniably occurred since the signing of the Peace Accords and the implementation of democracy-oriented reforms. However, I argue that official analyses of the transition, focused as they are on institutional and large-scale transformations, do not account for the nuanced continuities that surface in ordinary Salvadorans' experiences. In this book, I thus seek to trace the prewar and war legacies that prevail in the postwar era and illustrate how they work together with contemporary political processes.

The notion of 'transition' denotes a 'movement from something toward something else' (O'Donnell and Schmitter 1986: 65). As a period of 'liminality', a transition to democracy consists of a 'move from one status with its incumbent rights and obligations to another' (Wilson 2001: 19). The limitations of the transition paradigm that has informed peacebuilding operations and democratization studies lie in its definition of the teleological direction of change from an initial point of departure to a certain future destiny. Implicit in this definition is a sense of rupture and disjunction between the initial and final stage. Critics of the notion of transition—mostly anthropologists examining postsocialist transformations—have noted that transformations actually occur in much more gradual (sometimes imperceptible), uncertain, and contradictory ways (see O'Donnell and Schmitter 1986: 3–5; Pine and Bridger 1998: 3; Burawoy and Verdery 1999: 14–15). El Salvador's postwar moment cannot be understood unless analyzed against the background of the past and with an acknowledgment of the inherited prewar and war legacies. As I have expounded in the introduction to this book, the reference to 'legacies' does not deny change; instead, it attempts to highlight the historical foundations and continuity of certain prewar and wartime problems and processes, such as the relationship between violence and statecraft. As I will show in the following chapters, this relationship was prevalent in the wartime memories and postwar rumors and stories recounted by the left-leaning Salvadorans among whom I conducted research. Likewise, the understanding of change that underpins the official use of the notion of transition necessarily has implications for how we analyze postwar violence. By emphasizing rupture, the preeminence—identified by Kalyvas (2006: 21)—of violence as an event or outcome rather than a process is favored. The result is that the actions and mechanisms that precede violent events (e.g. repression prior to the war) and follow them (e.g. haunting war memories) are often overlooked.

Like path-dependence economic theories of modernization and development, transitions to democracy are by nature both normative and morally imbued. Given certain conditions and the observance of prescribed reforms of state apparatuses, a morally and technically superior future—one based on reconciliation and a respect of human rights—can be attained. Although transitions are modeled on specific Western political agendas (Whitehead 1986), they are defined as largely technical and depoliticized processes (cf. Buur 2002 and Wilson 2001 for the South African Truth and Reconciliation Commission as a technique of nation-state formation). In addition to their evolutionary connotations, transitions to democracy are clearly universalistic in their approach. Not only does the transition paradigm disregard historical continuity but it also overlooks accidents, local idiosyncrasies, and geopolitical circumstances. As a corollary, 'transitologists' are unable to predict the outcome of a transition or to recognize its contradictions and unintended consequences (Burawoy and Verdery 1999: 1). Indeed, El Salvador's democracy has been qualified by critics of the transition as 'low-intensity' (Stahler-Sholk 1994) or 'hybrid' (Karl 1995) to account for the divergences between the ideal-type of democracy that the Peace Accords set out to achieve and the actual result, which has been plagued by public and economic insecurity. While sharing their criticisms, I argue in this book that it is partly the limitations inherent in the uses of the transition paradigm and the notion of democracy by practitioners and scholars of peacebuilding and democratization that preclude a thorough accounting of El Salvador's postwar problem of violence.

By focusing in the following chapters on the nuances and contradictions of El Salvador's transformations since the signing of the Peace Accords, as conveyed by residents of Santiago and neighboring municipalities, this book contributes to the ongoing discussion about the limitations of transitions to democracy that have been premised on the post-Cold War blind belief in liberal market democracy as the panacea for both economic and social ills. I have thus focused on understanding the contradictions inherent in the transformations denoted by the transition paradigm. While the war and the postwar eras differ profoundly in terms of their forms of violence and violent actors, El Salvador's transition to democracy cannot be conceived as a rupture with the past; it is not possible to suggest that it has arrived at a final historical stage where legacies of the past in the form of political and economic structures, memories, and dispositions do not play a role. The high postwar levels of homicides and pervasive public and economic insecurity point to a certain degree of continuity, as, for instance, in the persistence of violence-as-possibility or in the interpretations offered by left-leaning Santiagueñas who explain this violence as political, even if the forms of violence and violent actors are not necessarily the same. The international community and former ARENA governments' emphasis on rupture seems to have buttressed the legitimacy of the democracy effected by the transition rather than facilitating an understanding of the contradictory transformations undergone by El Salvador since the end of the war.

Throughout the book, I focus on the continuation of violence in the postwar era, exploring how ordinary people relate violence to democracy as well as how this relationship unfolds through specific practices, processes, and events. Each of the chapters contributes to nuancing our understanding of the transformations triggered by the Peace Accords in El Salvador as they pertain to postwar subjectivities, statecraft, and citizenship. The chapters show that violence cannot be subsumed in the dominant processes of the period in which it occurred. Depoliticized forms of violence, after all, have appeared in the wartime accounts of residents of Las Ánimas as well as central Santiago. On the other hand, Santiagueños, along with residents of other La Paz municipalities as well as the capital, have drawn explicit and implicit links between postwar forms of violence and El Salvador's political life, albeit differently, depending on their political alignment.

CHAPTER 3

The Postwar Gray Zone of Politics

On 13 August 2009, as a few friends and I were about to leave Santiago to have dinner in Zacatecoluca, we received calls on our mobile phones regarding the assassinations of the two teenage boys in central Santiago mentioned in Chap. 2. Although the sun had already set, we could sight from where we were parked on Anastasio Aquino Avenue a mass of people surrounding the site and the glare of police car headlights. We left for Zacatecoluca amidst pleas from distraught relatives to return home early. During dinner, my friends could not resist speculating about the motives behind the assassinations. Someone suggested that the two boys might have been asked by gang members to carry out a task and then not fulfilled it: 'Perhaps they kept some money that they should have delivered and the *mara* (gang) went ahead and killed them.' However, as my friends gathered more information through phone calls about the identity of the two boys, whose family some of my friends knew, they dismissed the possibility that they were *mareros* (gang members) or related in any way to *maras*. As noted in the previous chapter, during the next few days, rumors circulated throughout the municipality that the assassinations had been a mistake and that someone else had been the intended target. Residents of Santiago's central neighborhoods suggested that the actual target might have been members of a local gang—at the time distinct from the infamous MS 13 and 18th Street transnational gangs—that enjoyed covert support from the local PCN mayor, thanks to its electoral loyalty. Yet

© The Author(s) 2018

A. Montoya, *The Violence of Democracy*, Studies of the Americas,
https://doi.org/10.1007/978-3-319-76330-9_3

nobody ventured to suggest that this was a conclusive explanation. A sentiment predominated that 'these days you can be killed at any point, anywhere, for any reason', as an acquaintance of mine put it.

As this opening vignette illustrates, unintelligibility and uncertainty have characterized Santiagueños' perceptions of postwar violence. El Salvador's main media and its former ARENA governments have consistently portrayed the country's postwar violence as being perpetrated by dehumanized youth who belong to the MS 13 or 18th Street gangs. Yet, even as gang-related explanations have remained salient among ordinary people, rumors sparked by several homicides that occurred in Santiago in 2009 challenged the gang trope while simultaneously struggling to pin down the meaning behind the violence. In contrast to the rightwing media and ARENA governments, both of which offered reductive and clearcut explanations for cases of postwar homicidal violence, ordinary people across the political spectrum perceived the identity of the perpetrators and their motives as fundamentally ambiguous.

Moodie's (2010: 20) ethnographic research in the capital city of San Salvador likewise identified a pervasive sense of 'not-knowing' among San Salvadorans vis-à-vis the postwar violence of the 1990s. While retrospectively they embraced clear-cut scripts of the country's wartime violence, they struggled to understand and cope with the violence of the postwar era. In this process, Moodie argues, San Salvadorans' narration of crime stories served as an effective means of knowledge production about the postwar era, even as these stories contributed to performing the resignification of violence promoted by the ARENA governments. The definition of postwar violence as delinquency and crime involves a misrecognition, or what Moodie (2010: 173) designates as a process of 'un-knowing', of the systemic elements underpinning the persistence of this violence. My own fieldwork, including the many conversations I had with Santiagueños of all political persuasions and the many rumors I recorded, indicated that a sense of 'not-knowing' remained prevalent at the end of the following decade. Nevertheless, there were also attempts, especially among left-leaning Santiagueños, to make sense of the postwar violence with interpretations that moved beyond the gang trope to hint at the persistence of 'political violence'. As explained in Chap. 2, in invoking political violence, ordinary Salvadorans referred to ideologically motivated, state-sponsored violence but often also pointed to the existence of relatively diffuse links between criminals and the country's political life.

This chapter examines how Santiagueñas have attempted to make sense of postwar homicidal violence. In so doing, it explores why left-leaning Santiagueñas' attempts to explain the persistence of this violence suggest the ongoing existence of covert 'political violence'. Part of the answer, I surmise, lies in left-leaning Santiagueñas' resort to wartime knowledge to explain the postwar homicides. In the face of the seemingly unintelligible homicidal violence that persisted under ARENA rule, wartime knowledge offered a lens through which to interpret at least part of this violence as state sponsored. In this sense, I argue that haunting war memories have made their way into left-leaning Santiagueños' explanations for postwar violence even though these memories may not be explicitly acknowledged. These memories have implicitly exposed left-leaning Santiagueños' belief that the categorization of postwar violence as 'social' and 'depoliticized' is inadequate to represent the postwar complexity. In this chapter I illustrate this point through radically different interpretations of the same postwar event by members of two different generations. I go on to argue that, in making sense of the postwar 'murk'[1] that surrounds incidents of violence, left-leaning and disaffected Santiagueños point to a complex interplay of onstage and backstage dynamics within the country's political life, from which state actors are not necessarily as absent as the category 'social violence' implies. By examining an episode of death threats that occurred shortly after I had completed my fieldwork—an episode documented through long telephone conversations with one of the people affected—the chapter teases out the connections lurking among this specific episode, violent actors, and the country's political life. My close friendship with the person subjected to the death threats gave me access to a level of insight that had been difficult to obtain about the violent episodes that had occurred in Santiago during my fieldwork.

I draw on the notion of the 'gray zone' to denote the ambiguity of El Salvador's postwar political life. The term 'gray zone', coined by Primo Levi in reference to the blurriness that he perceived between victims and perpetrators in the 'prisoner-functionary' of a Nazi concentration camp, was subsequently developed by sociologist Javier Auyero (2007). As I will explain later, just as Auyero observed regarding the post-2001 lootings in Argentina, I suggest that left-leaning Santiagueñas' interpretations of

---

[1] I take the notion of 'murk' from Moodie (2010: 20) who, based on Taussig, employs it to refer to the sense of confusion that has characterized El Salvador's postwar violence and how ordinary people have made sense of it.

postwar violence in El Salvador conjure up a 'gray zone' of politics in which different kinds of actors (violent and non-violent or state and non-state) and activities (political and everyday or licit and illicit) seem to coalesce. While the notion of the 'gray zone' does not describe a physical space, I consider the spatial analogy useful for denoting a domain of convergence. Santiagueñas' struggles to explain postwar violence seem to stem from the same lack of clarity that characterizes a gray zone per se. To illustrate this, the chapter draws on the growing body of anthropological literature on the opacity of political democracies.

FROM WAR TO SEEMINGLY UNINTELLIGIBLE VIOLENCE

Julio, a 50-year-old unemployed peasant who has led a grassroots development association in La Paz in which a number of Santiagueños have participated, mentioned to me at the end of a Sunday association meeting in May 2009 that his 17-year-old son had been arrested in March and was still in prison. The hearing was to take place the following morning at the courthouse in San Luis Talpa, a municipality in La Paz located on the road that leads from Santiago to San Salvador. Julio looked dispirited as he explained that for two months he had been trying in vain to get his son out of prison. I decided to accompany him to San Luis Talpa. On Monday morning, a number of people, mostly women, had gathered at the entrance of the courthouse—a small house invigilated by a police officer—to await the release of their relatives. Despite the barrage of questions directed at the police officer by those waiting, he provided no information as to whether their relatives had arrived, what the process would entail, or whether it was guaranteed that they would be released that day. Two hours after our arrival, three young men—one of them Julio's son—arrived in a police van and were taken inside the courthouse, with shackles on their hands and feet. Given that Julio was unemployed and his former wife did not have a stable job, a public defender had been assigned to the case. However, Julio had obtained no information from this lawyer throughout the entire process. All that Julio knew about the case was what he had gleaned through an acquaintance of his, a lawyer who worked for a Salvadoran human rights NGO and had managed to access the police report. This was the court's third attempt to hold the hearing insofar as the judge had not shown up for the two previously designated court dates, thereby extending Julio's son's stay in prison for over two months. Aware as he was that Salvadoran prisons are the sites in which much of the country's crime and homicides are orchestrated,[2] he could not wait to see his son out. The lack of information and support from state institutions throughout this period had only increased Julio's feelings of abandonment and disenfranchisement.

While we waited for hours outside the courthouse, Julio described to me the violent and improper way in which his son had been arrested at home, as recounted to him by the boy's mother. One evening at 10 pm, six military personnel had forcibly entered the house where Julio's son lives with his mother and brothers and taken the 17-year-old away. 'When his mother requested a warrant, the military officers replied that they didn't need one', Julio explained. 'She said that the military officers took my son to a nearby esplanade and placed a gun in his mouth—but then a police vehicle appeared and the officers rushed my son back out into the street.' Clearly, this episode resembled Salvadorans' wartime stories of the late 1970s and early 1980s, when people were taken from their homes at night by police officers or death squads and later disappeared—either imprisoned or killed. The police report, Julio explained, contradicted the mother's account. It stated that the arrests had been made much earlier on a street near the scene of a robbery and that the arrestees were carrying weapons at the time of the arrest.

Julio held his own view of the motives for the arrest. He explained that his son lives in a 'red' neighborhood, an area whose color classification—an allusion to the distinctively red FMLN flag—signifies that most residents publicly endorse the country's leftwing party. Julio believed that his son, along with other young people, had been imprisoned a week before the presidential election so as to reduce FMLN voter turnout. While this interpretation struck me as an implausible and inefficient way to decrease the FMLN share of the vote, it was consistent with the repertoire of rumors about ARENA's fraud strategies that had circulated before and after the 2009 presidential election. More importantly, the attribution of the arrest to the ARENA government resonated with rumors and stories—especially, though not exclusively, among leftwing Santiagueñas—that sought to explain many of the country's postwar homicides, such as the rumored assassination of FMLN leaders by state-sponsored gunmen

---

[2] It has been extensively reported how the overcrowding of prisons resulting from the enactment of *mano dura* policies since 2003 has enabled the flourishing of organized crime from within (see Chap. 4 for more details about this).

during the 2009 elections (see Chap. 5), as being rooted in persistent wartime political cleavages.

Since my first visit to Santiago in 2001, left-leaning Santiagueñas have frequently recounted wartime stories about selective assassinations, the display of dead bodies and severed body parts in the streets and on the bridges of Santiago, and the frequent *cateos* (house searches) conducted by the National Police in central Santiago and by the National Guard in Santiago's rural areas such as Las Ánimas. Although not every detail was unambiguous, these recollections denoted, for the most part, clear boundaries between good and bad violence; between political violence and crime (the latter often said to have barely existed during the war); and between the FMLN guerrillas, on the one hand, and the army, police forces, and state-sponsored paramilitary groups on the other. In short, left-leaning Santiagueños' wartime stories seemed, in hindsight, crystal clear to them. This apparent clarity, I argue, is a result of both the ability to make sense of wartime recollections retrospectively and of the lack of any public discussion that might have lent complexity to the formulaic wartime scripts that framed the memories of the two opposing sides. Interestingly, left-leaning Santiagueños have consistently insinuated that much of the country's postwar homicidal violence remains 'political' and implied that members of the former ARENA governments may be involved. The uncertainty that generally surrounds El Salvador's postwar episodes, in other words, dissipated slightly, as left-leaning Santiagueños explained certain high-profile episodes or mobilized the past to speculate about the possible political motivations and perpetrators underlying the problem of postwar violence.

Even as I was conducting fieldwork in 2007—outside of an electoral campaign—a few left-leaning Santiagueños insisted that the ARENA government remained repressive and that it was thus risky to voice political views publicly. 'You should even be careful about making inquiries about wartime violence for your research', I was warned by a man after our interview at his home. These kinds of fears increased during the 2009 electoral period, most likely due to the heightened hostility between members of ARENA and the FMLN that characterized that year's disputed elections. It was within this atmosphere of political tension that the head of my host family suggested that if Rodrigo Ávila won the elections there would be *matazón* (see Introduction). Given the electoral challenge that the FMLN posed to ARENA during the 2009 electoral season, a sentiment predominated among left-leaning and disaffected Santiagueños that ARENA, if reelected, would persecute those who had supported the FMLN.

The episode of Julio's son's arrest, which occurred just before the 2009 presidential election, epitomizes the prevailing sentiment among leftwing Santiagueñas who had lived through the war. Yet the episode, which Julio's son interpreted quite differently than his father, also highlights the different perspectives of two generations. In explaining the arrest as the result of persistent war-related political hostilities between ARENA and FMLN, Julio mobilized the wartime past to make sense of the murk surrounding his son's arrest. Julio's mobilization of the past became all the more evident when contrasted with his son's interpretation of his own arrest. Julio's son was released following his appearance in court. Afterward, I joined Julio, his son, and the mother for lunch at a nearby eatery. The son seemed terrified, insisting to his mother that he would be killed if he returned home. After his mother had calmed him down, he shared the details of his arrest. He explained that he knew about a local police officer's involvement in drug trafficking and thought the arrest had been a means of silencing him. The night he was taken away, he was told by the military that he would soon be freed from prison but that they would come back for him. Julio, who had listened silently to his son's account, suggested when his son had finished that he should file a report of the case. His son said categorically that he would not. As in most of the cases of extortion and other forms of menace that I encountered throughout my research, the son's unwillingness to report the case rested on a two-pronged attitude toward police officers that was shared throughout the political spectrum: first, cynicism about their ability or even willingness to do anything about the predicaments in which ordinary people found themselves, and, second, an awareness of police officers' plausible involvement in illicit activities.

In Julio's narrative, the wartime past made a subtle appearance in the present. He implicitly explained his son's arrest as the result of the ongoing confrontations, rooted in wartime, between ARENA and the FMLN, and ARENA's resort to repression to maintain its grip on power. While I do not wish to underestimate the validity of Julio's interpretation, the appearance of the past in his explanation suggests that the country's postwar era is informed by a haunting, traumatic past with which its citizens have not yet come to terms. This is not surprising given that the transition from war to peace has been limited to institutional reforms, most of which have proved disappointing, as evidenced by Julio's frustration with the scant support he obtained from the Public Prosecutor's Office and by the unaccountable acts of the police and military personnel involved in his son's arrest. Building upon Gordon (1997), I suggest that an acknowledgment of the haunting nature of the past—that is, its troublesome persistence in the present—can shed light on the operations of change that have occurred throughout El Salvador's transition. Specifically, such an acknowledgment can help identify the continuities, both material and ideational, that exist between El Salvador's prewar and wartime eras and that have been overshadowed by the postwar reform of institutions and de facto economic transformations. Yet I would suggest that Julio's narration of his son's arrest brought back the past in a more subtle and less overtly instrumental way than do explicit comparisons between present-day predicaments and wartime El Salvador. Using Connerton's terms (1989: 25), I suggest that, through his interpretation of his son's arrest, Julio was not merely 'remembering' but also 'acting out' the past; he was reliving the past in the present through a compulsion—rather than a deliberate effort—that rendered the past immediate and familiar without his even being aware of it.

The lack of coordinated attempts among Salvadorans to publicly address the wartime past, along with the persistence of daily homicides and the corruption or inefficiency of state officials, have imbued the past with a haunting nature most often revealed in the fine interweaving, whether explicit or implicit, of past and present. In this vein, it is also necessary to consider the symbolic reverberations of 20 years of rule by ARENA, itself a war-haunted party. Although ARENA did not make its way to the government until 1989, the party was founded in 1981 as an alliance between former military personnel and members of the agrarian elite. As noted in the Introduction, the party's main founding leader, Major Roberto D'Aubuisson, was cited by the Commission on the Truth as the founder of some of El Salvador's wartime death squads and the intellectual author of Archbishop Romero's assassination (United Nations 1993: 180, 185). Given the party's origins, I surmise that 20 years of ARENA-elected governments must have been a troubling presence for many of the Salvadorans who lived through the war. It is not surprising, then, that Julio and his son held such different interpretations of the son's arrest given that Julio had lived through the civil war, whereas his son presumably learned about it through predominantly formulaic postwar accounts. Yet, the distance between Julio's and his son's interpretations of the arrest notwithstanding, both hint at the existence of a 'gray zone' defining El Salvador's political life, where actors, motives, and forms of violence are ambiguous and the boundaries between the licit and illicit blur in the manner described by Auyero (2007). In the following sections, I describe a 2009 episode that occurred during, but mostly after, my fieldwork, in which this postwar gray zone and its web of clandestine connections emerged more clearly.

THE 2009 ELECTION AS A CATALYST OF CHANGE

On 21 October 2009, after I had returned to the UK, I received a phone call from Elena, a close friend I met on my first trip to Santiago in 2001 and with whom I have kept in touch regularly. As soon as I picked up the phone I sensed an unusual degree of emotion in her voice: 'I need to talk to you, Ainhoa. I've gotten myself into some trouble and don't know what to do'. At the time, Elena was a 40-year-old social worker at the state-funded Santa Teresa National Hospital in Zacatecoluca, where she had worked for 12 years. Elena lived in Santiago and commuted daily to Zacatecoluca, a 20-minute bus trip. She had actively participated in the local FMLN since 2000. Because of her unconditional support for this party and her popularity in Santiago, she had been informally sounded out as a possible municipal FMLN candidate on two occasions. Part of her popularity stemmed from her having spent four years coordinating the group that ran the El Calvario Catholic Church of Santiago, where Father Óscar—who embraces Archbishop Romero's thought and liberation theology[3]—served from 2006 to the end of 2010. In addition to her participation in these two groups, Elena and some of her colleagues at the hospital—all of them aligned with the FMLN but only a few working actively for the party—determined after the March 2009 presidential election that the new FMLN government would provide a friendly milieu in which to undertake reforms of their hospital. They believed the FMLN victory opened an opportunity to put an end to years of corruption within their workplace, beginning with the removal of *areneros* (ARENA loyal-

---

[3] Liberation theology is a Catholic doctrine that originated after the Second Vatican Council and derived from precepts laid down at the Conference of Latin American Bishops in Medellín, Colombia, in 1968 (Kirk 1979; Planas 1986; Mainwaring and Wilde 1989; Rowland 1999; Peterson et al. 2001). Based on a critical interpretation of the Bible and political life, liberation theology proposes a denunciation of injustice and human rights violations, an advocacy of and alignment with the poor, and a stimulation of their awareness of their unjust situation and the possibility of transforming it. For more information on its impact in El Salvador, see Chaps. 6 and 7.

ists) from the high administrative positions they had held in the hospital for several years while ARENA was in power.

In May 2009, Elena and her colleagues informally founded the Committee for the Development of Health. The committee's first intervention was to petition El Salvador's new Health Minister, María Isabel Rodríguez, to elect Tito Hernán Gámez—a doctor already working at their hospital—as the new director of the institution. The committee members met with both El Salvador's health minister and vice-minister and handed them hundreds of signatures collected from the hospital personnel. They finally achieved their goal: Dr. Tito Hernán Gámez was officially appointed as the new hospital director on 10 August 2009. Dr. Gámez requested that committee members continued working hand-in-hand with him by making suggestions on how to improve and transform the hospital. When I left El Salvador in mid-August, after more than a year of fieldwork in Santiago, Elena was excited about the possibilities for change that she anticipated once the hospital was no longer directed by an *arenero*. Until then, she had frequently complained about the pilfering of medications by hospital personnel and the resultant shortages for patients; the substitution of patients' new prostheses, for which they had already paid, with used ones by a doctor who kept the new ones for his private practice; and the arbitrary fees charged for surgeries and stays in the hospital that were theoretically free. Even more notorious was the fraudulent diverting of public funds designated for the reconstruction of the hospital building, which had been virtually uninhabitable since the 2001 earthquakes.[4] In 2009, with the funds spent and the work unfinished, the hospital operated out of portable cabins whose conditions were far from ideal for surgeries, x-rays, and patient welfare; some patients were reduced to sharing beds. However, Elena's and her colleagues' initial excitement about the prospects for improving these conditions gradually turned into an overt conflict between the FMLN and ARENA loyalists within the hospital—a conflict indicative of the persistence of wartime political cleavages in the postwar era.

Upset, Elena recounted to me in her 21 October phone call that she and other committee members had received death threats for their participation in the reform-minded group. It had all started, she explained, with an official announcement by the Ministry of Health that, as of 1 November, hospital employees who had held high-level administrative

---

[4] 'El terremoto que duró 10 años', *El Faro*, 9 August 2010.

positions during the ARENA administration would be demoted to lower positions with correspondingly lower salaries. Elena mentioned that those holding these positions were all active ARENA members who had benefited from their political affiliation and their participation in the ARENA political clientele—something that members of all political parties enjoy, albeit with a particular advantage for ARENA members given that their party held the presidency, and hence the administration of the country's resources, for over 20 years.[5] Not only did ARENA members protest the news of their being replaced, but they also blamed committee members for their future replacement. After the announcement was made, the disgruntled employees began holding meetings to plot their opposition to the decision to demote them while insidiously harassing committee members. Elena herself had been warned that if the committee did not manage to get their demotions reversed, Elena and her colleagues would suffer the consequences. Initially, Elena and the other committee members disregarded these threats. More recently, however, Elena said that she had felt deeply unsettled by comments made by hospital personnel. One day, for instance, a nurse approached her and said, 'Elena, you should be careful; many people have been killed in this country for talking too much or meddling in others' affairs.'

Gangs Enter the Picture

The episode did not end there. Elena continued to recount how it unfolded in further phone conversations detailing the latest threats. Two days after our first conversation, Moisés, an orderly at Santa Teresa and a member of the aforementioned committee, arrived at the hospital on his day off and told committee members some alarming news. The previous night, while Moisés was on duty at the hospital, a youth in loose-fitting gang-style clothes had asked for him at the entrance. The young man, unknown to Moisés, informed him that Jaime, one of the hospital employees soon to be demoted, had visited the Colonia El Quinto Patio, a sector of

[5] Postwar administrations led by ARENA from 1989 to 2009 entailed the perpetuation of bureaucracies through clientelism, enabling a degree of state capture that allowed the party to retain the presidency for four consecutive terms. Indeed, the Civil Service Law reform (Decreto Legislativo No. 10, *Diario Oficial*, 25 May 2009) passed before the FMLN took office in June 2009 was aimed at protecting ARENA's long-established civil servants from being immediately fired and replaced by individuals associated with the incoming FMLN government.

Zacatecoluca known to be gang-controlled. According to this youth, Jaime had met with a member of the 18th Street gang in this area and had given the gang member a folder in which were enclosed ten photographs of committee members. Jaime had then paid him US$600 with the understanding that 18th Street members would kill three of these committee members. One of the three people targeted was Moisés; the other two were Elena and Xiomara, another active committee member. The youth explained that the 18th Street members would phone a gang member at the San Vicente prison, who would in turn send someone to do the job. He told Moisés that not much could be done to halt this.

Committee members tried without success to find out more information about the alleged gang member who had arrived at the hospital to warn Moisés about Jaime's hiring of gangs. Simultaneously, rumors circulated in the hospital suggesting that the people on the verge of losing their positions were going to make their own attempts on committee members' lives. Members of the committee, along with the recently appointed hospital director, asked for help from an active FMLN member, a former mayor of Zacatecoluca personally acquainted with certain gang members in the municipality. When the committee members met with him, the former mayor confirmed that the 18th Street gang was the one ruling in Zacatecoluca and that its main leader was imprisoned in San Vicente. He was, however, surprised to learn of gang members' involvement in a plot against the committee, since according to him the gang members in Zacatecoluca had always respected FMLN members. He noted how difficult it was to halt this kind of job once it had been set in motion. The gang members would have to be paid US$1000, and even then it would be unclear whether the job had truly been halted. Furthermore, if the job was not accomplished by one gang, it could always be accomplished by another; that is, there was always the possibility that someone else would be sent to do the job. The former mayor also observed that whomever was sent to do the job would try to link the assassination with a robbery so as to disguise the real motive and perpetrator. He suggested to committee members that they not use their mobile phones in the street or wear any sort of jewelry, since a theft of those items could be used as a pretext for an assassination.

The meeting with the former mayor of Zacatecoluca left committee members even more shaken than they already were. His remarks and his apparent nonchalance at the scenario described to him by committee members seemed to indicate that the hiring of gang members to carry out the assassinations of committee members was entirely plausible. Postwar violence in El Salvador is officially depicted as being perpetrated more or less exclusively by and against rival gangs. This belief is fed by the fact that a large majority of the victims of violence in present-day El Salvador are males between the ages of 15 and mid-40s (IML 2009: 14–16). The media have contributed to corroborating this view. The major newspapers and television channels, most rightwing and supportive of ARENA, devoted relatively little attention to homicides until the FMLN victory in the 2009 presidential election. Never front-page news, coverage of homicides was until then limited to a list of the people killed on a given day or weekend, including their ages, places of origin, and where they were killed or found dead. Most often, homicides news would go unnoticed in the departmental sections of major newspapers, unless accompanied by a sensational headline stressing the number of homicides in the past month or invoking a term like 'massacre'. After the 2009 FMLN victory, however, homicidal violence became front-page news in the most widely read Salvadoran newspapers, the rightwing *La Prensa Gráfica* and *El Diario de Hoy*. The front pages of these newspapers were emblazoned with headlines such as 'Homicides, a Real Threat' and 'Businessmen and Citizens Alarmed'; figures, graphs, and statistics about the homicides; and quotes from public figures stressing the problem of security.[6] 'It is going to be extremely difficult to reactivate the national economy … if we don't have a climate of security appropriate for business' were the words of the executive director of the National Association of Private Enterprise (ANEP).[7] 'Insecurity is a national trauma that requires an extraordinary effort', the Archbishop of San Salvador declared in the same newspaper. Yet even as homicidal violence began to be represented as a problem of national security, gangs continued to be foregrounded.[8] The 2009 shift in the media's approach to covering violence is likely related to the concentration of the main print media and TV channels in the hands of a few elite families (see Wolf 2017: 79–83).

---

[6] 'Se eleva a 13 el promedio diario de homicidios', *El Diario de Hoy*, 17 June 2009; 'Temen que ola de asesinatos se incremente', *El Diario de Hoy*, 17 June 2009.

[7] 'ANEP demanda un freno inmediato a la violencia', *El Diario de Hoy*, 18 June 2009.

[8] See, for instance, 'El Plan 503: Maras ordenan secuestros exprés y chantajes', *El Diario de Hoy*, 21 May 2009.

Worried about whether Elena was taking enough safety precautions and knowledgeable of the risk of using collective transport,[9] I asked her in one of our phone conversations how she was commuting to Zacatecoluca. She was still taking the bus, she replied, but a nurse, a colleague of hers, drove her from the hospital to the bus station in the evenings. She was also changing bus routes from one day to the next, so that it would be difficult for anyone to predict which bus she would be on. Elena had even stopped engaging in regular activities such as going to the gym, at least until the situation calmed down. I chided her for continuing to travel by bus, where she could be an easy target, and encouraged her to find people who could drive her to the hospital for the foreseeable future. She concurred that it was necessary to be careful but insisted that she did not want anyone to drive her: 'You know how they are here, they just shoot anyone. They don't even care whether or not he or she is the right person. Remember what happened to the two boys killed near my home in August?' Her mention of the assassination of the two young cousins in central Santiago worried me all the more, and I urged her to avoid walking in the streets of Zacatecoluca and Santiago as much as possible. Elena's utterances in one of our conversations spoke to the anxiety that she and her family members felt: 'My mom wants me to report the whole thing to the police or the Public Prosecutor's Office. She is so worried! We don't even pick up the phone now unless we recognize the number. My mom says I should leave for the United States and stay with my brother, but I don't want to. What would I do there without a job? I can't even speak English!'

THE NOT-SO-VISIBLE

The connection between gangs and political actors unearthed in Elena's episode of death threats is one that manifested episodically during my fieldwork in different ways and through various means, both during and outside electoral periods. In Santiago, local gang members have consistently joined the PCN mayor on her campaign visits to various sectors of the municipality. Santiagueñas from various positions on the political spectrum mentioned to me that during electoral campaigns prior to 2009, these gang members allied with the PCN had attacked groups of *areneros* (ARENA loyalists) and *efemelenistas* (FMLN loyalists) while these groups

---

[9] At the time, many reported homicides—a great number of them related to extortion—occurred in buses.

were painting walls and house fronts with their party's colors at night. Indeed, two ARENA members were killed in such circumstances during the 2004 presidential election. ARENA leaders alleged that those killed had been run over by a PCN member driving a pick-up truck, but the case never went to trial. While I did not hear of any similar incident during the 2008/2009 electoral season, I was present when members of the local gang allied with the PCN threatened *efemelenistas* at an FMLN rally preceding the 2009 municipal election.

That FMLN rally, mirroring public gatherings of this party's loyalists in municipalities throughout the country, consisted of a colorful caravan of pick-up trucks slowly traversing Santiago's central streets. The backs of these pick-up trucks were crammed with FMLN loyalists—men, women, and children of all ages—dressed in red and waving FMLN flags while slogan-shouting, singing, and dancing. The vehicles participating in the caravan played famous *bachatas* and *merengues* with lyrics altered to anticipate an FMLN victory in the presidential election or to critique the previous 20 years of ARENA rule. The two-hour caravan ended in Santiago's central plaza, between the municipality council building and the market, where a mass of people and vehicles convened. FMLN loyalists, excited by that day's massive rally, jumped onto the stage, located in front of the market and opposite the council building, from which they waved large red FMLN flags. Gang members who supported the PCN, watching the spectacle from within the municipality council building and clearly irritated by the FMLN's massive and colorful occupation of Santiago's plaza, made their way onto the stage and began beating up some of the party's loyalists. The response of the FMLN leaders was to immediately evacuate the plaza so as to forestall any violence; those who remained fighting on the stage were finally separated, and the initially tense incident ended without further complications. Yet this incident, in which gang members did not hesitate to assert their control over the public space of the plaza, made visible the connections that have existed for years between the PCN mayor and local gangs.

A second occasion on which the connection between gangs and political actors manifested during my fieldwork was an interview I conducted with a police officer who worked at a subdelegation in the periphery of San Salvador. I was introduced to him by a friend and managed to obtain an interview to find out about his personal experiences of violence between political opponents during elections. At some point during the interview, he interrupted his enumeration of the cases of this kind of violence reported during the months prior to the 2009 elections at his subdelega-tion and recounted to me an anecdote about an arrest he had recently made of several gang members. On the way to the police subdelegation, the oldest gang member among the arrestees, a man in his early 30s, implored that his face be covered before they left the vehicle. 'I was not paying him much attention, so the man explained to me that if certain ARENA members of parliament learned of his arrest, they would order his assassination while he was in prison to prevent him from divulging that they had hired him to kill FMLN members', the police officer remarked. 'I don't know what happened after that since it was not my job to follow the case, but we are aware that gang members often act as *sicarios* (hired assassins) targeting leftwing political leaders.'

This police officer's anecdote was corroborated by Tutela Legal's late 2000s annual reports on the results of this organization's investigations of a small number of unresolved homicides. These reports suggested that gangs have sometimes been hired for 'social cleansing' or 'political' pur-poses. In other words, the reports stated that there is reason to believe that some gang violence may be rooted in motives unrelated to inter-gang conflicts (Tutela 2006: 13–16; 2007: 9; 2008: 14). I did not document any further cases in which a link between gangs and political actors mani-fested in the late 2000s, and such links were rarely discussed publicly. However, these episodes pointed to the clandestine connections between violent actors and political actors, and between licit and illicit activities, that frequently surfaced in my conversations with disaffected Santiagueños and that would become public when in 2016 the digital newspaper *El Faro* published evidence of electoral alliances between the country's main polit-ical parties—both ARENA and FMLN—and gangs (see the Epilogue for further details about these alliances). These connections have been men-tioned by people across the political spectrum, with those on the Left tending to associate them specifically with ARENA. Yet Zilberg's (2007) research in the early 2000s explored rumors spread by the Right that assimilated the FMLN with gangs.

In a different vein, criminal activities such as drug trafficking have been linked with El Salvador's political life as well as with gangs. Since the late 2000s, rumors spread by Salvadoran citizens and media outlets alike have suggested that the country has increasingly become a part of drug-traffickers' route toward the north. Relative to Guatemala and Honduras, not much of the overall drug smuggling that occurs through territorial routes crosses El Salvador. Yet rumors, backed by police intelligence, have related certain Salvadoran political actors to drug trafficking in the Northern Triangle. An incident that sparked an impassioned public discussion in El Salvador of this issue was the brutal assassination of four Salvadorans—three ARENA members of the Central American Parliament and their chauffeur—in Guatemala in 2007 (PNUD 2009: 143). These assassinations, which rumors and investigations linked to drug trafficking, attracted a polemical response, especially given that all the Guatemalan anti-narcotics policemen arrested for alleged involvement in the assassinations were themselves assassinated while in a Guatemalan prison.[10] News and investigations in recent years have only confirmed the links between political actors and drug trafficking.[11] They have likewise shed light on the corruption and involvement in organized crime of PNC high officials.[12]

Another frequently invoked link during Funes's government was between Salvadoran gangs and Mexican drug cartels such as the Zetas.[13] It was suggested that increasing vigilance by authorities in the Pacific has led to increased activity along the route through the Central American isthmus together with a resort to preexisting criminal networks such as gangs. More recent reports have suggested that these are ad hoc relationships and that to date Salvadoran gangs are instead involved in local drug distribution, with extortion rather than drug trafficking serving as their main source of income (Dudley 2010; see Chap. 4 in this book).[14] El Salvador's role in the drug-trafficking business is largely as a money-laundering site due to its dollarized economy, such that dollars obtained from drug

[10] See 'CICIG determinó que asesinato de diputados fue por drogas', *El Faro*, 15 November 2010.

[11] See, for instance, 'El Cártel de Texis', *El Faro*, 16 May 2011; 'Autoridades salvadoreñas vuelven a ignorar pistas sobre nexo entre diputado y narcos', *InSight Crime*, 12 April 2013; 'ONU: Narcos con nexos políticos en El Salvador', *La Prensa Gráfica*, 4 July 2013; 'Exdiputados vinculados en redes de narcotráfico', *La Prensa Gráfica*, 13 September 2013; 'Cinco exdiputados salvadoreños que han sido involucrados en delitos', *El Diario de Hoy*, 7 October 2015.

[12] See 'Infiltrados', *El Faro*, 14 May 2014; 'Infiltrados, un año después', *Revista Factum*, 13 May 2015.

[13] See, for instance, 'Funes alerta de la presencia de Los Zetas en El Salvador para sellar una alianza con las maras locales', *Europa Press*, 16 April 2010; 'Organised Crime in Central America: The Rot Spreads', *The Economist*, 20 January 2011.

[14] See 'Las pandillas, los nuevos actores en la venta de droga', *El Diario de Hoy*, 28 June 2015; 'Algunos empresarios y los pandilleros trabajan para los narcos en la región, confirma GAFIC', *La Página*, 27 November 2014; 'Cartel de Sinaloa contrató a MS para vengar robo de droga', *La Prensa Gráfica*, 8 May 2014; 'MS-13's 'El Barney': A Trend or an Isolated Case?' *InSight Crime*, 11 June 2013.

trafficking in Central America travel in the opposite direction from drugs.[15] However, all this evidence, hinting as it does at clandestine entanglements, serves to confirm the wide currency of the idea of a 'gray zone' of politics in El Salvador—an idea frequently conjured by disaffected Santiagueñas and similar to the one described by Auyero in Argentina.

THE POSTWAR GRAY ZONE

Auyero (2007) set out to investigate the supermarket lootings that had occurred in Buenos Aires in the context of the 2001 Argentinean economic crisis. By unpacking how these lootings developed, he sought to answer how and why these extraordinary acts of violence occurred in the first place. The Argentinean media had depicted the lootings as clear-cut acts of desperation by citizens who had publicly expressed their inability to feed their families in the face of the unemployment stemming from the crisis. However, Auyero's investigation of the lootings as well as of the actors participating in them and their connections to political actors yielded the image of a 'gray zone' in Argentinean politics. Auyero (2007: 32) suggests that a 'gray area [exists] where the activities of those perpetrating the violence and those who presumably seek to control them coalesce'. He adds: 'I conceive of the gray zone as both an *empirical object* and an *analytical lens* that draws our attention toward a murky area where normative boundaries dissolve, where state actors and political elites promote and/or actively tolerate and/or participate in damage-making' (Auyero 2007: 32, emphasis added). Interestingly, Auyero's research of the 2001 lootings revealed several insidious elements: the coordination of the lootings by political party brokers and their not wholly overt clientelistic practices that linked both formal and informal realms of politics with everyday life, the ambiguous role played by police officers in the lootings, and, more generally, the entanglement of politics and violence. Looters and looted alike identified *punteros* (party brokers)—and, in at least one case, a political leader of the Peronist Party and mayor of Moreno (a district in Buenos Aires)—as having encouraged the lootings of small supermarkets and stores while the police remained inactive or focused only on protecting large supermarket chains or those stores whose owners had paid for protection (Auyero 2007: 97–130). The disclosure of the clandestine relationships underlying the 2001 lootings revealed, more broadly,

---

[15] 'Maras y narcotráfico', *El Faro*, 19 March 2014.

the linkages that existed in Argentina between routine politics and extraordinary acts of collective violence.

I suggest that the notion of the 'gray zone' is likewise pertinent to the analysis of El Salvador's postwar violence. While once again I do not intend to suggest a systematic link between gangs and political actors in postwar El Salvador, my research points to the existence of clandestine connections between violence and politics—as revealed in the death threat incident in which Elena got involved as well as the arrest of a gang member described by the police officer. Rumors, crime stories, media scandals, and Tutela's investigations about gangs acting as violent entrepreneurs—whether for political actors, Mexican cartels, or anyone wishing to settle a problem—suggest that these connections have become relatively recurrent. Indeed, as mentioned earlier, in 2016, clear evidence would emerge that both ARENA and FMLN had engaged in negotiations with gangs to gain their electoral support. In this sense, the postwar episodes described in this chapter, along with ubiquitous rumors, point to the existence of a 'gray zone' in which these connections, whether ephemeral or systematic, are plausible. In this gray zone, the boundaries among actors, domains, activities, and various forms of violence become blurred.

Part of the ambiguity of gray zones stems from the hybrid actors who populate them, such as the Brazilian 'police-bandits' who embody the connection between police and drug gangs so pervasive in the *favelas* of Rio de Janeiro (see Goldstein, cited in Auyero 2007: 36; see also Misse and Vargas 2010) or, in the United States, the 'criminal cops' who both enforce and transgress the law as they police immigrant neighborhoods (Zilberg 2007: 45–47). An example of how this ambiguity manifests in El Salvador is Julio's son's explanation for his arrest, which presumed that a police officer was also a drug trafficker. Drug trafficking is likewise connected to gangs and political actors through rumors and anecdotal scandals that make their way into the media, such as the assassination of the three ARENA members of the Central American Parliament and their chauffeur in Guatemala. In a different vein, the incumbent Santiago mayor's promotion of 'good governance',[16] with the support of NGOs and foreign development organizations, masked her association with political clienteles, and

---

[16] Commonplace in the lexicon of international public policy since the 1990s, the term 'good governance' has become prominent in neoliberal agendas as a means of stipulating how power should be exercised in relation to the management of economic and social resources—as though this were a mere technical problem (Leftwich 1994).

with a local gang, during elections (see Chap. 5). This corresponds to what Zilberg (2007: 39) has described as the logic of '*doble cara*' (two-faced), a Salvadoran expression noting that 'things are never as they appear or as they are presented.' In invoking the 'doble cara', Zilberg points to the widespread suspicion among Salvadorans that seemingly different things, such as gangs and political actors (in her work FMLN members), may be converging in the postwar era.

El Salvador's postwar political life plays out through a dynamic interplay of onstage and backstage processes or a combination of hyper-visible and shadowy elements. Buur (2002) has examined the relationship between onstage and backstage dynamics in the work of the South African Truth and Reconciliation Commission (SATRC) established in 1995, after a negotiated settlement put an end to the apartheid regime. The SATRC sought to present itself as a depoliticized and impartial body that would arrive at a scientific or technical outcome. As Buur (2002) has described, the success of this ostensible separation of politics and science involved, on the one hand, the suspension of the SATRC in both place and time so as to underline its distance from political institutions and, on the other, backstage processes in which ambiguous information was suppressed. I consider that processes akin to Buur's description of the suppression of ambiguity involved in the work of the SATRC have also played out in El Salvador's political life.

In El Salvador, gangs have been foregrounded as the primary postwar source of violence despite indications that not all of the country's homicides can be attributed to gangs.[17] Indeed, gangs seem to have become the scapegoat in El Salvador's democracy (Zilberg 2007: 44). Until recently, the hyper-visibility of gang members' marked bodies[18]—gothic tattoos, shaved heads, and hip-hop style baggy clothes—has allowed the country's rightwing media and former ARENA governments to manage the problem of postwar violence through a sort of 'biospectacle' consisting of the visual displays and criminalization of marked bodies (Moodie 2009). The hyper-visibility of these displays has its counterpart in the shadowy areas of

---

[17] Between 2002 and 2008, the Salvadoran IML found that the motives behind 55.7 percent of homicides were unknown, 28.8 percent were due to common delinquency, and only 10.6 percent were attributable to gangs. The PNC, however, determined that between 60–70 percent of homicides during that period had been perpetrated by gangs (IML 2009: 69, 72).

[18] Although this aesthetic is associated with gangs, it has in fact been widely adopted by young Salvadorans embracing a hip-hop style.

the political domain that they favor. The ARENA government's gang-abatement policies along with the media's deployment of gang images have played a major role in creating an onstage portrayal of postwar violence that eclipses the many backstage activities and clandestine relations that contribute to the country's postwar endemic violence, for example, gang members acting as violent entrepreneurs for political actors, a link that has surfaced anecdotally through rumor, media scandal, and investigative journalism.

Whether or not fully intended, a 'politics of (in)visibility' is at work in this interplay of onstage and backstage processes, similar to what, Nordstrom (2004) argues, played out after the 1983 riots in Sri Lanka. In comparing her field experience with official accounts of the violent 1983 anti-Tamil riots, she found out that significant details—most notably the involvement of priests in promoting the violence of the Sinhalese rioters against the Tamils—had been 'edited out' of official accounts because they strayed from straightforward and unambiguous depictions of violence and would thus have required further explanations (Nordstrom 2004: 31). In El Salvador, not only have the major media foregrounded gangs and their alleged violence over and above other details, but they have also presented postwar homicidal violence in a highly decontextualized manner. The almost anecdotal manner in which homicides have been described in the media has lent a semblance of unintelligibility to them, especially when details of the homicides do not quite seem consistent with gang violence. The seeming disorderly and anecdotal nature of violence, I thus argue for the case of El Salvador, is not entirely accidental. Indeed, the gray zone hinted at by Santiagueños is consistent with a politics of (in)visibility.

A gray zone has been conjured by Santiagueños of both Left and Right persuasions, with left-leaning citizens frequently asserting the existence of backstage state domains. In this sense, it seems pertinent to introduce the metaphor of the 'Shadow State' (Gledhill 1999; Reno 1995). The Shadow State, Reno (1995) has suggested for the case of postcolonial Sierra Leone, is the parallel authority that emerges out of state and political actors' participation in a country's informal economy. This metaphor is apt for postwar El Salvador given the opacity of some of its state practices and effects. Rumors by left-leaning Santiagueños have pointed to opaque practices that have in turn consolidated political and economic power, resulting in a sort of Shadow State. The opacity of the state, as conveyed by rumors, is not a postwar phenomenon but rather one that developed during wartime. During El Salvador's civil war, there existed state-sponsored violence perpetrated by proxies such as death squads and paramilitary groups (see United Nations 1993: 58, 180–189). Episodes of wartime violence, even those on the magnitude of massacres, were denied or attributed to the guerrillas, as in the case of El Mozote and nearby areas, in northern Morazán, in which more than a thousand civilians were killed between 11 and 13 December 1981 (see Binford 1996: 49–67). While I do not suggest that the postwar Shadow State is a mere reproduction of clandestine wartime relationships and activities, it is necessary to note the implication by left-leaning Santiagueñas that the advent of democracy has not dissolved existing backstage state domains but instead facilitated their reproduction. Yet, just as Auyero has suggested for the Argentinean case, the grayness of El Salvador's postwar era is not just a relevant *object of enquiry* but also a useful *heuristic device*. The next section expounds this point.

POSTWAR LAWLESSNESS

In a later phone conversation with Elena, she explained to me how unbearable the situation at the hospital had become for all committee members: 'Two committee members who were going to replace those holding high administrative positions have received phone calls at their homes. The callers threatened them, insinuating that something would happen to their relatives if they accepted the positions that had been offered to them. Both of them are so scared for their families that they have resigned. The situation at the hospital is really unbearable for all of us. Tomorrow the *areneros* have organized a protest at the hospital and threatened not to let us in, so we are travelling to San Salvador to explain the situation to the Minister of Health'. In yet another phone conversation, Elena sounded downhearted. Tearfully, she told me that nobody had received her and her colleagues at the Health Ministry, even though they had arranged an audience days in advance and sent a letter explaining the situation at the Santa Teresa Hospital.

Skeptical that the police would intervene and preferring not to stir up any more resentment among the ARENA members at the hospital, Elena's fellow committee members chose not to report the threats against them. Elena was the only one determined to make a report. However, once at the Public Prosecutor's Office, she was denied the opportunity to file one: 'I was told that I could not report because I had no evidence, and that I could be sued by the very people I was seeking to report. I was so mad at them! I had to call my cousin Mario, who is a lawyer. Only when he arrived did they allow me to file a report. Even then, I was told that there was nothing to be done with my case. My mom says that even if nothing is done, at least if something happens to me there will be a report indicating what was going on'. Elena's episode continued with threats that persisted for over a year but never materialized. Perhaps terrifying her and her colleagues in the committee was the only outcome actually sought by those affected by the demotions. The episode nonetheless revealed three important aspects of El Salvador's postwar era: the plausibility of clandestine relations between political actors and gangs; the lack of institutional support for victims; and the ways in which the grayness of El Salvador's postwar political life works as a heuristic device for ordinary people.

The sequence of events in which both Julio's son and Elena became involved revealed the plausibility of clandestine connections and activities involving state or political actors but also the lawlessness that has characterized El Salvador's postwar era. This lawlessness is evident in the arbitrariness with which the rule of law is enforced and with which state institutions of order intervene. Julio got no support or information from the lawyer in the Public Prosecutor's Office who had been assigned to the case of his son's arrest, and his son had spent over two months in prison simply because the judge missed two court dates. As for Elena, she was first denied the opportunity to report at the Public Prosecutor's Office the death threats to which she had been subject at the hospital. Only when a relative of hers, himself a lawyer, accompanied her was she allowed to file a report, albeit with the caveat that nothing would be done about the case. Significantly, both Julio's son and Elena's colleagues at the hospital opted not to report the threats that they had received—underreporting being a trend that has come to exacerbate El Salvador's problem of postwar impunity.

Lawlessness is not new in El Salvador; rather, it is an aspect of the impunity and violence that have extended beyond the war and into a period of democracy. By 'lawlessness' I do not mean to imply that the law does not exist, but rather that it is characterized more by its lack of enforcement than by the resort to it.[19] Yet at specific moments of the postwar era—most notably when the *Plan Mano Dura* (Iron Fist Policy) and the Antiterrorist Law were implemented in 2003 and 2006, respectively, and continued by the ensuing governments, or when it comes to protecting business

---

[19] For instance, out of the 1020 homicides perpetrated in El Salvador's three main municipalities in 2005, only 3.8 percent were solved (Acevedo 2008: 76–77).

activity—the law has been enforced, however harshly and discriminatorily at times. These heavy-handed policies, which mimic policing strategies in the United States (see Zilberg 2007), have been denounced by human rights organizations for their repressive outcomes and attendant increases in homicidal violence as well as police corruption.[20] By their very nature, these policies conform to Benjamin's (2007) and Derrida's (2002: 233) thesis that the enforcement of the law is a form of violence, yet an authorized one. The coexistence of both lawful and lawless processes in El Salvador engenders particular zones of ambiguity in which the undermining of the law occurs at the very moment and in the very space in which the law is fetishized (see also Comaroff and Comaroff 2006: 5, 21; Taussig 2003). These zones of ambiguity are in turn beneficial for the emergence and consolidation of a gray zone of politics.

As noted earlier, the grayness of El Salvador's postwar political life has also worked as a heuristic device for ordinary people, who have interpreted and strategized accordingly. The advent of democracy, alongside the formal establishment of the rule of law, has thus not succeeded in fostering trust toward the country's institutions of order among ordinary Salvadorans (Cruz et al. 1998: 16–17; IUDOP 2009b: 94–96, 106–107; Latinobarómetro 2011: 34, 36). Haunting prewar and war memories of repressive police forces have certainly taken their toll in the postwar era. However, rumors suggest that in postwar political life, the boundaries between political actors and criminals, as well as the licit and the illicit, have often collapsed. As noted earlier, shadowy practices and connections have led a great number of ordinary Salvadorans to circumvent state institutions (for a more in-depth discussion of the impact of the grayness of El Salvador's political life on citizenship practices, see Chap. 7).

Most people who confided in me about their subjection to death threats and extortion did not report these incidents to police because they sensed that authorities would not do anything and might even be involved. It was, for instance, Julio's son's fear of retaliation that kept him from reporting the death threats by the military officers who had arrested him. While Julio had urged his son to file a report, Julio explained in subsequent conversations that he had never considered filing a report through the police; instead he would have gone through the regional ombudsman, with whom he was personally acquainted through his work in the grassroots

---

[20] See Hume (2007a) and Wolf (2017) for the case of El Salvador, and Misse and Vargas (2010) for the case of Brazil.

organization he led. As this example makes clear, distrust of the state has not impelled Salvadorans to detach themselves definitively from the state but rather to engage with state officials they know through personal networks. The grayness of political life, conjured up by rumors, has led ordinary people of various political persuasions to circumvent state institutions of order and navigate their way around them via personal networks perceived to be more trustworthy than the official channels of the institutions themselves. Santiagueños are thus haunted not only by wartime memories but also by the grayness of the postwar era in which they live. There and yet not clearly there, the postwar gray zone haunts Santiagueños of all political orientations, although it is mainly leftwing Santiagueños who have attributed to ARENA state actors a main role in it.

While not the focus of this book, there is yet an additional layer to the (in)visibility characterizing El Salvador's political life. Hume's (2009b) feminist perspective on El Salvador's postwar violence has shed light on the high levels of violence that have affected women[21] and children in El Salvador and the scant attention this has received relative to the violence that occurs in the public sphere—a by-product, she suggests, of the lack of consideration received by the gendered dimensions of violence. Hume points to the generalized problem of underreporting evident in Julio's and Elena's stories, along with the lack or inconsistency of information and statistical data on non-homicidal violence and the patriarchal ethos of state institutions that trivialize and justify violence against women and children, as the main issues that deflect attention from these other dimensions of violence in El Salvador. The wide currency of the gang trope has therefore not just eclipsed the grayness of political life but also evacuated gender violence from public discussions about the politics of El Salvador's problem of postwar violence.

In postwar El Salvador, ordinary people across the political spectrum have consistently conjured up a gray zone of politics in which violence and political life are deeply enmeshed. Their difficulty in pinning down the problem of postwar violence seems to reside in the grayness of postwar political life, in which onstage practices and hyper-visible elements eclipse clandestine relations and practices. It is through rumor and scandal, which are per se anecdotal, that elements of the gray zone of politics manifest. In

---

[21] El Salvador exhibits some of the highest femicide rates. Indeed, between 2007 and 2012, it was the country with the world's highest average femicide rate (Isacson et al. 2017: 7).

the late 2000s, Santiagueñas suggested in their explanations for postwar violence the existence of clandestine relations between political actors and violent entrepreneurs, thereby challenging the gang trope so frequently mobilized by both the former ARENA governments and the rightwing media. Rumors, scandals, and personal attempts to make sense of El Salvador's postwar violence that point to grayness have coexisted with references to the wartime past that are considered less ambiguous, at least in retrospect. Frequent remarks along these lines by left-leaning Santiagueñas have also implicitly challenged the triumphalism that characterizes the official rhetoric about the country's transition from war to peace. In contrast to sub-Saharan African countries, where gray zones emerged during the 1990s as a result of transitions to multiparty politics (Kirschke 2000), in El Salvador a gray zone of politics already existed during the war. Yet, it would be inaccurate to assume that El Salvador's postwar gray zone of politics is simply a continuation of the gray zone that developed during wartime.

The existence of a gray zone where links between homicidal violence and El Salvador's political life are ambiguous and clandestine has allowed for a sanitizing of the country's public face and forestalled an outcry from the international community over its high levels of postwar homicidal violence. In eclipsing the linkages between postwar violence and the country's political life, El Salvador's gray zone has allowed the ARENA governments as well as international organizations to proclaim the ostensible success of the transition; as the gang trope suggests, the problem is after all one of dehumanized youth emerging from El Salvador's broken social fabric in the aftermath of a protracted and violent war. More importantly, ambiguity has also stemmed from the rule of law, which is repressively enforced against some citizens on the basis of zero-tolerance policies yet suspended in other instances because of inefficiency, ill-equipment, corruption, or disinterest. Under these circumstances, it is not surprising that many Santiagueñas of all political orientations have opted to circumvent the state institutions of order.

Another development that is associated to the existence of a gray zone is the collapse of boundaries among actors, categories of violence, and the licit/illicit. The next chapter addresses the apparent similarities that arise between realms that are nominally licit and illicit. I show how El Salvador's neoliberalization process has contributed to the development of new domains and circuits of accumulation, such as the private security industry, and how an ontological similarity seems to exist between the country's licit and illicit 'provisions of security'. As I will discuss in Chap. 7, the 2009 FMLN victory does not seem to have sparked a great deal of change with regard to El Salvador's gray zone. Fieldwork conducted among Santiagueñas during various trips since 2009 allowed me to document episodes of violence that pointed to this gray zone and, subsequently, to identify Salvadorans' twofold critique of it. Some people suggested that, despite the FMLN government, ARENA continues to control a captive state, while others implied that the FMLN itself has become part of the country's gray zone of politics. On the whole, ordinary people's attempts to make sense of postwar violence—attempts that point to the existence of a gray zone of politics—are simultaneously a critique of El Salvador's democracy and until 2009 a critique of the ARENA-ruled state's role within this democracy.

CHAPTER 4

Neoliberalization and the Violence Within

'They called home and said that they belonged to the *mara* and that I should pay US$800', said an acquaintance from Santiago. 'They said that if I didn't pay they would come to my house at night and kill someone, though they didn't want to do that.' This was just one of many episodes of extortion confided to me during my fieldwork in Santiago. During the 2000s, extortion rackets proliferated and consolidated in El Salvador. The success of extortion-related death threats was largely predicated upon fears of the ever-existing *possibility* of homicidal violence—fears fueled by the daily homicide count reported by the media, the circulation of rumors (founded or not) about various forms of violence and violent actors, haunting war memories, and speculation about the grayness of politics and the impunity thereof. However, exemplary assassinations have also been perpetrated by racketeers—most often, but not only, by gangs—so as to secure their pecuniary goals. Against this background of public insecurity and lawlessness, the country's private security industry has burgeoned in the postwar era, enabled by the parallel neoliberalization process. The juxtaposition of extortion rackets and the private security industry in El Salvador serves as the basis for an exploration in this chapter of the relationship between these twin facets of the 'provision of security',[1] the former an illicit activity and the latter purportedly licit.

---

[1] The designation of extortion in El Salvador as a 'provision of security' is not completely accurate. In contrast to examples of extortion elsewhere (e.g. Schneider and Schneider 2003), no offer of protection enters the language of racketeers in El Salvador.

© The Author(s) 2018
A. Montoya, *The Violence of Democracy*, Studies of the Americas,
https://doi.org/10.1007/978-3-319-76330-9_4

My aim in this chapter is to provide insights into how the gray zone conjured by Santiagueñas across the political spectrum, and the alternative circuits of accumulation and political authority that are rumored to be part of it, are related to political economies. El Salvador is an appropriate setting in which to explore this question given this country's historical interrelation of statecraft and coercion; as I have explained in the Introduction, since the early 1930s, the country's state apparatus repressed the peasant population on the basis of a 'communist threat' that the military had concocted, or at least exaggerated, so as to justify a military state in the eyes of the elite (Stanley 1996: 56–58). Since the embracement of a neoliberal agenda by the ARENA administrations from 1989 and the 1990s crisis of El Salvador's agrarian economy were concurrent with the country's transition from war to peace, I ask how these transformations are related, if at all, to the development of the postwar gray zone that characterizes the country's political life. As I have illustrated in Chap. 3, in postwar El Salvador, links between political actors and violent entrepreneurs have surfaced in various violent episodes described and rumored by Santiagueños as well as through investigative journalism, but they have generally been subsumed under the violence perpetrated by gangs by successive ARENA governments and the main media, all rightwing. In this chapter, I turn my attention to how neoliberalization might be related to the emergence and consolidation of the grayness of El Salvador's postwar political life. In so doing, I seek to contribute to discussions about the constitutive relationship between violence and capitalist political economies.

I argue in this chapter that neoliberalization has contributed to a collapse of boundaries between the licit/illicit domains that benefit evenly from the unintelligibility of violence stemming from El Salvador's postwar gray zone. Building my argument upon Comaroff and Comaroff's (2006: 5) thesis that neoliberalism has enabled criminal activities to adopt market-like or state-like forms, I suggest that in postwar El Salvador, the reverse seems to have occurred, inasmuch as the ARENA-governed state acquired a criminal-like guise in the eyes of large portions of left-leaning and disaffected Santiagueñas but also in light of the actions of various state actors and successive administrations. My argument is based on an exploration of the rise of extortion, an illicit 'provision of security', in Santiago in the late 2000s and on the juxtaposition of this trend with the rise of the country's private security industry. Lawlessness—which has, as I have suggested in Chap. 3, transcended the war and become entrenched in the postwar era—poses undeniable threats to Salvadorans. The few references that exist about El Salvador's private security industry, as well as the rampant rumors circulating mainly among left-leaning and disaffected Salvadorans, suggest that some prominent leaders of ARENA are owners of private security firms. A direct implication of this suggestion is that the neoliberal reforms of the ARENA governments—the privatization of security among them—yielded a disturbing equivalency between the extortion rackets and the ARENA-governed state, especially if we consider the parallel lack of law enforcement and rumored participation of ARENA political leaders in El Salvador's postwar gray zone.

As I expound my argument, I also demonstrate how El Salvador's neoliberal agenda and the coeval consolidation of a gray zone of politics have made economic and public insecurity work together in specific ways. While businesses were the initial target of extortion racketeers, Salvadorans across classes have been subject to extortion since the late 2000s. Even as security is nominally provided by El Salvador's democratic state institutions of order, police inaction vis-à-vis the reports of violent episodes by poor Salvadorans and the concomitant flourishing of a private security industry have increasingly turned access to effective security into a privilege. In this sense, the existence of a gray zone that renders violence unintelligible and unpredictable and the concomitant individualization of risk management have led to a situation in which economic and public insecurity reinforce one another. Although the bulk of the research on which this book focuses was mostly conducted before and during the 2009 political shift, further follow-up research trips allow me to suggest that the arguments in this chapter remain valid for the FMLN-governed state.

EXTORTION RACKETS IN POSTWAR EL SALVADOR

In part due to the United States 'War on Drugs' and the worldwide expansion of drug consumption over the last decade, there has been a displacement and proliferation of drug-trafficking routes in Latin America (Bagley 2012). In this context, Mexico and Central America, especially the so-called Northern Triangle, have increasingly become part of drug traffickers' route toward the north (Arnson and Olson 2011).[2] El Salvador's former President Mauricio Funes even publicly acknowledged that some

---

[2] Although most cocaine shipments from South America are sent directly to Guatemala and Honduras, some involvement has also been tracked down in El Salvador; those involved in drug trafficking in this country (as well as in Guatemala and Honduras) do so mainly as

members of the country's own police and judiciary institutions are deeply involved in drug trafficking (Farah 2011: 105; Meléndez Reyes 2016: 82). Yet despite evidence of El Salvador's involvement in drug trafficking through criminal organizations such as Los Perrones and Cartel de Texis, the country's main role in the drug business, given its dollarized economy, is as a drug-related money-laundering site, as mentioned in Chap. 3. Along with drug trafficking and the concomitant development of clandestine associations, several forms of crime have developed in the Central American region that further complicate the problem of public insecurity, including gun and human trafficking, kidnapping and extortion. Exploring public insecurity through episodes of extortion, I suggest in this chapter, is illuminating, as such episodes exemplify the ways in which public and economic insecurities reinforce one another.

Extortion rackets mushroomed throughout El Salvador during the 2000s (Hume 2009a: 104–105; Ellen Moodie, personal communication 2010; Gómez Hecht 2013), with extortion being the most prominent form of crime when I was doing fieldwork there in 2008 and 2009. Although I have visited Santiago since 2001, it was not until after the mid-2000s that I first heard about episodes of extortion from Santiagueños. Before arriving in El Salvador in June 2007, I had read in the news and been told on the phone by friends in Santiago about two kidnappings—one ending in assassination—that had resulted when extortionists' demands were not met.[3] In January of that year, a young woman from one of Santiago's wealthiest families, which owns a grain distribution business, had been kidnapped, with a ransom of US$50,000 demanded of her family. The family ultimately paid the ransom, and the woman was released a few days later. A month after this episode, the son of a family that owned a car wash was likewise kidnapped; he was assassinated soon thereafter, even though his family had paid a ransom of US$15,000.[4] Both these episodes of kidnapping and extortion made headlines and stirred great consternation among Santiagueños.

While I was visiting Santiago in 2007 to conduct my MPhil research, I was told by several Santiagueños that every single business, formal or infor-

---

transportistas (shippers) who temporarily store and transport the drugs toward the north (Dudley 2010).

[3] 'Santiago Nonualco pide paz', *Diario Colatino*, 13 February 2007.

[4] 'Sepultan restos de joven secuestrado y asesinado', *La Prensa Gráfica*, 17 February 2007.

mal, in the center of the municipality was a target of extortion. The owners of stores, canteens, market stalls, and buses, as well as street vendors, were all paying extortion money. When I returned in 2008 to conduct my PhD research, extortion was no longer mentioned as occurring in the municipality itself, although rumors continued about extortion in the bus sector nationwide. Then, after March 2009, Santiagueños once again began telling me about their recent experiences of extortion. It should be noted that extortion episodes, both in the mid- and late 2000s, were rarely raised in public conversation. It was only through gossip and personal conversation with neighbors and close friends that I heard the innumerable stories of local extortion and death threats. Yet despite the apparently dramatic rise in extortion, the media paid little attention to the issue in the first half of 2009; moreover, whenever extortion-related events were featured in newspaper or television reports, they were subsumed under the trope of 'gang violence' rather than treated as a phenomenon of their own. It was not until after the FMLN took office in June 2009 that systematic extortion, both gang-related and otherwise, began to be acknowledged by the most widely read mass media, all of them largely conservative and critical of the FMLN.

A marked shift in the pattern of extortion occurred along with its rise in 2009. While the extortion that affected Santiagueñas in the mid-2000s targeted business owners, it has since 2009 arbitrarily targeted Santiagueñas across classes, regardless of their assets or purchasing power. One of the first episodes recounted to me that directly affected an acquaintance of mine was that of Wilfredo's parents. They live in a *cantón* that extends westward in the lowland areas of Santiago. In May 2009, Wilfredo, a teacher at a local school, learned that his parents had been subjected to extortion. After beseeching me to be discreet, he told me that his mother had answered a phone call from a young man who threatened to kill two of her sons if she did not 'cooperate'. The man did not mention a precise amount and said he would call again to arrange for the payment of the extortion money. Wilfredo's parents, both in their 80s, were extremely worried for the safety of their sons—all the more so because they did not own anything apart from their house, made of adobe and aluminum sheeting, with which to pay off the extortionist. Indeed, they did not have any regular income or enjoy a state pension[5] and were supported economically

---

[5] It is worth noting here the limited coverage of El Salvador's pension system, which was largely privatized in 1996 and transformed from one of intergenerational distribution to one of individual capitalization. In 2008, a total of 84.2 percent of the population over 60 years

by their sons and daughters, two of whom were unemployed at the time and worked only on occasion.

Wilfredo shared his two hypotheses for who might be behind the extortion. Either gang members from the *cantón* were trying to collect money to help another gang member, whom rumors suggested had recently been imprisoned, or, alternatively, Wilfredo speculated, Santiagueños who had gained control of the local FMLN political party during the 2009 presidential campaign were trying to terrorize him because, as an FMLN member for several years, he had publicly condemned their clientelist politics and illicit use of party resources. He reported the case of extortion to the Santiago police. Skeptical that the local police would take action, he also reported the case to the regional police subdelegation in Zacatecoluca, where he was asked to make a cursory report on the phone and told thereafter that there was not much the police could do. Given the lack of support obtained from police, Wilfredo's parents decided to change their telephone number, thus managing to avoid further phone calls from the racketeers.

Soon after Wilfredo had told me about the extortion threat to which his parents had been subjected, I learned about innumerable cases of extortion affecting Santiagueñas from both the central *barrios* and the *cantones* surrounding them as well as acquaintances from other neighboring municipalities. A similar pattern characterized the extortion-related death threats that menaced the poor. Most often through phone calls, anonymous men[6] threatened to kill whomever had answered the phone, along with his or her relatives, should that person not meet the demands. Interestingly, the man calling sometimes referred to family details that betrayed a lack of knowledge about the targeted family. For instance, a widow living in a central *barrio* recounted to me that the caller demanding that she pay *la renta*[7] (the rent, as the extortion payments are popularly known, given their being demanded on a regular basis) had threatened to kill her husband if she did not pay. These cases led people to think that perhaps their telephone numbers had been randomly obtained from phone listings.

---

old was not receiving a pension, and in the rural areas, the number rose to 96 percent (PNUD 2010: 134–135).

[6] In all cases I learned about, the person calling was a male.

[7] Businesses in central San Salvador have also reported that extortion rackets demand the payment of *el aguinaldo* (the Christmas bonus), which in 2010 ranged from US$1000–3000. 'Maras acosan en el centro por aguinaldo', *El Mundo*, 16 December 2010.

Apparent arbitrariness was not always the case, however. I was also told of episodes in which the man calling knew enough details about the family in question to suggest that he had done some prior investigation. Even though in many cases the person calling identified himself as a gang member, Santiagueños remarked that this was more likely a way to scare people rather than a true indication of the racketeer's identity. Residents from Santiago also noted that the telephone numbers from which extortion demands were made were sometimes Guatemalan, suggesting that the organizational dimensions of extortion rackets may well transcend national boundaries. Given the frequency of homicidal violence in the country, extortion-related death threats were all the more effective in scaring people into making the payments. Indeed, assassination and kidnappings in Santiago and elsewhere in the country have followed on the heels of certain unpaid extortions to serve as a warning for what can happen to those who do not pay *la renta*. Rumors suggested that three homicides that occurred in the central neighborhoods of Santiago during one of my follow-up trips, in December 2009 and January and February 2010, were all extortion-related.

By the time I returned to Santiago in 2010, every Santiagueño I knew had received at least one phone call from an extortionist. The increasing demands of one-off payments via the phone suggested that people unrelated to organized crime had become involved in extortion on an opportunistic basis at a moment when the impact of the 2008 global economic crisis was starting to be felt by Salvadorans. El Salvador's rise in extortion did indeed coincide with a 10 percent decline of remittances relative to the previous year[8] as well as with the gradual closure and downsizing of various United States textile maquilas (foreign-owned assembly factories) in the nearby offshore zone of El Pedregal at the beginning of 2009—a development that affected thousands of employees from Santiago and the surrounding municipalities. In other words, judging by the shift in the pattern of extortion that occurred from the mid- to the late 2000s—that is, from a targeting of businesses to generalized victimization—it seems plausible that anonymous participants other than consolidated networks of organized crime had opportunistically engaged in extortion as a means of making a living in a time of recession; these new extortionists may have decided to

---

[8] 'Remesas registran caída promedio del 10% anual', *La Prensa Gráfica*, 17 August 2009.

exploit the anonymity afforded by the extended use in El Salvador of pay-as-you-go mobile phone SIM cards.[9]

Yet there were also cases of systematic extortion that required a certain degree of organization, indicating that gangs or other sophisticated organized crime groups might be involved. In El Salvador, the consolidation of systematic extortion over time has been epitomized by the country's bus sector. Buses are the only means of collective transport that travel throughout the country. After the collapse of the Salvadoran agricultural economy in the 1990s and an increase in employment in the capital and major towns as well as in the offshore zones where the maquilas are located, buses became a widely used resource for commuters as well as a primary source of income for bus owners and drivers. Bus transport in El Salvador is a service privately run by Salvadorans who own run-down United States school buses.[10] However, the successive ARENA governments provided major subsidies for the bus sector so as to maintain the low bus fares that allow ordinary Salvadorans to afford daily commutes, the resulting irony being that taxpayers have indirectly subsidized extortion.

From the 2000s, extortion demands have been increasingly made of bus owners and drivers on a weekly or monthly basis. A 40-year-old from Santiago who drives a bus in central San Salvador told me that bus owners were demanded to pay a fixed sum of a few hundred dollars per week or month, while drivers had to pay a portion of whatever they collected for every return trip they made. There are specific rendezvous sites where bus drivers' money is collected by extortion racketeers. Children are often sent to collect the money, which many of my informants remarked is a way for higher-ranked criminals to avoid being identified. Unpaid extortions have sometimes resulted in drivers or collectors being assassinated while operating the bus. In such cases, one or two young men have jumped onto the bus or stood up from their seat, walked toward the front of the bus, and shot the bus driver in the head, at which point they have fled the bus and vanished. During and after my fieldwork, several assassinations of bus drivers occurred on buses being driven along the Coastal Road that crosses

---

[9] This is consistent with trends in other regions of El Salvador. For instance, in Morazán in 2009, popular explanations for the rise of extortion also pointed to the proliferation of mobile phones, the means through which many had made extortion phone calls, and to individuals rather than gangs as the extortionists (Ellen Moodie, personal communication 2010).

[10] For an analysis of the relationship between the state of El Salvador's bus sector, which has experienced a high number of yearly fatalities, and neoliberalism, see Moodie (2006).

La Paz (see the highlighted road in Figure 2) or within this region's municipalities themselves. Using public transport myself, I observed how, after episodes in which bus drivers had been assassinated, police often separated male and female passengers and looked for tattoos on the men's bodies, signaling a search for the marked bodies of gang members. Given that the assassins had already left by the time the police arrived, this search could be interpreted as merely a public staging of police intervention—all the more effective if a few gang-like youths were actually arrested—rather than an efficient means of investigating the assassination.

Systematic extortion began affecting a bus cooperative in a municipality neighboring Santiago in 2009. One of the cooperative members living in Santiago confided the details of the case to me when I traveled to El Salvador in December 2010. The president of the cooperative, this member explained, had received an extortion-related phone call in the second half of 2009. A young man, identifying himself as a gang member, asked him to let the other cooperative members know that they should pay a monthly contribution of US$400. The president of the cooperative initially disregarded this phone call and did not mention it to anyone. A few weeks later, a 23-year-old who worked for the cooperative was gunned down by two men in broad daylight while driving a cooperative bus along the Coastal Road. Since his assassination, cooperative associates began to pay *la renta* on a regular basis. The person who recounted the case to me described how one of the cooperative members had been put in charge of collecting monthly contributions from all of the other cooperative members and then leaving the payment at a particular location on the Coastal Road, where it would later be collected by the extortionists or their proxies. By the end of 2010, the cooperative associates had not reported the case since they did not trust that police would do anything about it; indeed, rumors were circulating that local police officers were themselves involved in extortion. The bus cooperative members' unwillingness to file a report was no exception.

During my stay in Santiago in 2009, as well as during follow-up trips, I noted that most Santiagueños who told me of their extortion-related experiences were reluctant to report them to officials.[11] Also noteworthy was the high frequency with which police officers populated extortion-related

---

[11] A prior report by the IUDOP indicated that in El Salvador, an average of only 25 percent of victims of any sort of crime report the crime to the country's institutions of order (PNUD 2005a: 43).

rumors and imageries, some of these fed by memories of wartime police repression in the area. Rumors circulating in central Santiago in 2009 attributed the sudden rise in extortion to the return of a certain police officer formerly stationed in the municipality and allegedly involved in extortion episodes dating back to the mid-2000s. In addition, several episodes that occurred in northern Santiago in 2009—all involving men disguised as police officers who burst into Santiago homes, violently attacked family members, and looted their possessions—bore for some a disturbing resemblance to the violent nocturnal *cateos* (house searches) by police during wartime and stirred widespread distrust toward the police institution. Crucially, in 2010, when extortion was rampant in Santiago, the police officer in charge of the municipality's subdelegation denied that extortion existed in Santiago when I requested the figures of reported cases.

Extortion that extends over time with demands for periodic payments (*la renta*), as in the case just described of the bus cooperative in La Paz, by its very nature must involve a certain level of organization, insofar as it requires information about victims as well as a structure that facilitates committing acts of kidnapping and assassination with impunity. However, while El Salvador's media outlets typically link criminal organizations such as gangs with bus-related and other cases of systematic extortion, confusion has predominated regarding who has perpetrated the extortion that affects lower-class families. Since 2009, Santiagueñas' characterizations of the motives and perpetrators of extortion were miscellaneous and fragmented, varying over time and throughout the municipality, thus creating an image of extortion rackets that was far from cohesive. Their explanations for the motives underlying the extortion that has targeted poor families ranged from the personal to the political to the purely economic and have evoked a variety of suspected perpetrators, including neighbors, police officers, political opponents, gangs, and other transnational criminal networks.[12] The disparity of projected motives and perpetrators speaks to the sense of 'not-knowing' (Moodie 2010: 20) among Salvadorans regarding extortion as well as homicidal violence. What does stand out in cases of both systematic and episodic extortion is the negligence of police interventions, as in the episode reported by Wilfredo, and the consequent public sentiment of living in a lawless environment in which everyone must see to their own security.

---

[12] Aguilar Villamariona (2006: 91–92) reaches a similar conclusion when she suggests that police officers and criminal organizations other than gangs have also engaged in extortion.

Extortionists benefit from the fear instilled by the regularity with which homicides occur in El Salvador and the grayness that characterizes them. Ironically, the fear elicited by the daily homicide count is exacerbated by the rumors that try to make sense of it (cf. Caldeira 2000: 19–20). Regardless of their veracity, rumors about extortion-related death threats, criminal activities, and homicidal violence contribute to reproducing the very fears the racketeers seek to instill in the population. This was clear in the case of the death threats received by Jesús (see Chap. 2) and so many of Santiago's residents. While in Jesús's case extortion did not follow the death threats, the latent *possibility* of homicidal violence and the rumors about extortion-related death threats affecting other neighbors fed his relatives's fears and influenced their decision to change routines and sequester themselves at home. Lawlessness thus appears to result as much from police inefficiency and corruption as from the underreporting that results from the public's rampant distrust—reproduced by rumors—of the police force.

Further increasing the effectiveness of postwar death threats are wartime memories concerning violence and the related pervasive fears. Santiagueñas from both urban and rural areas alike have related to me that before and during the civil war in the 1980s, the country's police forces, death squads such as Nationalist Democratic Organization (ORDEN),[13] and civil defenses would perpetrate violence not just with impunity but with a brutality that left an indelible emotional imprint on the local population. The bodies of those assassinated as well as severed body parts were often disposed of in public spaces such as side roads, markets, squares, and bridges. A 'politics of fear' was thus at work, consisting of exemplary practices that terrorized the population so as to secure particular goals, such as dissuading the population from participation in political activity. While these practices and organizations were dissolved after the end of the war, episodes and rumors of corruption by police officers have revived memories of wartime atrocities and reinforced distrust of police in the postwar era. I thus surmise that Salvadorans' feelings of insecurity in the postwar era stem from the confluence of routinized unintelligible violence, rampant

---

[13] ORDEN was founded in the early 1960s as a 'grass-roots network of informants' under the command of local landowners and the National Guard and served as the PCN's electoral constituency; by the late 1960s, it was acting as a paramilitary group. It was composed largely of former military personnel who received concessions for their participation (Stanley 1996: 81–82). Once dismantled because of its involvement in human rights abuses, it turned, under the aegis of D'Aubuisson, to support ARENA while simultaneously acting as death squads (Font Fàbregas 1998: 138; Ramírez Fuentes 2017).

rumors, and haunting war memories. While a generalized feeling of insecurity and an official emphasis on the gang trope throughout the 2000s have legitimized El Salvador's endorsement of punitive measures, the distrust and perceived inefficiency of the country's police forces have simultaneously led Salvadorans to tend to their own security.

SECURITIZATION STRATEGIES

The 1992 Chapultepec Peace Accords, as explained in Chap. 2, essentially sought to end El Salvador's 12-year civil war and dissolve the country's military rule. Stanley (1996) has depicted the Salvadoran military state—which originated with the government ruled by General Martínez Hernández in the early 1930s, persisted through the move to civilian rule in the early 1980s, and lasted until the end of the civil war—as ontologically similar to a protection racket, insofar as it managed to retain its grip on power in exchange for protecting the country's economic elites against the contingent threat posed by class enemies that the military itself had created or boosted. In the face of the historical entrenchment of military rule, Stanley (1996: 7–8) has argued that the success of El Salvador's peace settlement rests on its dissolution of the country's protection racket through demilitarization, even as economic and social problems were sidelined or only secondarily addressed. To end military rule, the Peace Accords stipulated a set of reforms affecting primarily the military and military-controlled police forces. The Accords called for a purge of the military and its removal from the public domain; its functions were relegated to the protection of borders and the performance of external military operations (United Nations 1992a: 49–50). The police forces (National Police, National Guard, and Treasury Police) that had participated in the harsh repression of the population before and during the 1980s war were dissolved; in 1992, a new police force, the National Civilian Police (PNC), was created that absorbed demobilized excombatants from both sides of the war and recruited 60 percent of its members from civilians. Yet the success of those demilitarizing processes is questionable given the increasing toughening of approaches to security, the permanent employment of the military in public patrolling, and the remilitarization of the country's police, part of whose personnel as demobilized excombatants had been effectively trained during the 1980s conflict in repressive approaches akin to the ethos of postwar *mano dura*.

As noted in the previous section, homicides and crime, of which extortion is an important part, have stirred fear and feelings of insecurity throughout the Salvadoran public during the postwar era. These feelings have in turn led ordinary Salvadorans to demand protection and welcome *mano dura* approaches to security from the state. Yet, public support for *mano dura* policies did not just precede these policies; it mounted after they were enacted. Indeed, *mano dura* policies were ARENA's electoral strategy at a juncture at which the party was losing popularity and votes to both the FMLN and the PCN (Holland 2013).[14] These policies were modeled on its United States analogues; just as the United States increasingly deported gang members to Central America—thereby contributing significantly to the spread of a gang culture originally rooted in Los Angeles—it also exported zero-tolerance policies as part of the promotion of its so-called War on Terror and War on Drugs (Zilberg 2007, 2011; Wolf 2017: 67–71).[15] In El Salvador, a securitization discourse of transnational character has set in motion processes by which collective notions of threat or danger (e.g. the transnational gang[16]) have been constructed, thereby legitimizing certain extraordinary actions, notably the enactment of *mano dura* policies and an increase in public militarization and private security (van der Borgh and Savenije 2014; cf. Buzan et al. 1998, Gledhill 2009, and Goldstein 2010). Rather than a new phenomenon, these policy imports amount to a continuation of United States intervention in a region where the Cold War 'communist threat' rationale for hardline policies has been replaced by the post-Cold War suturing together of 'terrorist' and 'gang' categories (Zilberg 2011: 17–18).

El Salvador's rightwing ARENA government headed by President Francisco Flores implemented the *Plan Mano Dura* (Iron Fist Policy) in 2003, right before the 2004 presidential election, so as to secure electoral

[14] By basing its 2004 presidential electoral campaign on *mano dura* propaganda, ARENA managed to attract votes across classes and ideologies, especially as the FMLN did not have a clear proposal for how to address insecurity and the PCN was attracting rightwing voters aligned with ARENA's agrarian faction by focusing its campaign on agricultural and public security policies (Holland 2013).

[15] *Mano dura* policies differ from their North American models in their reduction of due process rights de jure, which zero-tolerance policies have maintained or even augmented, if only on paper (Holland 2013: 47).

[16] While the MS 13 and 18th Street gang brands are present throughout the Northern Triangle as well as in the United States, and a certain level of communication exists among some of their members, its actual transnational character has been questioned (see Zilberg 2011: 12–13).

advantage vis-à-vis the increasingly popular and rival party FMLN.[17] Identifying gangs as the only source of El Salvador's endemic violence, the *Plan Mano Dura* (underpinned by the Ley Anti Maras[18]) enforced the display of joint military-police operatives, area sweeps and rapid mass arrests based on subjective evidence (most often appearance), and the reduction or even suspension of the due process rights of alleged gang members.[19] Along with the subsequent *Súper Mano Dura*[20] implemented during President Elías Antonio Saca's administration, this policy allowed ARENA to manage the problem of postwar violence through discretionary measures such as the criminalization and repression of gang-like bodies.[21] In this vein, El Salvador's printed media played a critical role in publicly magnifying gangs as well as eulogizing, and creating the grounds for popular support of, *mano dura* policies (see Wolf 2012a, 2017: 74–118). While after 2006 these *mano dura* policies were putatively discontinued, the repressive methods they had set in place outlived them (Wolf 2017: 65).

The government's employment of military forces to enforce security in public areas contravened the mandate of the 1992 Peace Accords, which had relegated El Salvador's military solely to functions relating to border-patrolling and external security. Since the early 2000s, the military has increasingly assumed police functions, as exemplified by the patrolling of public areas by *Grupos de Tarea Conjunta* (Joint Task Groups) consisting of one police officer and four or five military personnel. During my fieldwork, these patrolling groups were present in both the center of Santiago and in *cantones* where major landowners had requested their presence. It is not just through a stepped-up military presence that the remilitarization of public life has been achieved but also through the militarization of the country's police forces via the appointment of former military personnel

---

[17] The first attempt at *mano dura* legislation occurred in 1996, but the law was repealed only a few months after it had been passed (Holland 2013: 48–49).

[18] Decreto Ejecutivo No. 158, *Diario Oficial*, 10 October 2003.

[19] This policy, like similar ones that followed, was met with strong opposition from the Salvadoran judiciary, who considered it unconstitutional (Wolf 2017: 50–51).

[20] The *Súper Mano Dura* policy included prevention and rehabilitation components (*Mano Extendida* and *Mano Amiga)* that were, however, sidestepped or limited in practice (Wolf 2017: 53–63).

[21] As noted in the Introduction, the indiscriminate arrest of gang-like youth has increasingly led gangs to avoid their previously hyper-visible appearance in order to go unnoticed (Aguilar Villamariona 2006: 83–84).

to high-ranking positions as well as the founding of military-geared and military-equipped police units (Zilberg 2011: 177–204; Silva Ávalos 2014; Wolf 2017: 42). Even more alarming have been reports of extermination groups within the PNC itself since the 1990s (FESPAD and CEPES 2004a: 118–119). Tellingly, it has been not just ARENA but also the subsequent FMLN governments that have contravened the Peace Accords' mandate to demilitarize public life and foster law-abiding institutions of order.

The victory of the country's leftwing party and former guerrilla organization FMLN in the 2009 presidential election heralded the prospect of a novel citizen-focused and integral approach to security that would include prevention, rehabilitation, judicial reform, and victim support as its chief pillars, and that had been elaborated with the participation of various sectors of Salvadoran society (Hoppert-Flämig 2013). President Funes and the FMLN had themselves heartily critiqued the *mano dura* approach of the ARENA administrations, and focused instead on a more comprehensive understanding of organized crime, drug trafficking, and corruption rather than concentrating only on gangs (van der Borgh and Savenije 2014: 161–162). However, the FMLN administration soon began following ARENA's punitive and gang-centered blueprint.

In 2009, the number of annual homicides dramatically increased even before the FMLN took office, reaching 4349—a homicide rate of 70.6 per 100,000 inhabitants and a 37 percent increase vis-à-vis the previous year (OAS 2012: 17–18). Faced with mounting pressure from ARENA, the country's main rightwing mass media, and the business elite regarding the rising homicide rates, in October of that year the FMLN administration, through two decrees,[22] increased the number of military personnel involved in the patrolling of public areas in El Salvador just six months after taking office and entrusted the guarding of maximum-security prisons to the military another six months later (Wolf 2012b; Hoppert-Flämig 2013). Less than a month after, a fatal incident occurred in San Salvador in which gang members doused two buses with gasoline and set them on fire. Passengers were trapped inside one of the buses, leaving 17 people dead and 11 gravely injured. In response to the ensuing public outcry, the FMLN administration consolidated the previous administration's *mano*

---

[22] Decreto Ejecutivo No. 70, *Diario Oficial*, 4 November 2009—a reform to the previous Decreto Ejecutivo No. 60, *Diario Oficial*, 9 October 2009—and Decreto Legislativo No. 371, *Diario Oficial*, 17 June 2010.

dura policies through the similarly repressive 2010 *Anti-Gang Law*[23] that punished gang membership based on appearance (Wolf 2010; Hoppert-Flämig 2013). Data on public expenditures have only confirmed the emphasis that the successive administrations have placed on penality in postwar El Salvador: in 2010, the public budget for the country's institutions of order surpassed the budget designated for public healthcare (PNUD 2010: 276).

Nor did the gang truce reached in 2012 signify a departure from previous *mano dura* approaches. This truce between the leaders of El Salvador's main rival gangs—for which the head chaplain of the military, a former FMLN combatant, and members of the FMLN government served as facilitators—yielded a significant reduction in the country's homicide rate until its collapse at the end of 2013. As a tradeoff, government representatives accepted moving gang leaders from a maximum-security prison to penitentiaries with standard security measures. However, the government was not transparent about this strategy and only admitted it a few months after it made the headlines in the digital newspaper *El Faro*.[24] The government's opaqueness, along with its failure to manage the truce with any clear, long-term strategy, foreclosed any opportunity for the truce to represent a move away from the hardline approach to public security that successive administrations had hitherto maintained (for more details about the truce, see Cruz 2012; van der Borgh and Savenije 2014). Indeed, the negotiation of the truce in the months leading up to the 2012 municipal and legislative elections has prompted suggestions that it was actually an electoral strategy rather than an attempt to foster a shift in security policy (see Holland 2013).

Crucially, the first of El Salvador's *mano dura* policies were implemented at a moment in which homicide rates had declined relative to the 1990s; indeed, 2002 registered the lowest homicide rate of the previous five years (Aguilar Villamariona 2006: 90). Meanwhile, El Salvador's gang-abatement laws have served to legitimize military-led solutions, 'stop-and-frisk' measures, mass arrests, and prisons' overcrowding with gang-like citizens—many of whom have not been sentenced—rather than to curb homicidal violence and organized crime. Since 2005, the prison population has virtually doubled in El Salvador, resulting in the highest

---

[23] Ley de Proscripción de Maras, Pandillas, Agrupaciones, Asociaciones y Organizaciones de Naturaleza Criminal, Decreto Legislativo No. 458, *Diario Oficial*, 10 September 2010.

[24] 'Gobierno negoció con pandillas reducción de homicidios', *El Faro*, 14 March 2012.

prison occupancy rate in Latin America (Carranza 2012: 39, 35; OAS 2012: 112, 122). Although El Salvador's prisons have a maximum capacity of 8187, in 2011, they held up to 24,399 inmates—with all the added administrative, logistical, and medical deficiencies that this excess implies (Carranza 2012: 34; Wolf 2012c). Prisons, as described by Wacquant (2009a) with regard to the United States, have become sites for warehousing criminals and citizens deemed undesirable rather than implementing any sort of rehabilitation. Yet, in contrast to the United States, where high rates of incarceration have correlated with a reduction in crime, the overcrowding of prisons in El Salvador has only deepened certain problems, such as organized crime from within[25] and upheavals or confrontations resulting in the deaths of several inmates.[26]

The punitive measures endorsed by the Salvadoran governments since 2003 and the concomitant overstatement of the gang trope have in turn contributed to the structural sophistication, consolidation, and professionalization of gangs as well as their increasing participation in criminal activities such as the aforementioned systematic extortion (Aguilar Villamariona 2006; Hume 2009a: 142–143). Additionally, these measures have not been conducive to increasing the efficiency of the country's institutions of order. Out of the 1020 homicides perpetrated in El Salvador's three main municipalities in 2005, only 3.8 percent were ever solved (Acevedo 2008: 76–77). In this regard, human rights organizations have reported repressive outcomes of zero-tolerance laws and a subsequent increase in homicidal violence, crime, and police corruption in El Salvador (Aguilar Villamariona 2006; Hume 2007a; Wolf 2012a, 2017). Homicides indeed have only increased since 2002, albeit with some fluctuation, and the exception of the sizeable decline during the 18-month interlude is rooted in the 2012 gang truce.

Increasing militarization and a fetishization of the law have coexisted with lawlessness in postwar El Salvador.[27] Their coexistence is not paradoxical insofar as remilitarization and policing strategies appear to be more of a public staging than an actual means of improving citizens' secu-

[25] 'Prisons in Latin America: A Journey into Hell', *The Economist*, 22 September 2012.

[26] Twenty-seven prisoners died as a result of a fire at a young offenders' institution in Ilobasco, Department of Cabañas, on 10 November 2010. See 'Muere el preso número 27 de los quemados en Ilobasco', *La Página*, 17 November 2010.

[27] This pattern of parallel fetishization and transgression, or lack of enforcement, of the law is a characteristic of Latin America that is rooted in the region's colonial past (Gledhill 2004a: 166).

rity.[28] Furthermore, perceived police corruption and lack of accountability, alongside haunting memories of prewar and war violence and impunity, have contributed to a widespread distrust of police forces and an under-reporting by victims. Not reporting is not just a cost–benefit decision; it is motivated by pervasive fears and distrust. Reactions to extortion have ranged from changing daily routines to relocating, when it can be afforded, to other Salvadoran municipalities or, in the last few years when relocation has proved inefficient, even seeking asylum in the United States, Europe, or neighboring countries.

Significantly, reports in El Salvador of the kinds of collective responses to violence that have proliferated in other places where insecurity, lawless-ness and police corruption, or inefficiency are the rule have been rare (e.g. vigilante violence, see Abrahams 1996; Godoy 2002; Goldstein 2004; Pratten and Sen 2008). In general, social cleansing practices in postwar El Salvador have most often been police-linked, as noted in Chap. 3. The handful of reported cases of civilian-led cleansing practices could be due to a number of factors: damage to the country's social fabric in the aftermath of war, which has led to a generalized decay in collective responses; the pervasiveness of fear stemming from both war memories and daily homi-cides; the conjuring of a gray zone that has made the source of postwar violence relatively diffuse; and the increasing individualism associated with neoliberalization (on this last aspect, see Moodie 2010: 110). Yet it could well also be the case that there are more cases of Salvadorans organizing to take justice into their own hands than it is publicly admitted (Wolf 2017: 73); a few such cases recounted to me in 2017 by Salvadorans from differ-ent departments would point toward this hypothesis.

The Affinities Between Extortion Rackets and Private Security Firms

In the context of the persistent, or even increasing, subjective feeling of insecurity that has plagued Santiago, those who can afford it have increas-ingly turned to the private security industry. This trend is starkly visible in the landscape of this municipality's center. The entrances to every public building have for years been flanked by private armed security guards—the City Council, the local Justice of the Peace, and the only public high

---

[28] Note that only 5 percent of those arrested in the first year after the enactment of *mano dura* were judicially charged (FESPAD and CEPES 2004b).

school are just a few examples. A foreign NGO, the local supermarket, the only credit institution, and any small business in central Santiago that can afford it have also followed this trend. In addition to security guards, barbed wire, high walls, electric fences, and metal bars have become commonplace—notably in public buildings, successful businesses, and those houses whose dwellers receive remittances from migrant relatives, typically based in the United States. Yet, for the large majority of Santiagueños employed in agriculture or the maquilas—sectors in which the daily minimum wage during 2010 was US$3.24 and US$5.79 respectively[29]—these kinds of security services were not affordable. Perhaps in part as a result of the access to private security enjoyed by affluent families and successful business owners, extortionists have increasingly tended to victimize poor citizens unable to access protection.

An increasingly securitized landscape is hardly unique to Santiago, a location in which homicide and other crime rates have not been particularly high relative to those in other Salvadoran municipalities. Throughout El Salvador, a similar trend of rising private security has yielded a pattern of strict spatial segregation between highly protected areas and no-go zones. San Salvador's streets—especially leisure areas like the Zona Rosa, replete with hotels, restaurants, clubs, and shopping centers, or residential and business areas like the Colonia Escalón—are saturated with armed security guards. Gated communities and condominiums have also proliferated in the northwest and southwest of San Salvador, the capital city, providing an oasis of security for their upper- and middle-class inhabitants (Baires 2006: 68). This segregationist trend has been observed in other Latin American countries with a problem of rising public insecurity. In her ethnography on the rise of private security in São Paulo, Brazil, in the 1980s and 1990s, Caldeira (1996, 2000: 256–296) describes how increasing demands for security have brought about socio-spatial segregation and exclusion, epitomized by the proliferation of 'fortified enclaves'. This socio-spatial delineation has emulated the so-called Fortress America, that is, the highly securitized gated communities that have proliferated in the United States since the early 1980s in response to an increasing subjective feeling of insecurity (Blakely and Snyder 1997; Low 2003).

The development of El Salvador's security industry is coeval with that of similar industries in other Latin American countries (Arias 2009). Although a few security firms appeared in El Salvador during the country's

---

[29] Decreto Ejecutivo No. 133 and No. 135, *Diario Oficial*, 22 December 2008.

civil war, the country's security industry grew exponentially in the 1990s, expanding from 14 registered private security firms in 1994 to 295 in 2000 (Carballido Gómez 2008: 20–21; Melara 2003: 56–57).[30] These figures do not include the estimated 200–300 illicit suppliers of private security (Arias 2009: 27). One need only consult public opinion polls to realize that El Salvador's security industry has expanded in direct response to an increasing demand for personal safety and the protection of private property—not to mention an increasing distrust of the state institutions of order (Melara 2003: 58, 60). In 2007 alone, Salvadoran families spent an estimated US$160 million (0.8 percent of the GDP) and businesses an estimated US$384 million (1.9 percent of the GDP) on private security— well over the 1.5 percent of the GDP spent by the government in public security functions and the administration of prisons (Acevedo 2008: 84–85). Indeed, the demand for private security has increased to such an extent that the country's private security industry personnel outnumber police personnel,[31] the weaponry and technology of the private industry are distinctly superior, and spending in the private security industry far surpasses that of all the country's institutions of order put together (Arias 2009: 52; Carballido Gómez 2008: 16, 21–22).

Although not attributable solely to the privatization of public functions and the shaping of individuals' conduct thereof, security and protection have become highly profitable commodities in El Salvador as well as much of Latin America. Their commoditization raises a number of ethical and political concerns about the role of the country's security industry, the vested interests that this industry might have in the persistence of public insecurity, and the sorts of inequalities that develop when physical security becomes a privilege. In addition, the commoditization of security begs questions about the state's role in this process. On the one hand, as in other countries, El Salvador's prodigious private security industry amounts to a sort of parallel military force that could potentially challenge the state's monopoly on the legitimate use of violence. On the other hand, the private industry does not necessarily stand in opposition to the public realm: its personnel consist

---

[30] I should note that the existing national regulation in El Salvador ('Ley de los servicios privados de seguridad', Decreto Legislativo No. 227, *Diario Oficial*, 24 January 2001) allows for the suppliers of private security to assume a range of forms, from individuals to private firms to authorized vigilante associations (Melara 2003).

[31] This is actually the case throughout the Latin American region (Ungar 2008: 22) as well as in countries as variegated as the United States, the UK, Bulgaria, and India (Abrahamsen and Williams 2009: 2).

largely of former or active military and police personnel, and its owners and shareholders are often part of the public administration or governing political elites. Job vacancies are available for active police members to work as security guards for private firms, even using their official uniform and weapons; public institutions have increasingly outsourced security functions; and available reports on the country's security industry have noted that a large number of private security firms are owned by former military personnel or active ARENA members (see Melara 2003: 65–66; Carballido Gómez 2008: 22; Arias 2009: 24; Godnick 2010: 460–461).

For the purposes of this chapter, it is interesting to explore the synergies that result from the affinitive relationship between violent actors such as extortion rackets and the country's private security industry. Homicides and death threats, along with the fears that these instill in the Salvadoran population, have stimulated demands for and offers of protection from which both extortion rackets and the private security industry benefit, albeit in different ways. In producing private profit from violence, both extortion and security contribute to coproducing an 'economy of violence'. Although the metaphor of the 'economy of violence' does not quite convey the disaggregated nature of the circuits of accumulation that postwar violence has stimulated, I consider it a useful means of depicting the consolidated nature of these circuits and their market-like form. Economies of violence, war economies, and organized crime are often qualified as non-state, illegal, invisible, and non-formal. Yet as existing studies on violence-nurtured economies expound, these economies often lie on the boundaries between (il)legality and (in)visibility (Heyman 1999; Nordstrom 2004). Nor is the state completely absent from economies of violence (Tilly 1985; Heyman 1999; Schneider and Schneider 2003).

As examples of organized crime elsewhere have shown, the state has been integral to these economies historically. Gaio (2006: 154) has, for instance, coined the notion of the 'delinquent state' to describe how in contemporary Brazil the scale and scope of illicit activities by public officers is such that 'corruption' and 'white collar crime' are no longer useful terms to describe the dynamics of the nexus between politics and crime. In El Salvador, a defense attorney for gangs suggested to me in an interview that much of the country's crime may be gang-related, but gave a broad hint that gang members necessarily maintain connections with elites that allow them to manage the large sums of money they gather through extortion: 'The extortion money has to go into the bank account of someone for whom deposits of US$2000 are not a big deal and their origin won't be checked'.

In distinguishing between extortion and private security in El Salvador, we could note the illicit character of extortion versus the purportedly licit nature of the private security sector; theoretically, this distinction would correlate with the invisibility of extortion versus the visibility of the security sector. While the characterization of El Salvador's extortion rackets as illicit and relatively invisible seems indisputable, the definition of the country's private security industry as licit and visible is less clear. A regulation exists that renders legal the private provision of security. However, as I found out through some wealthy families from Santiago, protection is sometimes sought extra-legally through the hiring of men who do not work for an approved security firm and have not received official authorization. More importantly, the transparency of the security industry is dubious. The guards who work for a security firm do not appear, in practice, to be accountable for the violence they effect. Nor do they always receive adequate training. Additionally, while armed and uniformed private security guards are part of everyday life in any Salvadoran municipality or town, there is virtually no publicly available information on the ownership or management of many of the firms that employ these guards. As mentioned earlier, ordinary Salvadorans and news outlets have consistently suggested that a number of prominent ARENA leaders and ex-military personnel own or are shareholders of private security firms (Carballido Gómez 2008: 22). I thus suggest that in order to discern how the licit and the illicit work together in an economy of violence, it is necessary to turn our attention to the role of state actors—even as the country's lawlessness and increasing privatization would seem to suggest otherwise.

In his study of the Sicilian mafia, Gambetta (1993: 15) contends that a demand for protection can create a supply of protection. The Schneiders (2003: 103–126) and Humphrey (2002b: 101) offer a more complex historical explanation in their study of the Sicilian and Russian mafias, highlighting the cultural traditions characterizing the eras in which these mafias originated—that is, during the transitions from feudalism and socialism, respectively, to capitalism. Whereas the Sicilian mafia was able to turn networks of friends and acquaintances linked by reciprocal obligations into a resource, the Russian mafia benefited from the predatory techniques and structures of control rooted in the Soviet era. I share the Schneiders' and Humphrey's view that a mere examination of how the supply of protection and the demand for protection coalesce cannot on its own explain the emergence and success of an economy of violence. While it is necessary to examine how El Salvador's rampant crime and homicidal violence have stimulated demands for protection from the private security industry, the influence of the country's wartime legacies should not be overlooked.

Lingering war-related issues include the country's large number of readily available weapons, many of them remnants of the war in the 1980s, others having emerged out of postwar economies such as the security industry and drug trafficking; the large number of middle-aged Salvadorans trained in the use of violence during the war, whether in guerrilla organizations, the army, police forces, or local paramilitary groups; and the inefficiency and corruption of the police force and the judiciary. The war has therefore indisputably yielded conditions that have nurtured organized crime and its twin facet of private security. In the 1990s, for instance, as violence was being resignified as common and apolitical, stories proliferated suggesting that military-trained, demobilized army and guerrilla combatants were nurturing organized crime (Moodie 2004, 2010: 71–73). Civil wars in African countries such as Angola, South Africa, and Zimbabwe (Nordstrom 2004), along with those in Eastern European countries such as Bosnia (Andreas 2004), have likewise fostered organized crime and war economies that have gone on to flourish in peacetime. While in the Salvadoran case everything seems to indicate that an economy of violence has emerged in peacetime, the relative temporal proximity of the war and the ongoing presence of war-related problems and actors have unquestionably contributed to its success. Yet, as the next section explains, the influence of neoliberalism in processes of statecraft has laid the groundwork for the licit and the illicit to coalesce.

The State as Racketeer

The commoditization of security is just one aspect of the broader process of marketization that occurred in El Salvador throughout the 1990s. Despite the militarization of public life and the toughening of zero-tolerance laws, the ARENA-governed state ostensibly withdrew from various economic sectors (see Segovia 2002). As described in the Introduction, after coming to power in 1989, when the war was ongoing but peacebuilding operations were underway, the successive ARENA governments gradually emulated neoliberal reforms elsewhere. The pro-market think tank FUSADES, established with USAID funding in 1983 by members of the Salvadoran elite, prescribed economic policies for the ARENA government to undertake in order to recover from the economic impasse

effected by the war. While El Salvador's United Nations-monitored political transition was underway, the country made a concomitant transformation to a finance, manufacturing, and non-traditional exports economy
and introduced an aggressive privatization program. Even though the latter might imply a declining or increasingly weakened state, the state actually reshaped and retasked while reproducing itself in shadowy ways.
Likewise, it is worth noting that an agenda of aggressive privatization and
state reduction has for years existed alongside policies anathema to liberal-
izing ideologies, such as state subsidies for transport, gas, water, and electricity, as well as an increasing display of police and military forces.

To better convey the implications of the process of neoliberalization,
even while acknowledging the disaggregated nature of the Salvadoran
state, it is also worth looking at the idea of the state as a relatively coherent
subject (cf. Mitchell 1991). In El Salvador, this idea of the state stems
from a process of concentration, both historical and contemporary, that
has contributed to its representation as a long-lived bloc that has reconfigured over time yet maintained a high degree of coherence despite major
economic changes. Throughout the twentieth century, the Salvadoran
state was entrepreneurial in nature. Even during the decades of military
rule that followed the coup by General Martínez Hernández, economic
policies were oriented to protect the national coffee industry (Stanley
1996: 59). The historical concentration of economic and political power
by a relatively cohesive economic elite in a symbiotic alliance with the military[32] has justified popular references to the Salvadoran state as an independent subject that have continued even after the war. Exemplary among
these references is the denomination of the country's elite as 'the fourteen
families', a commonly used phrase, even though it does not accurately
describe its referent, which is far more extensive and disaggregated. With
the transition to civilian rule in 1984, the military and the elite were displaced from political power. Yet ARENA's victory in 1989 allowed for the
return of the elite, and once again for a concentration of power.

As indicated in the Introduction, powerful groups within the governing party—whose wealth originally stemmed from export-led agriculture
and reproduced over time through marital alliances but has shifted to new
economic sectors by the end of the war—have benefited from the neoliberal policies implemented from 1989 by the ARENA governments.
ARENA's deregulation and privatization of state-owned sectors—includ-

---

[32] This military–elite alliance was nonetheless not free of tensions (Stanley 1996: 57).

ing banking and finance, healthcare, public utilities, telecommunications, and protection—have allowed state actors within ARENA and foreign corporations to acquire these sectors (Segovia 2006: 528). As Paniagua Serrano (2002) has illustrated, a comparison of the boards of directors of privatized service firms and the kinship diagrams of El Salvador's wealthiest families shows how both marital and corporate alliances have allowed a few families to control the country's main firms. The adoption of a neoliberal agenda by the ARENA government, in short, created the conditions for profitability by the elite affiliated with ARENA. Even ordinary Salvadorans across the political spectrum have considered the dollarization and privatization of public utilities introduced by ARENA to have benefited that party's ruling elite (see Chap. 7). This description of neoliberalization in El Salvador is consistent with more general critiques of neoliberalism as the project of a particular class (Duménil and Lévy 2004; Harvey 2005: 19). In El Salvador, however, this aspect of state formation does not substantially differ from previous forms of statecraft, whether military- or civilian-led.

There are therefore reasons to question the extent to which there has been a turn in El Salvador's public policy at all. On one level, a welfare state, as conceived from a Western perspective, has never developed in El Salvador, and indeed public expenditure has actually increased since the 1990s, thereby suggesting a rather different point of departure relative to countries in the Global North. From 1950 to 1980, successive Salvadoran administrations, beginning with President Óscar Osorio, developed a system of universal social protection enshrined in the 1950 Constitution and influenced by international blueprints of social protection systems (PNUD 2010: 283–300). Its implementation in El Salvador coincided with a period of modernization, urbanization, and prosperity. Yet the Salvadoran system covered only a minimal portion of the country's population and excluded the majority of rural inhabitants (PNUD 2010: 253, 292).[33] Since 1989, this integrated system of public expenditure was dismantled and later on transformed into one that targets vulnerable populations through specific piecemeal programs, such as *Red Solidaria* (Solidary Network).[34] In light of

[33] For instance, in 1979, only 14 percent of Salvadorans, most of them from urban areas, enjoyed public healthcare and pensions.

[34] This is a program that began in 2005, under the administration of President Saca, aiming to alleviate rural poverty (PNUD 2010: 61, 296). It consisted of conditional cash transfers to families living in extreme poverty. The program continued under President Mauricio Funes but was renamed *Comunidades Solidarias* (Solidary Communities) and expanded to the urban areas.

the country's paltry public finances, these programs have been funded with loans and funds from international financial organizations such as the WB and the IDB.

The Salvadoran state did, however, nationalize various sectors during the 1980s, as part of an attempt to curtail civilian support for the FMLN. As mentioned earlier, these sectors were subsequently privatized after the war. The withdrawal of those sectors from the public domain has been accompanied by a strengthening of the coercive and surveillance functions—whether through public or private means—required to protect private industries and businesses.[35] In his study of United States neoliberal state-craft, Wacquant (2009a, b) describes the shift from an emphasis on social programs to the expansion of the penal apparatus as 'the punitive policy turn'. It would thus seem that in reducing state intervention, for instance in the supply of basic utilities, El Salvador has proceeded by mimicking the United States. Nevertheless, there has not actually been much of a turn in El Salvador. Not only was a welfare state never fully developed, but also historically policing strategies were already oriented toward the protection of the economic elite and the criminalization of the poor by their identification as 'subversives' (Stanley 1996: 56–58). Postwar state transformations have nevertheless marked a turn vis-à-vis the ethos of the Peace Accords, the enactment of which, as noted earlier, sought to reduce the number of police and military personnel and limit military functions to the patrolling of borders and participation in external military operations.

Yet, in postwar El Salvador, the state's 'strong hand' is most often either unable or unwilling to enforce the rule of law. As discussed earlier, what the *mano dura* policies have done instead is criminalize the aesthetics and bodies of certain young men rather than certain acts (Moodie 2009: 83). These policies, which have encouraged mass detentions of gang-like youth, crammed prisons and thereby facilitated the coordination of organized crime from within, motivated the Funes government to entrust the military with the monitoring of prisons. The lack of police intervention and law enforcement, as exhibited in the few reported cases of extortion in Santiago, may, I suggest, be due partly to the fact that postwar violence

---

[35] This increase of the state's 'strong hand' reveals a contradiction in the practice of neoliberalism *vis-à-vis* neoliberal doctrine. Neoliberal doctrine prescribes the curtailment of state intervention; in practice, however, neoliberal governments have increased their intervention with regard to security so as to protect the business environment (Harvey 2005: 64; Peck et al. 2009: 101, 103–104).

does not destabilize the state as it did during the war—it disrupts primarily the lives of ordinary Salvadorans who are no longer needed as a labor force. Indeed, despite the shift toward a strong-handed state, the institutions of order have been deeply underresourced and lacked investigative capacity. Yet police inaction also points to the possibility that some police officers are themselves involved in corruption or collaborate with criminals, as rumors have suggested and investigative journalism and research confirmed.[36] The prevailing lawlessness has given way to private strategizing and the burgeoning of a private security industry, thus encouraging those who can afford it to find individual solutions to the management of public insecurity.

As noted earlier, the flourishing private security industry is rumored by ordinary people and the media to be controlled partly by ARENA leaders and former military personnel. In the face of these rumors, and inspired by Tilly (1985), I suggest that the analogy of the state as racketeer serves to denote the extent to which the state and extortion rackets have seemed commensurate in postwar El Salvador. While extortion rackets have demanded that Salvadorans pay *la renta* to ensure that they or their relatives are not killed, the ARENA-ruled state consistently failed to provide the nominal protection that a liberal democratic state typically offers its citizens. Meanwhile, rumors and the media have it that prominent ARENA leaders have been supplying protection via the private security sector, but only to those who can afford it. Both the rackets and the security industry—the latter rumored to be not so neatly separable from the ARENA-governed state—therefore have benefited from insecurity.

Tilly explains how power-holders in sixteenth- and seventeenth-century Western Europe extracted resources from citizens in exchange for military protection, while the war-making sustained by this extraction became an essential part of state formation. Ironically, the war-making in turn posed the very threat that had legitimized extraction for military protection in the first place. Tilly's analogical analysis has heuristic value insofar as it evinces that the rumors about the private security industry have come to imply that the ARENA-governed state has, to a certain degree, operated 'in essentially the same ways as racketeers' (Tilly 1985: 171) by neglecting the police and judiciary, while, as a secondary consequence, members of the governing party have profited by supplying protection. The rumored

[36] See, for instance, 'Infiltrados', *El Faro*, 14 May 2014; 'Infiltrados, un año después', *Revista Factum*, 13 May 2015.

existence of a sort of Shadow State and the participation of state actors in El Salvador's gray zone is indicative of the extent to which left-leaning Salvadorans conceive the state to be part of the very same threat that justifies increasing militarization or extraction by the private security industry. In this analogy, the difference between the state and the extortion racketeers is that the latter 'operate without the sanctity of governments' (Tilly 1985: 171).

Far from challenging the state monopoly on legitimate violence, as Caldeira (2000: 2) puts it for the case of twentieth-century Brazil, El Salvador's private security sector allowed for its reproduction during the years of ARENA government, albeit in ways that precluded transparency and accountability. Similar to Stanley (1996: 219–220), I argue that in the case of El Salvador, the state did undergo a major ontological shift in the last quarter of the twentieth century. El Salvador's twentieth-century military state, intentionally run as a protection racket, was dismantled with the implementation of the 1992 Peace Accords reforms. Yet rumors and the media have implicitly suggested that neoliberal restructuring and endemic violence have allowed ARENA's political network to profit from a problem of postwar public insecurity that appears manageable given that it does not threaten the state itself or the interests of the economic elite. Neoliberal restructuring has thus contributed to state-crafting and retasking in ways that have yielded equivalency across licit and illicit domains. While I do suggest that the ways in which prominent ARENA leaders have benefited from postwar insecurity are tantamount to the ways in which racketeers have profited from extortion and public fear, I surmise that this resemblance is the result of the convergence of a number of processes and conditions rather than a wholly intentional project of government. Interestingly, the resemblance between the licit and the illicit is a pattern found elsewhere in contemporary Latin America (see Rodgers 2006; Holston 2009).

SECURITY AS A PRIVILEGE

The resemblance between the licit and the illicit—the effect itself of structural processes and intended actions—has contributed to deepening a particular expression of structural violence. 'Structural violence', Farmer (2004: 307) explains, 'is violence exerted systematically—that is, indirectly—by everyone who belongs to a certain social order.' It is the expression, often embodied, of social inequalities. Via the Salvadoran state's disinterest in protecting ordinary Salvadorans and its simultaneous privatization of protection, structural violence becomes discernible in the restriction of security only to those Salvadorans who can afford protection as well as in the emergence of safe and unsafe zones. The interrelatedness of economic and public insecurity is palpable—both in the intensification of the risk of violence for impoverished Salvadorans who cannot access security or legal services and in the embodied fears, anxieties, and sense of vulnerability that so often accompany this violence. In this sense, inequality not only organizes space—as in Caldeira's (2000) description of São Paulo in the 1980s and 1990s—but also the lives of poor Salvadorans who cannot afford protection and consequently modify their routines and activities in public places and even, if they can afford it, relocate their residences or flee the country altogether.

Another dimension of structural violence is that poor people end up demanding the same zero-tolerance policies that criminalize the members of their own class (see IUDOP 2009b: 52–53, 63). In sum, even as extortion is inflicted across classes, it simultaneously accentuates class differences (Caldeira 2000: 12). The analysis of the dynamics of securitization, in which the state plays a critical role, thus proves to be one way of illuminating the existing correlations between economic insecurity and crime (see Gledhill 2009). Likewise, the analogy of the state as racketeer allows us to identify the origin of the infliction of this expression of structural violence. Even if the ontological equivalency between the state and the racketeers is the result of not wholly intentional actions on the part of political actors associated with the former ruling party ARENA, the profitability of the private security industry in a climate of public insecurity could be viewed as an added bonus for ARENA to have maintained a particular social and political regime.

The preceding exploration of El Salvador's postwar economy of violence—of which extortion rackets and security firms have become an integral part—has allowed me to illuminate the ways in which political economies and endemic violence are intimately linked. In short, there are at least two ways in which El Salvador's gray zone and the country's neoliberalization process are related. First, according to rumors as well as evident through my analysis, neoliberal statecraft has contributed to the coalescing of some actors, relations, and actions across the licit/illicit boundary. A direct implication of these rumors and the condition of lawlessness is that El Salvador's neoliberal state, during ARENA rule, bore a disturbing resemblance to the postwar racketeer: both had vested interests in the existence of (or even participated in) a gray zone that renders violence unintelligible and fosters feelings of insecurity. While this country's state has historically been the equivalent of a protection racket, the ontological equivalency between the postwar state and the extortion racket is the effect of a complex play of processes. In postwar El Salvador, neoliberal statecraft has permitted the flourishing of a licit security industry which, like extortion rackets, benefits from the combination of persistent homicidal violence and the inefficacy of the rule of law. In this sense, it becomes clear how 'law and lawlessness ... are conditions of each other's possibilities' (Comaroff and Comaroff 2006: 21) in El Salvador's liberal market democracy.

In examining the conflation between the licit and the illicit, the relationship between neoliberalization and El Salvador's gray zone has also manifested in the fact that economic and public insecurity have worked together and reinforced each other. Neither the Peace Accords nor the postwar governments have addressed the pervasive socio-economic insecurity that, alongside state-sponsored repression, lay at the root of the political dissidence of the 1970s and the outbreak of war in 1980. This failure, along with broad postwar economic transformations such as the collapse of the agrarian economy in the 1990s, the subsequent transition to a service and export manufacturing economy, and the country's government adoption of a neoliberal agenda, has maintained El Salvador's problems of inequality. Meanwhile, forms of violence like extortion-related death threats and homicides affect Salvadorans regardless of their purchasing power. Since security and the management of risk have increasingly become individualized and dealt with through the market, those who cannot afford security have remained at risk and live with anxiety over the *possibility* that the threat of violence might materialize.

The statements made in this chapter largely concern El Salvador's state until 2009, when the FMLN took office. Despite the Salvadoran state's efforts to militarize public life during ARENA rule, the security of ordinary people did not seem to be a priority in its agenda. Indeed, the state's management of violence transformed from counterinsurgency warfare in the 1980s to limited policing intervention coupled with a high level of routinized inaction—with private security offered as the alternative for those who can afford it—in the postwar era. When police have intervened, the focus has been on repressing potential gang members rather than adopting a more comprehensive approach to crime and security and acknowledging other violent actors. These interventions ignore in turn the structural roots of the country's high levels of crime and homicidal violence. This chapter has thus shown how left-leaning and disaffected Santiagueñas have made sense of violence not only as the resource of specific violent actors but also as an element built into the operation of a liberal market democracy still led by political and economic elites. In light of this, I suggest that there is a need to repoliticize the study of violence beyond the confines of the category of 'political violence', narrowly defined as harm or assault perpetrated on the basis of a political ideology (see Bourgois 2001: 7).

While evidence has not emerged that there are owners of private security firms who belong to the FMLN, this party's approach to security and social programs has not differed significantly from ARENA's, and the blurring between the licit and the illicit has remained after the 2009 shift. Funes's administration initially demonstrated a volition to develop a citizen-focused approach to security. Yet pressure from elites and the media soon led his administration to continue the same punitive approach. Indeed, the administration's participation in the gang truce of March 2012 seems to have represented a strategy to canvass electoral support rather than a clear departure from the hitherto dominant punitive paradigm. More importantly, as I will discuss in the Epilogue, despite the 2009 presidential handover, the state capture by ARENA members over the years has allowed the party, to some extent, to exert pressure on the FMLN government to enable the continuation of previous policies, thereby suggesting that the arguments in this chapter have held beyond 2009.

CHAPTER 5

War Reenactment Through Elections

In 2009, for only the second time since the end of El Salvador's civil war, Salvadorans would be called upon to cast their votes in municipal, legislative, and presidential elections within the same year.[1] Municipal and legislative elections would be held on 18 January and the presidential election on 15 March. As the two election days approached, the political parties' activities intensified. One day in January 2009, aware that an FMLN electoral committee meeting was scheduled for that afternoon, I arrived early at the new FMLN headquarters, centrally located on Anastasio Aquino Avenue and recognizable for its red façade and the white logo painted on its bottom left corner. At this small one-room property, I found the party's local leaders, all men, gathered around a large table on which a map of Santiago Nonualco was spread out. As I approached the group, I overheard their conversation, which revolved around which *cantones* were FMLN strongholds and which would require intense work in order for the FMLN to gain influence and overtake them from ARENA; which areas had a certain FMLN presence, and which were dominated by ARENA loyalists to such an extent that FMLN members had been violently attacked in previous electoral seasons and would not dare set foot there again. For a second, the image of these men poring over the map and studying their next move to gain control

---

[1] Since the end of the war, all three elections had only coincided once, in 1994. That year's elections were designated by the press as the 'elections of the century' for having inaugurated El Salvador's democracy (see Alcántara Sáez 1994; Cruz 1998; Vilas 1998: 311–312).

© The Author(s) 2018
A. Montoya, *The Violence of Democracy*, Studies of the Americas,
https://doi.org/10.1007/978-3-319-76330-9_5

of more municipality areas conjured up fictional images of similar territorial strategizing by senior military officials fighting a war.

This snapshot from my fieldwork offers a glimpse of the ways in which El Salvador's 2009 elections were still suffused with wartime memories and conflicts. In this chapter, I examine the unfolding of these elections in order to explore how the archetypally democratic practice of voting and participating in electoral campaigns and events was influenced by political cleavages rooted in wartime. These cleavages, as shown in Chap. 3, have persisted and retained salience in the postwar era, notably in the explanations given by left-leaning Salvadorans for the persistence of homicidal violence and public insecurity in the war's aftermath. Yet postwar presidential elections have also seen these cleavages reemerge with vigor. Relying on literature on ritual and affect, I suggest that El Salvador's postwar elections have amounted to a reenactment of the cleavages, tensions, and conflicts of its civil war. In the new millennium, elections became increasingly important for ordinary people because they constituted one of the few moments in which the war and the problems thereof were dealt with publicly. Rather than simply suggesting that Salvadorans who voted were manifestly demonstrating their confidence in elections as potential instruments of change, this chapter examines the war-related rhetoric, symbols, and ritualized practices that elections encapsulate in order to investigate more closely why so many Salvadorans participated in electoral events and voted in the 2009 elections and why they voted in the ways that they did.

More than other arenas of Salvadoran political life, electoral politics have recreated the divisions of the past, thereby reintroducing unresolved wartime frictions into public discourse. The campaigns for the 2004 and 2009 presidential elections, I argue, impelled Salvadorans to engage—publicly and in a relatively controlled manner—in wartime conflicts with which many of them had not yet come to terms. Hostility and recriminations between the governing rightwing ARENA party and the leftwing FMLN opposition party had characterized the postwar elections ever since 1994 (Ramos 1998: 5; Garibay 2005; de Zeeuw 2010: 1191). In 2004 and 2009, however, ARENA's politics of fear, enacted through a mass media propaganda campaign that resuscitated wartime conflicts, arguably made the ongoing political frictions all the more palpable to Salvadoran society at large. In addition to evidencing how postwar elections have accommodated various forms of violence, ARENA's resuscitation of wartime memories and rhetorics, I argue, may explain why voter turnout virtually doubled in 2004 and then again in 2009. In this respect, it is important to note that the 2009 elections were a showdown solely between FMLN and ARENA.[2]

Yet an additional relevant question is what moved so many Salvadorans to vote for the FMLN in the 2009 elections given the continuity of the politics of fear that ARENA had employed since the 2004 elections.[3] Even as this chapter explores the persistence of El Salvador's political divide, it yields an understanding of the country's political life beyond the Cold War imagery so often invoked by ARENA. The FMLN victory in the 2009 presidential elections was possible, among other things, because this party's candidate spoke to pressing social and economic problems, appealing to disaffected Salvadorans on both the Left and the Right. In a different vein, the sharp distinction between the results of the municipal and the presidential elections that same year points to the ability of clientelistic practices and internecine factional disputes to override the political cleavages of wartime.

My fieldwork before, during, and after the 2009 elections revealed how Salvadoran political life is pervaded by the country's haunting past. Although Santiago is not considered a former war zone, it nonetheless reflects the historical wartime divisions that have manifested nationwide. Indeed, Santiago, whose population strikes a representative balance between the country's Left and Right wings, is better suited for a study of political division than most municipalities in former war zones, whose populations tend to support the FMLN in overwhelming numbers. Yet even as this municipality can be seen as a microcosm of the polarized conflict that persisted in the country during the 2009 presidential elections, it also possesses local specificities, not least the presence of the PCN, that allow for further study of the publicly unacknowledged ambiguities of the country's persistent wartime divide. Since 2000, Santiago was governed by the PCN, a minority party since the war and one that has largely supported ARENA

---

[2] The PCN and the PDC, the other two major parties, had presented a presidential candidate initially. In the 18 January 2009 municipal and legislative elections, the FMLN increased its share of the electoral vote and edged past ARENA despite losing in the capital city, thus demonstrating its ability to win the presidential elections. In light of these results, ARENA negotiated with PCN and PDC leaders a strategic removal of these parties' presidential candidates so as to concentrate the rightwing vote.

[3] Even though the 2004 presidential election was highly disputed, ARENA won by a large margin over the FMLN, with 57.71 percent of the vote share in a first round. The result of this election can be consulted at Georgetown University's Political Database of the Americas: http://pdba.georgetown.edu/Elecdata/ElSal/pre04.html.

in the Legislative Assembly. The differences between Santiago's postwar municipal and presidential elections—attributable in large part to the presence of the PCN—have offered crucial insights into El Salvador's postwar political divide as well as the question of how Salvadorans have voted in postwar elections and participated in party politics.

IN THE ABSENCE OF A PUBLIC DISCUSSION

As expounded in Chap. 2, the 1992 Peace Accords that marked the end of El Salvador's 12-year war included the creation of a truth commission to investigate and clear up wartime human rights violations that had been denied or left uninvestigated. Immediately after the signing of the Peace Accords, the truth commission on El Salvador began investigations. Its report, published in 1993, included basic information on certain high-profile cases, such as the El Mozote massacre and Archbishop Romero's assassination, and pointed to those responsible. Although the truth commission was not endowed with judicial jurisdiction, its report propounded that further investigations on human rights violations would have to be conducted in order for Salvadorans to reconcile. These future investigations, the report assumed, would in turn provide the grounds for adequate moral and material reparations (United Nations 1993: 256). The report did not specify the terms of the investigations, leaving this decision to the Salvadorans themselves.

Only five days after the commission's recommendations were put forward, El Salvador's ARENA government, headed by President Alfredo Cristiani, passed the 1993 General Amnesty Law for the Consolidation of Peace[4] that, until it was declared unconstitutional on 13 July 2016, enforced silence on the subject of wartime crimes and hindered accountability for these crimes. Given the enactment of a blanket amnesty and the limited reform of the country's judiciary post-Peace Accords, accountability was scarcely pursued for more than two decades (see Collins 2010: 168–208). Neither did the country's two major political parties, ARENA and FMLN, facilitate a public discussion that might have provided a forum for reconciling the war's opposing sides. Until 2009, consistent efforts to introduce a discussion of the past into the public domain had been largely limited to the work of El Salvador's human rights and victims' organizations (see Chap. 6). Only during electoral periods have ARENA and the FMLN,

---

[4] Decreto Legislativo No. 486, *Diario Oficial*, 22 March 1993.

which correspond to the war's opposing sides, publicly and consistently addressed what the war was about. Their explanations, however, echoing their political propaganda, have been stereotypical and caricatured.

Since my fieldwork coincided with the campaigns for all 2009 elections, it provided me with insights into how Salvadorans perceived and experienced postwar electoral politics. The electoral season had not officially started when I arrived in El Salvador in August 2008, and yet all parties had already been campaigning for months, some even for over a year. While my initial focus was not on elections, the fact that party politics had taken over so much of the country's political and social life meant that I ended up closely observing the electoral campaign. Given the heightened animosities characterizing the 2009 presidential election, informal conversations about electoral politics cropped up constantly in mundane situations and among people not formally involved in the various campaigns. During the campaign, I attended countless regular meetings and rallies of all political parties, held informal conversations with their leaders and constituents, analyzed their propaganda, and participated as an international observer with the PDDH on both election days. That said, I gained more access to the meetings and members of the FMLN than I did to any other party given that I lived with a family that actively supported it.

The polarized nature of the election meant I had to be as cautious as possible in how I handled my participation in political parties' meetings and events, and the information I learned or was shared with me. This included not showing allegiance to any party, both for research purposes and to demonstrate compliance with the Salvadoran electoral law that prohibits the participation of foreigners in electoral campaigning.[5] Party politics being a male-dominated activity, at least in rural areas, and parties' meetings often being held after sunset when most women were tending to domestic chores and in areas remote from the municipality center, I faced limitations to my ability to attend those meetings when no one I could trust was able to join me. I could more easily attend FMLN evening meetings, in which close friends and some young women participated, than I could those of any other party.

This chapter focuses on the procedural element of political democracy that an election constitutes so as to explore aspects of Salvadoran politics that do not otherwise surface so conspicuously in everyday public life.

[5] Article 247 of El Salvador's Electoral Code stipulates that any foreigner who participates directly or indirectly in political activities will be immediately expelled from El Salvador.

Although the local meanings, discourses, and practices of democracy have been widely explored by anthropologists, its procedural aspects—the mechanisms and procedures that legitimize a democratic regime—have been largely neglected and have thus remained the purview of political scientists, whose work tends to employ sophisticated quantitative analyses and emphasize rational-choice approaches, political institutions, and structural changes (for the case of El Salvador, see, for instance, Wantchekon 1999). In contrast to rational-choice approaches to elections, which privilege explanations of voters' decision-making process as guided by the maximization of self-interest, symbolic approaches have largely studied the ritualized aspects of elections as purely performative, non-utilitarian acts that nevertheless contribute to maintaining and restoring social cohesion (Banerjee 2007: 1556). There are, however, a number of recent ethnographic studies on elections that have highlighted the relevance of symbolic elements and affective dynamics in elucidating the complex processes by which people decide to participate in elections (see McDonald 1997; McLeod 1999; Lazar 2004; Banerjee 2007). These works, which eschew the dyadic division between the rational and the symbolic, are my source of inspiration for understanding how Salvadorans have experienced postwar electoral processes. Memories and experiences of the war, I argue, delineate basic party constituencies to such a degree that postwar elections represent expressions of historical divisions and conflicts that do not overtly manifest in other circumstances.

Postwar Elections as War

On the eve of ARENA presidential candidate Rodrigo Ávila's visit to Santiago on 19 September 2008, groups of ARENA loyalists covered the municipality's central neighborhoods with ARENA flags and posters of Ávila himself. That afternoon, I watched from the window of the house where I was living a group of ARENA members, identifiable by their party T-shirts, plastering the Anastasio Aquino Avenue with their party propaganda. Half an hour later, neighbors arrived at the house to comment on an incident that had just occurred a few houses away. An ARENA loyalist had ripped a poster of FMLN presidential candidate Mauricio Funes off a housefront and replaced it with one of Rodrigo Ávila. The owner of the house complained vehemently to the ARENA loyalist, ceasing only when another ARENA loyalist pointed a gun at him.

Other residents of the central *barrio* where I was living were likewise upset that their neighborhood had been flooded with ARENA propaganda. Overnight, a group of FMLN loyalists undid the work of ARENA in the central *barrios*. As I was told the following day by FMLN loyalists themselves, they had waited a long time, since some ARENA loyalists had stayed in an effort to ensure that their work would remain untouched. Finally, just before midnight, FMLN loyalists, equipped with red paint and brushes, a ladder, glue and posters of Mauricio Funes, painted and plastered over the ARENA posters and slogans that covered the Anastasio Aquino Avenue. 'This is a liberated zone', an FMLN loyalist explained to me as he recounted their overnight raid. This expression, which I had heard before in Santiago residents talk about FMLN strongholds during the war, served to underline that his *barrio* was aligned with the FMLN. As this ethnographic vignette illustrates, the disputes and strategies of the 2009 election amounted in some respects to a reenactment of wartime enmities and passions.

Elections and their mechanisms constitute highly ritualized events, the observance of which is considered to yield a qualitative democracy. Their periodical repetition, discrete durability, and sets of rules and procedures support the ritual analogy. Coles (2004: 554) has suggested that the study of elections as ritual tends to divest people's practices of utility and reflect merely their symbolic dimension. In describing elections in Bosnia-Herzegovina, she has accentuated the relevance of electoral mechanisms, knowledge, and techniques in order to elucidate how elections are culturally and socially, as well as politically, embedded. Yet, in postwar El Salvador, the ritualized aspects of elections include both calculative practices and heightened feelings. Specifically, elections have become highly ritualized in ways that are expressive of Salvadorans' past experiences as well as their motivations for participating in the elections themselves. The ritualized nature of elections has allowed the two major political parties and their constituencies to confront one another in a relatively controlled manner that nonetheless evokes war-related concerns and animosities. The reenactment of war that elections constitute partly explains why parties' basic constituencies care to vote in postwar El Salvador. Particularly for people who campaign actively, the elections allow for a vital and performative reaffirmation of identities and a reliving of war-related passions.

My observations of the unfolding of the 2009 municipal, legislative, and presidential elections in Santiago confirmed the persistent salience of the historical FMLN/ARENA divide. In Santiago, party allegiances in the *barrios* and *cantones* were largely predicated upon war experiences and family ties. The central *barrios* and northern Cantón Las Ánimas—where the population was harshly repressed during the war—massively supported the FMLN, whereas the remaining northern *cantones*—where local populations had joined paramilitary groups during the 1980s—zealously supported ARENA. Party allegiance was reflected throughout the municipality's landscape with murals, flags, and portraits of the preferred candidate. Housefronts, entrance doors, lamp posts, pavement, and even trees were decorated either in red in support of the FMLN or in the blue-white-red evoking ARENA's tricolor flag. Interestingly, just as Salvadorans supported the FMLN or ARENA on the basis of their own war experiences, the parties' leaderships devised electoral strategies reminiscent of tactics used during wartime. In attending both parties' meetings and accompanying these parties' constituencies for months during the electoral campaign, I observed their fixation with territorial control as elucidated through this chapter's initial snapshot; death threats, confrontations, and physical aggressions perpetrated on the basis of party allegiances; secrecy and rumors about spies; and a refusal to acknowledge the possibility of neutrality, ambiguity, or alternative positions.

Territory was a critical factor in the electoral strategizing of all parties. Both the FMLN and ARENA were structured around a local hierarchical leadership that was then decentralized via the establishment of support groups or leaders in as many *barrios* and *cantones* as possible. This structure already existed in areas where the parties enjoyed large basic constituencies but had to be created anew for the 2009 elections in others. While the FMLN sought to found 'base committees' in each municipality sector, ARENA identified specific leaders supportive of their party who would manage to attract other residents from their area. In both party's meetings, discussions revolved around the *barrios* and *cantones* that each party controlled, where FMLN base committees or ARENA leaders were located, and what strategies should be devised vis-à-vis those in control of the opposing party. As illustrated by the vignette that opened this section, the dispute over territory was evident in the competition between parties to cover streets, houses, and roads with their respective colors; often one party's contingent painted and plastered a street or road during the day, only to have their work painted or plastered over by members of the opposing party that very night. The flags of both parties were sometimes stolen or burned overnight, with accusations flying back and forth between their members. ARENA's headquarters walls were doused in burning oil one night, ruining the blue-white-red flag painted on its front. At the subsequent weekly meeting of ARENA leaders, this was deemed indisputable evidence of an attack by the FMLN. These types of territorial disputes were not unprecedented; in previous elections, disputes over territory had likewise led to clashes between FMLN and ARENA loyalists as they plastered streets with their parties' propaganda.[6]

Although election rules and ritualized features allowed for a relatively controlled unfolding of the confrontation between ARENA and the FMLN, physical aggression was not absent during the 2009 electoral campaign. Several FMLN members told me that as they were trying to found a base committee for the first time in the mountainous northern Cantón San Antonio Arriba in September 2007, the committee's leader was beaten up by three hooded men, resulting in a hospital stay, with a few months' recovery time. Other residents who showed an interest in joining the FMLN received death threats. FMLN members were confident that all these cases were attacks by ARENA. One explained,

> The two San Antonios, Arriba and Abajo, and Santa Cruz Loma are all *areneros*, so it is dangerous for us to set foot there dressed in our red T-shirts. Until 2007, the FMLN leadership had not even tried to visit these *cantones* during electoral campaigns. It was there that the Comandos Chencho Beltrán[7] [paramilitary groups] were active during the war.

During FMLN meetings, rumors about the persecution or assassination of party members during elections were a constant. At one such gathering, a police officer who had befriended members of the local FMLN leadership shared with them news from his subdelegation about unlicensed cars and taxis whose drivers had been hired to drive around the neighboring Department La Libertad, assassinating FMLN members. He provided

---

[6] 'ARENA denuncia a alcalde viroleño', *La Prensa Gráfica*, 3 March 1999. The most notable case of inter-party violence occurred during the 2004 presidential elections, when two ARENA members were killed while mounting party propaganda throughout the Costal Road that crosses Santiago. In hindsight, ARENA members have interpreted this as a PCN attack, which adds a new layer to the understanding of political cleavages in El Salvador, as I will show in the last section of this chapter. See 'Un muerto durante cierre de campaña', *La Prensa Gráfica*, 19 March 2004; 'Entierran activista arenero', *La Prensa Gráfica*, 20 March 2004.

[7] Chencho Beltrán was well known in Santiago for having led a local paramilitary group (civil defense) and orchestrated numerous assassinations during the early 1980s, until guerrillas attacked his group in 1985.

details of the colors and makes of the reported vehicles so that people could keep an eye out for themselves. Faced with this kind of threat in a country in which homicidal violence makes the daily news, FMLN members either walked home in groups after evening meetings or, more often, dropped each other off in pick-up trucks. Several FMLN loyalists even confessed to me their fear of participating in any political activity at all during elections.

Secrecy was another feature common to both the 2009 electoral campaign and wartime. Both ARENA and FMLN leaders were extremely suspicious of people they did not know or trust who attended their meetings. They became fixated on the possibility that the opposing party was infiltrating these meetings, or that someone from within their own leadership was leaking information about their electoral strategies. This distrust was not groundless, since all parties gathered intelligence, based not just on rumors but also on information passed on by members who had been sent to meetings of the opposing party. As I attended public meetings of all the different parties, I frequently ran into Santiagueños whom I recognized from the meetings of more than one political party, and often I could not be sure which party they actually supported and which party they were spying on. Even among their own relatives, party loyalists tended to remain secretive about their party's electoral strategies; this same kind of secrecy had existed during the war, when, as some women told me, their own husbands would not share information concerning political and military activity.

Neither FMLN nor ARENA leaders conceived of neutrality as a possibility. Santiagueñas often knew their neighbors' and relatives' allegiances or thought they could guess them. As during the war, religious leaders in Santiago were no strangers to electoral competition. The priest who ran Santiago's El Calvario Church was popularly dubbed 'the guerrilla priest' by ARENA loyalists. This identification rested on his Archbishop Romero-inspired preaching, which attracted leftwing Santiagueños to his services, and his having granted permission to FMLN constituents to congregate in El Calvario Church until they got their own headquarters in the run-up to the 2009 elections. The party affiliations of the country's Evangelical churches were likewise widely known. For instance, the Tabernáculo Bíblico Bautista's head minister publicly endorsed ARENA, while the FMLN received unconditional support from the head minister of the Elim Church.

Since I was attending electoral events and staying in Santiago throughout the elections, even I was sometimes viewed through a polarizing political lens. The ARENA leadership assumed that I sided with the FMLN because the family I was living with supported this party. The father of this family had been killed at the beginning of the war for allegedly collaborating with the guerrillas, and one of the sons had to go into exile for the same reason; another family member had been involved in the FMLN leadership during the 2009 electoral campaign, while others helped out the party during the weeks preceding election day. The family's house was decorated with a poster of Funes, and an FMLN flag, visible from the street, hung from a tall mango tree in the backyard. Several times I was publicly accused in ARENA meetings of having been sent by the Venezuelan and Cuban governments to gather information about ARENA's electoral strategies and pass the intelligence on to the FMLN. These experiences could be terrifying, especially when accompanied by threats in front of an audience of deeply conservative rural populations from northern areas of Santiago, some of whom had belonged to paramilitary groups during the early years of the civil war. Nor was I free from the suspicion of the FMLN leadership, given my scrupulous silence about what I had heard at ARENA meetings. I thus had to repeatedly justify to everyone why I was interested in the elections. I was as open as possible about my attendance of the public meetings of all parties, and I avoided leadership meetings to which I had been invited so as not to raise suspicions that I was gathering intelligence for the opposing party.

On more than one occasion I was chided by friends who supported the FMLN for interacting with members of an ARENA-affiliated family. This happened, for instance, as I returned from an event at the Jesuit Central American University (UCA) in San Salvador in a microbus crammed with university students. I spent the journey chatting with two 20-year-old girls who had seen me in Santiago and were curious about what I was doing there since that municipality is rarely visited by foreigners. A friend who was accompanying me, himself an FMLN loyalist, remained silent throughout the journey. When we got off the microbus in Santiago, he told me that the two girls were from families supportive of ARENA and admonished me for having told them details about myself. Immersed as I was in the polarized atmosphere of the elections, I found it stressful simply to have conversations with locals since I could not always sense people's political affiliations and the extent to which I needed to be careful. With members of both parties, ARENA in particular, I felt a constant pressure to prove my neutral position with regard to the elections. While this was possible during the municipal and legislative elections, my relationship vis-à-vis ARENA members became more difficult to manage during the month leading up to the presidential election. In that period's atmosphere of heightened animosities and increasing distrust, I received serious verbal death threats from ARENA members and decided that it would be safest not to continue attending the activities of any political party for the remainder of the campaign.

An examination of the ritualized strategizing of political parties during the 2009 electoral campaigns reveals not only the continuing salience of wartime divisions, but also the extent to which FMLN and ARENA have acted as mirror images of one another. Looking solely at the symbolic and performative elements of electoral competition, one could infer that El Salvador's postwar elections had become a struggle unto themselves, in which both sides mimicked the other while the motivation at the root of conflict had dissipated. This reproduction of the wartime divide and its per-petuation in peacetime seemed to suggest that both parties had entered a spiral of violence in which they had lost sight of the object of their initial contention—just as Girard (1977, 1996) says occurs when a conflict persists over time through the mimesis of violence. Yet even by 2009, and despite the transformation of ARENA and the FMLN over time, their mimicry of each other's performative elements had not fully dissolved the ontological alterity that existed between them. During the war, both parties were argu-ably the products of a fusion of political and military elements. The FMLN structured itself as an army yet had originated in mass political organiza-tions. ARENA, albeit a political party clearly diverging from the PCN, the formerly country's military party, publicly presented itself as being protected by its own army (Martín-Baró 1991: 295, 298) and was linked to wartime death squads (United Nations 1993: 184–186). However, the two parties have differed radically in ideology. Tracing the genealogy and ideological underpinnings of the two main political parties can thus shed light on the ongoing frictions between their basic constituencies. The persistence of alterity through the mimetic play involved in the reenactment of war during elections illustrates that 'mimesis registers both sameness and difference, of being like, and of being Other' (Taussig 1993: 129).

The FMLN, born in 1980 as a coalition of the five main political-military organizations of the 1970s, was founded in an effort to wage a 'final offensive' against the Salvadoran state in 1981 that turned out to be merely one of the events precipitating the country's 12-year civil war. The five organizations—albeit differing in their political interpretations and strategies—shared a Marxist–Leninist ideological orientation. All the organizations rejected democracy and the electoral system as a mere façade for El Salvador's authoritarian and oligarchic regime, and believed in armed revolution led by a vanguard as the means of taking over the apparatus of the state and setting up a one-party system that would enact the transformations necessary for a socialist society to flourish (Martín Álvarez 2006, 2010). The FMLN had come into existence as a reaction to the contraction throughout the 1970s of the country's already limited arenas for political participation and had a close relationship with popular organizations and social movements, many of whose members would eventually become their mid-level and rank-and-file cadres.[8] During the war, it became the largest Latin American revolutionary group—with nearly 30 percent of its members being women—and managed to control about a third of El Salvador's territory (Martí i Puig 2006; Martín Álvarez 2010). The FMLN converted to a legal political party, with the 1992 Peace Accords and the denouement of armed struggle. Its supporters in the postwar era have comprised largely ex-guerrillas, residents of repopulated areas, and members of social movements and popular organizations, largely due to the party's origins and the fact that it has become the main leftwing electoral option. Indeed, since its transformation into a political party, more precisely from the 1997 municipal and legislative elections, the FMLN became ARENA's main electoral rival by gradually increasing its party share in subsequent legislative and municipal elections. It managed to win San Salvador's council during four consecutive elections since 1997 as well as the majority of parliament seats in the 2000 and 2003 legislative elections.[9]

ARENA was founded in 1981, as the war was escalating, by military and elite sectors along with the support of some segments of poor, rural populations. A nationalist, anti-communist, and pro-capitalist party, in its origins ARENA represented the interests of a faction of the country's elite disgruntled over the reformist PDC-led junta erected after the 1979

---

[8] In their first few years of existence, the organizations that would later comprise the FMLN recruited large numbers among the PCS, Christian Democrat sectors, university organizations, and later unions (Martín Álvarez 2006, 2010; Sprenkels 2014: 83–84). Yet the success of these organizations was due to their ability to obtain the support of rural populations that, influenced by liberation theology, organized in peasant organizations and, as early as in the 1970s, joined or supported revolutionary struggle (Sprenkels 2014: 87–95).

[9] Despite being the party with most seats in the Legislative Assembly during those years, the rightwing ARENA, PCN, and PDC, despite their historical differences, together amassed a majority and therefore were able to control legislative reform and marginalize any FMLN initiative.

coup—particularly its nationalization of the banking and export sectors and its implementation of an agrarian reform program which, although limited in scope and technocratic in orientation, negatively affected elites' interests (Martín-Baró 1991: 297; Font Fàbregas 1998). Yet, although founded by members of the elite and the military, ARENA soon expanded its original constituency into rural areas. It did so by maintaining the ORDEN paramilitary structures that had been officially dismantled in 1979, which facilitated the party's successful development of patron–client relationships,[10] and by discursively emphasizing the problem of security and the need for a heavy-handed approach by which to crush the insurgency. The party's success in the 1989 election made ARENA leaders appreciate the advantages of democracy for their economic interests, at which point the party agreed to peace negotiations with the FMLN. In the postwar era, ARENA has represented itself as the party that brought peace to El Salvador and promoted democracy and economic development.

Both ARENA and the FMLN underwent important transformations throughout and after the war. The initial electoral failures of ARENA led to changes in the balance of power within the party, with new business sectors of the elite taking over the leadership from the agrarian, more authoritarian faction (Font Fàbregas 1998; Robinson 2003). In partnership with FUSADES, ARENA—as described earlier in the book—gradually developed a liberal market ideology and promoted neoliberal economic measures conducive to the consolidation of accumulation by the country's elite. This party managed to win four successive presidential elections by expanding its political base, which remained broad in rural areas due largely to clientelistic practices and among upper-class Salvadorans but also expanded to professionals and new urban middle-class sectors (Font Fàbregas 1998: 129–130). Despite its modernized face, ARENA has remained characterized by strong intra-party discipline. In addition, in 1997, when it started to lose votes and members to the PCN, ARENA shifted to more conservative rhetoric and proposals so as to cater to its traditional electoral basis (Robinson 2003: 97–98; Holland 2013).

By contrast, the FMLN, as stated in its charter, maintained after the war its aim to radically transform the status quo via the establishment of a socialist state (see FMLN 2006). In practice, however, the collapse of the Soviet Union, the electoral defeat of the FSLN in 1990, the geopolitical marginalization of Cuba, and, more generally, the erosion of their atten-

---

[10] For a discussion of ARENA's clientelistic practices, see Chap. 7.

dant ideologies and referents contributed to gradually dissipating the FMLN's socialist agenda and triggering increasing internecine divisions (Martín Álvarez 2010). In the aftermath of war and until 2003, the FMLN experienced internal struggles over the control of the party, split between advocates of maintaining a Marxist–Leninist ideology (*ortodoxos*) and those ascribing to Center-Left views (*renovadores*). The control of the party apparatus by the orthodox wing from the early 2000s may explain why the party has, to a certain degree, maintained a structure and political strategy inherited from the past and expelled members critical of the party's functioning. Yet it has also increasingly tempered its public discourse and sidelined the goal of socialism so as to attract a greater electorate. After taking office in 2009, as I will discuss in Chap. 7 and the Epilogue, the FMLN has improved or enacted a number of programs and policies to alleviate poverty without aiming for structural transformation. Meanwhile, it has struggled with the material limitations posed by El Salvador's exiguous public budget.

Given the war reenactments and attendant emotions that so pervaded the 2009 presidential elections, Salvadorans' party loyalties and electoral participation were largely motivated by their war positionalities and experiences. In this sense, electoral campaigns were one of the main public instances where what Sprenkels (2011) has called 'militant memories'—memories informed by the country's political divisions and aimed toward engendering party identity and discipline—were (re)produced and acted out. As I have already stressed, the rules governing the rituals of the elections allowed for a relatively controlled public forum in which to elicit and vent publicly wartime hostilities that had heretofore been left unaddressed. During the 2009 campaigns in Santiago, both parties enjoyed the participation of significant numbers of young people. In general, these young people had joined the parties to which their elder kin were loyal, and they readily embraced that party's symbols and outward signs—hence the relevance of 'militant memories'. Both parties cultivated such loyalty through meetings, popularly known as 'political schools', at which leaders from San Salvador or Zacatecoluca sought to indoctrinate constituents. Ideologies did remain relevant at these meetings. FMLN leaders continued to issue systemic and class-based explanations for Salvadorans' economic predicaments, albeit formulated in dogmatic and anachronistic forms. Yet, in their 2009 program, both local and national FMLN leadership conspicuously avoided addressing the establishment of a socialist regime, strategically distancing the party from its original guerrilla face. By contrast,

ARENA leaders continued to disseminate a fiercely anti-communist message, now predicated upon the alleged risk that the FMLN would establish a totalitarian regime mirroring those of Venezuela, Nicaragua, and Cuba.

THE POLITICS OF FEAR AND MEMORY: THE WARTIME DIVIDE UPDATED

Abstentionism in El Salvador has been consistently high since the late 1980s, with only the 1994 elections surpassing a 50 percent turnout (Artiga-González 2004: 38). After the 1994 elections, voter turnout decreased once again. This decreasing turnout has been interpreted as a symptom of ordinary Salvadorans' disillusionment with the postwar era and skepticism about the potential of elections to effect change (Cruz 1998, 2001), which does not seem surprising in the face of the persistent economic and public insecurity described in previous chapters. Yet turnout at both the 2004 and 2009 presidential elections was virtually twice that of previous years (IDHUCA 2004: 23; Artiga-González 2009: 13). The remainder of the chapter addresses this surge in electoral participation and explains why so many Salvadorans voted and participated in campaigns and other related events in 2009. I argue in this section that at least that year, the symbolic and affective components of the elections managed to mobilize many. It should not be discounted, however, that the 2003 introduction of the Unique Identity Document (DUI), a national identification card that facilitated registration in the electoral roll, preceded the rise of voter turnout in 2004 (Wade 2016: 76).

While flying to El Salvador in August 2008 to begin my fieldwork, I met a Salvadoran professor from a Honduran university. Our animated conversation somehow ended on the topic of the 2009 presidential election: 'I have not voted since I left the country in 1998', he declared. 'I only did so in the first democratic elections. I identify myself with the conservative Right, but one with a social component. None of the parties in El Salvador represent that political orientation. My mother, however, supports the FMLN and will vote for that party in the coming elections. She still lives in El Salvador. She repeatedly says that this time they are going to win, so she will surely leave the country'. At first I did not understand his mother's apparently contradictory attitude, but it made sense once I had arrived in El Salvador and immersed myself in the polarization, hostility, and fears that pervaded the electoral period. In addition to understanding elections as highly ritualized events, one needs to look at their affective component in order to explain the doubling of voter turn-out in 2004 and again in 2009 despite the country's widespread political disaffection and disillusionment.

A 'campaign of fear' orchestrated by ARENA and waged via mass media characterized El Salvador's 2004 presidential election (García Dueñas 2006; Wolf 2009: 447–454). In addition to making security vis-à-vis gang vio-lence, rather than economic policies, the core of its electoral program, ARENA's campaign was rooted in two threatening scenarios that the party claimed would materialize if the FMLN won: first, the consolidation of a communist regime similar to those of Cuba and Venezuela, and, second, the enactment by the United States government of a policy prohibiting Salvadorans in the United States from sending remittances to their relatives in El Salvador (García Dueñas 2006: 376; Wade 2016: 98–102).[11] The invoking of a communist threat was hardly new; this strategy had been widely deployed by the Salvadoran governments during the prewar and war years—when El Salvador became a Cold War battleground—to legitimize the counterinsurgency violence that often targeted civilians (see Binford 1996). Recourse to 'the communist threat' can, indeed, be traced all the way back to El Salvador's 1932 peasant rebellion, which the government blamed on the PCS, and the army's ensuing repression of 10,000 peasants (Anderson 1971; Alvarenga 1996; López Bernal 2007; Gould and Lauria-Santiago 2008). In the 2004 election, ARENA updated the communist threat to coincide with ordinary Salvadorans' present-day concerns, such as remittances, while invoking long-lived but still fearsome communist imag-eries. In this vein, the communist threat served ARENA's political interests by activating memories of war violence, which in turn triggered fears among ordinary Salvadorans. This conflation of calculative and affective elements in a politics of fear likewise characterized the 2009 presidential election.

As mentioned earlier, ARENA has fiercely and indeed proudly self-identified as an anti-communist party. Yet ARENA leaders' use of the term 'communism' has been vague enough to encompass anyone and anything that threatens the country's status quo and elite interests (Martín-Baró 1991: 296). During the 2004 and 2009 elections, ARENA's anti-communist rhetoric insinuated that the FMLN would seek to establish a totalitarian and military state if it won the presidential elections. The effec-

---

[11] The latter threat was indeed reinforced by the public declarations of several United States civil servants along those lines (Garibay 2005: 40).

tiveness of this rhetoric on El Salvador's rural population became evident when I accompanied FMLN constituents on their visits to the *cantones* of Santiago during the 2009 electoral campaign. Especially where residents had participated in paramilitary groups during the war, people were often quite hostile to visitors from the former guerrilla organization, now turned party. A barefoot woman in her 70s who received the FMLN leaders at the entrance of her adobe house in San Antonio Abajo did not want to hear their explanations of their party's electoral program. She declared emphatically that she knew what the FMLN would do in the event of an electoral victory:

> I have heard that we will be given a single dress and a single pair of shoes. And it doesn't matter if they are not our size because we won't be given any more of them. I am poor but I do have a few dresses. I also have my own house, and I know that I will have to share it with another family if they win. I also know what they intend to do with the old people, just because we are no longer able to work like the young people. And the coupons—we will be rationed and given weapons as during the war. What can you expect of the people who destroyed the country during the war?

This woman's statement exemplifies how the symbolic and discursive strategies of ARENA leaders, which did play on actual memories and experiences of the country's civil war as well as more propagandistic images of communist austerity, percolated through to ordinary Salvadorans and succeeded in alienating them from the FMLN.

The hostility against FMLN constituents and manifest fear of communism prevalent in areas of northern Santiago stemmed partly from ARENA's deployment of Cold War rhetoric at public meetings during the campaign. ARENA's public meetings, held every Sunday at the party's headquarters in central Santiago, were attended mainly by men and a few women in their 50s and 60s, most of them peasants. Men donning peasant hats and women in aprons predominated, their garb indicative of their humble origins. Every meeting began with ARENA's anthem, which everyone had to sing with his or her right fist raised so as to avoid public accusations by ARENA leadership of being an FMLN spy or showing insufficient enthusiasm. The anthem expresses overt hostility toward FMLN members: '*El Salvador será la tumba donde los rojos terminarán ...*' [El Salvador will be the grave where the reds—meaning FMLN members—will end]. Speeches by ARENA leaders followed, repeatedly describing how FMLN guerrillas had destroyed the country through their attacks on pylons, bridges, and other infrastructure during the war. These speeches also portrayed the FMLN as a present-day and future threat given the party's alleged alignment with Hugo Chávez and Fidel Castro. The utterances of a local ARENA leader at a weekly meeting encapsulated this updated version of the communist threat:

> Why is communism so interested in El Salvador? Because this is a country of development. ARENA supports agriculture, the church, sports ... ARENA is the party of peace, freedom and progress. We live in a democracy but let's make good use of this democracy. Let's give our children a free country like the one we have enjoyed. If we do not defend ourselves, we might be in great *danger*. The FMLN will hand the country over to Chávez. We should not make the same mistake as the Nicaraguans, who are now *slaves* of Venezuela and Cuba. These elections have to make history. We need to fight for a fifth ARENA government that allows for a perpetuation of freedom and democracy. You are the soldiers who must defend the peace against the *threat* of international communism, which is the origin of the current economic crisis. ARENA promotes freedom, economic development, and foreign investment. The FMLN only wants *war*. The change proclaimed by the FMLN is one of *war* and communism. [emphasis added]

ARENA's electoral strategy hinged upon a Manichaean representation of postwar political life in which the FMLN epitomized threat, destruction, totalitarianism, economic collapse, and violence. By contrast, ARENA was depicted as righteous, involved in the reconstruction of postwar El Salvador, and a guarantor of freedom and democracy. Democracy, in the rhetoric of ARENA leaders, is the antithesis of communism; it allows the individual freedom to hold private property and undertake profit-driven economic activity. In these meetings, ARENA leaders aggressively emphasized the FMLN threat in hopes of maintaining a fear-based loyalty.

According to ARENA's rhetoric, political change effectively threatened all postwar achievements: democracy, freedom, and private property. For instance, in February 2009, following the closure of several *maquilas* in El Pedregal, in the La Paz Department, as a byproduct of the financial crisis in the United States, and the consequent loss of thousands of jobs that severely impacted residents of Santiago and the neighboring municipalities, rumors spread that these changes had occurred in response to the prospect of an FMLN victory in the upcoming presidential election. Indeed, during the electoral campaign, ARENA leaders continually invoked the threat of disinvestment in the event of an FMLN victory. Whatever possessions citizens had, ARENA leadership warned, a communist FMLN government might seize them. Violence was thus legitimized and encouraged, or declared ineluctable, in the event of an FMLN victory. This rhetoric cannot be considered a mere strategic ploy on the part of ARENA leaders. On 26 October 2008, when I met with the 15 men and 1 woman who composed the local ARENA leadership in Santiago to explain my interest in attending their meetings, I noted that some seemed genuinely concerned about the prospect of an FMLN victory. After I had described the details of my research and addressed their concerns, a man in his late 30s told me: 'Everything you have explained to us seems reasonable to me, but you have to understand that our worries are not unfounded. Our country is under the threat of communism, so we cannot trust anyone right now'.

The mass media, being largely pro-ARENA, played a key role in drawing attention to the threat that the FMLN allegedly posed to the Salvadoran nation, and hence in sparking widespread fear. During the 2009 campaign, daily advertisements on El Salvador's television channels 2, 4, and 6 (all owned by the same ARENA-linked media mogul, Boris Esersky) asserted both the violent nature of the FMLN and the presumed alliance between FMLN presidential candidate Mauricio Funes and the Venezuelan government—an alliance so strong that the country would be handed over to Hugo Chávez in the event of an FMLN victory. One of these television ads suggested the following:

> Mauricio Funes is a presidential candidate backed by the FMLN, a communist party and an ally of Hugo Chávez. Chávez is the number one *enemy* of the United States. The United States is an ally of El Salvador. Millions of Salvadorans live there, send their remittances and thousands have benefited from the TPS.[12] Therefore, if Funes and the FMLN take office we will be subjected to Chávez. Your remittances and the TPS are in *danger*. In *danger* are your freedom, your job, and prices will truly rise sky high. Risky? It is more than that. Funes and the FMLN are a *danger* for your pocketbook and a *real danger* for El Salvador. [emphasis added]

---

[12] The Temporary Protected Status (TPS) is a program that grants legal residency in the United States to victims of natural disasters or civil wars. In March 2001, after the two earthquakes that devastated El Salvador, the United States granted the TPS status to 260,000 Salvadorans, and has since successively extended it (PNUD 2005b: 432–433). Yet the TPS has amounted to a sort of 'legal limbo' given that those benefiting from it could not leave the United States or reunite with their kin and have lived with the uncertainty that stems from an unresolved status (PNUD 2005b: 432–433). The temporary nature and economic ponderance of the TPS explain why ARENA has been able to deploy it as a threat during presidential elections.

These advertisements were either anonymous or signed by the organization Fuerza Solidaria, heretofore unknown in El Salvador, which had originated in Venezuela to delegitimize Chávez's government. Associations were made in these ads between the FMLN and the Venezuelan, Cuban, and Nicaraguan governments, and even Islamist terrorism.[13]

On 13 December 2008, the newspaper *La Prensa Gráfica* reported that the Salvadoran Ministry of Defense was investigating the existence of armed groups in different parts of the country, most of them FMLN strongholds during the war.[14] Concrete details were offered to lend credibility to the charges:

> At the coordinates 13°59'07.7" North and 89°13'34.76" West is an area of military training, northeast of the Cinotepeque mountain, in the jurisdiction of El Paisnal, a zone that was under the territorial and military control of the Popular Liberation Forces (FPL) during the war.

This news precipitated a widespread discussion in the country's mass media about the ties between these alleged armed groups and the FMLN. Photos of a commemoration held annually on 12 and 13 December in the municipality of El Paisnal, in the San Salvador Department, to pay homage to the deceased guerrilla commander Dimas Rodríguez were published by the media. In this commemoration, ex-guerrillas simulated a military march dressed in uniform and carrying plastic or defunct rifles. The presence of FMLN members in the photos of this simulacrum of a military march was used by the rightwing media and ARENA government as evidence that the FMLN was arming and training new guerrilla groups.

'The FBI and Interpol could help us with the technical and scientific investigation'—these were the words of the country's attorney general regarding the issue of armed groups. 'We need to have scientific verification that the photographs are authentic in order to sustain a potential accusation'.[15] This insistence on the scientific nature of the investigation seemed to aim at depoliticizing the issue in the eyes of the Salvadoran public. According to this rightwing newspaper, the investigation simply sought to verify the existence of organizations receiving paramilitary training with

---

[13] See, for instance, the documentaries 'Hugo Chávez: Una amenaza real' and 'No entreguemos El Salvador', which are available at: http://fuerzasolidaria.org/?p=583 and http://fuerzasolidaria.org/?p=723. These documentaries were shown on Salvadoran television and at ARENA's political rallies.

[14] 'Defensa indaga existencia de grupos armados', *La Prensa Gráfica*, 13 December 2008.

[15] 'Fiscalía pide ayuda al FBI y a Interpol', *El Diario de Hoy*, 16 December 2008.

the goal of destabilizing the state. Although the ARENA government suggested that the gravity of the issue was such that it had to be reported to international organizations,[16] after a few days of front-page coverage by rightwing newspapers, the issue was dropped. In Santiago, however, incidents in the municipality were interpreted in light of the news about the rearming of the FMLN. A relative of my host family recounted to me a rumor that had spread throughout the Cantón San Sebastián Abajo, where she lived. According to the rumor, guerrillas might well have been training in Santiago's mountainous *cantones* given that residents had sighted armed men who were not from the area. As this rumor indicates, the inimical mass media's coverage of the FMLN had managed to sow seeds of doubt about the nature of this party's political project.

Similar symbolic and discursive strategies were deployed in Mexican electoral politics during the 1990s by the Institutional Revolutionary Party (PRI) to preserve its hegemony and delegitimize the opposition (McDonald 1997; García Dueñas 2006). McDonald (1997) has described how, during Mexico's 1994 presidential election, the PRI implemented a 'campaign of everyday fear' that discredited the Democratic Revolutionary Party (PRD). This campaign elicited feelings of fear and danger by alleging the PRD's violent nature and suggesting that—given the party's lack of experience and acknowledgment of the new conditions provided by the global economy—economic and political instability could result from the PRD's outdated social welfare program, which included measures previously promised by the PRI and proven inefficient (McDonald 1997: 271–273). In 2004 and 2009, ARENA, like the PRI, resorted to a politics of fear and memory in an effort to forestall the erosion of its dominance—an erosion rooted in the unfulfilled promises of the Peace Accords and aggravated by the corrosive impact of neoliberal economic policy on ordinary people's livelihoods. This type of campaign also allowed ARENA to capitalize on existing fears while showcasing the quality of the Salvadoran democracy to an international community less supportive of overtly repressive tactics than it had been during the 1980s, when the United States provided the Salvadoran government with financial, military, and moral support. What is distinctive about the Salvadoran case is the prominence of Cold War rhetoric during an era in which such rhetoric had practically disappeared from both international and Latin American politics. Although the Left/Right divide is still widely invoked in Latin America, it has, over

---

[16] 'Saca llevará a ONU pruebas sobre armas', *La Prensa Gráfica*, 17 December 2008.

time, become associated with new ideologies, such as Chávez's 'twenty-first century socialism' in the 2000s.[17]

Aside from the performative aspects described in the previous section, which were largely reflective of war experiences and the emotions thereof, ARENA's politics of fear also put emotions to work in specific ways. Ahmed's (2004) notion of 'affective economies', I surmise, is useful in understanding the affective component of the electoral processes and practices that were activated by ARENA's politics of fear. Ahmed's economic analogy suggests that 'emotions work as a form of capital' (Ahmed 2004: 120). 'Some signs … increase in affective value as an effect of the movement between signs: the more they circulate, the more affective they become, and the more they appear to "contain" affect' (Ahmed 2004: 120). The power of the communist threat thus rested on the ability of fear to circulate and adhere to signs as well as to slide from one sign to another. According to Ahmed (2004: 127), fears do not reside in specific bodies and signs but circulate among them, and in their circulation produce the very bodies and signs that are feared.

It was through the circulation of signs of fear that the FMLN and any signs thereof became fearsome. ARENA's free-floating signifier of 'the communist' slid sideways among FMLN guerrillas, the Cuban, Venezuelan, and Nicaraguan regimes, and Islamist terrorists. The country's rightwing media and ARENA leadership also deployed historical and contemporary associations of 'threat', 'danger', 'war', and 'terrorism' that increased the affective value of the communist threat. An economic analogy helps explain how the signs in circulation during the 2009 elections became commonplace currency for Salvadorans across the political spectrum. In this sense, it no longer seems contradictory that an FMLN loyalist such as the mother of the university professor whom I met on my flight to El Salvador would want to leave the country in the event of an FMLN victory. Her determination to do so was consistent with the milieu of fear in which Salvadorans, regardless of their political allegiance, partook during the 2004 and 2009 elections. Indeed, during the 2009 presidential election, numerous FMLN loyalists expressed their fear that ARENA would react violently to an FMLN victory.

[17] For instance, the 2009 coup in Honduras against the government of President Manuel Zelaya is illustrative of how the Left/Right divide was at the time expressed on the basis of an alignment with or against Venezuela's regime.

WHAT CHANGE?

During my research, the country's 2009 electoral season constituted one of the few occasions on which Salvadorans publicly aired wartime frictions; yet discussion was hindered by campaign rhetoric and political ideologies. Wartime memories were elicited not to promote dialogue, but rather to evoke fear, exacerbate hostilities, and gain electoral advantage. As described in the previous section, ARENA disseminated propaganda serving a particular politics of memory that conflated the country's wartime violence with the Venezuelan government's political project and the countries aligned with it. Yet, when faced with accusations like the one against the FMLN's vice-presidential candidate and former guerrilla commander Salvador Sánchez Cerén—widely considered responsible for the FPL guerrillas' internal purge during the war via the torturing and assassination of hundreds of alleged army collaborators by FPL commander Mayo Sibrián—the FMLN's response on wartime crimes was largely silence.[18] When articulated, FMLN leaders' perspectives on the war simply reproduced the moral hierarchies of wartime, which rest on a clear-cut divide between 'good' and 'bad' violence. FMLN's moral hierarchies echoed, albeit inversely, ARENA's discursive representations. In this sense, neither the FMLN nor ARENA satisfied Salvadorans' need to explain how the war managed to divide the entire population of ordinary Salvadorans, rather than merely the rich few and the poor majority. Indeed, the FMLN's ideological dogmatism and personal as well as internecine disputes only magnified the effects of the politics of fear that ARENA leveled against it.

Within this divisive and confrontational electoral politics, Salvadorans' views on the appeal of the elections were also highly polarized. Many ordinary people did not seem to conceive of elections as a plausible means of substantial change, other than the political change that replaces one party with another in the administration of the country. Even though the majority of Salvadorans stated in polls that they believed the country would improve with an FMLN victory and deteriorate with an ARENA victory in the 2009 presidential elections (see IUDOP 2009a: 70–72), in Santiago

---

[18] FPL commander Mayo Sibrián's execution of hundreds of guerrillas suspected of treason and infiltration until the organization's leadership ordered his execution in 1991 is one of the most renowned episodes of FMLN's human rights violations (Sprenkels 2005: 71). FPL excombatants who witnessed the purge have suggested that Sánchez Cerén as then-head of the FPL political commission was aware of it and even authorized it (see Galeas and Ayala 2008).

and neighboring municipalities, views predominated even among the left-leaning population that any improvement would be minimal, especially in the short term. This is similar to what Banerjee (2007: 1558–1559, 1561) found to be the case in elections in contemporary rural India. Poor people's enthusiasm and respect for elections, along with their high voter turnout, reflect their understanding of elections as an opportunity to remind governments that they count, rather than a means of effecting any substantial improvement in their lives. In postwar El Salvador, I suggest, core constituencies voted according to their ideologies, which in turn had been largely shaped by their families' wartime experiences. The heightened animosities stemming largely from ARENA's politics of fear stimulated voting by disaffected Salvadorans in the 2004 and 2009 elections. It was thus wartime political cleavages and experiences that motivated many people to vote. However, as we will see, Funes's candidacy in 2009 created the possibility of associating the FMLN with new agendas.

While Santiagueñas on both the Left and Right had difficulty envisioning substantial long-term change occurring during their lifetimes, they harbored different attitudes about the nature of the political change that elections were likely to effect. Two polarized views of change could thus be observed in Santiago. Those who appropriated and reproduced ARENA's anti-communist discourse considered political change a potential threat that could substantially affect their lives. Rather than being motivated to vote by the prospect that the ARENA governments would alleviate their economic insecurity, they were instead motivated by the perceived need to preserve what they owned—no matter how minimal—and prevent it from being seized by a communist regime. Those who endorsed the FMLN, by contrast, embraced political change as an urgent necessity. Whether or not an FMLN government might substantially improve their lives in the short term, FMLN loyalists feared that the continuation of an ARENA government after 2009 would only exacerbate their state of economic insecurity and lead to political repression. The adoption of the dollar back in 2001 and its gradual replacement of the *colón* (the previous national currency), part of the ARENA government's unpopular neoliberal agenda intended to facilitate trade liberalization and foreign investment, had exemplified the economic insecurity resulting from ARENA policies. In converting prices to dollars and cents, many business owners had 'rounded up', which in turn had a strong inflationary effect that disproportionately impacted the poorest Salvadorans (see Towers and Borzutzky 2004: 47–49). Indeed, Santiagueños from urban and rural areas alike, both during and outside electoral periods, repeatedly voiced how sharply they felt the impact of dollarization on the family pocketbook. Yet, during the 2004 and 2009 elections, discussions about the parties' economic agendas among core constituencies were largely sidelined by the 'affective economies' at work.

These polarized views of change were not merely expressed rhetorically; they manifested in several instances, both during and after the elections. During the 2009 electoral campaign, I was consistently urged by friends to leave the country if ARENA won the elections, because 'even foreigners were assassinated during the war'. The head of the family I lived with would remind her sons and daughters, all of them openly supportive of the FMLN, that they should all obtain their passports so that, in the event of a victory by former police chief and ARENA presidential candidate Rodrigo Ávila, they could leave the country before the violence began. By contrast, after the FMLN victory, stories circulated about old women who were terribly frightened of 'the communists' victory'. A relative of the family I lived with mentioned an 80-year-old neighbor in the Cantón Santa Cruz Loma who had become physically ill in response to the election results. Another neighbor had told her that the daughter of this old woman had asked for help with her mother. The frightened woman had been crying ceaselessly and did not want to leave her bed. When asked why she would not get up, she explained tearfully that the new communist government was going to turn her into liquid soap because of her age, just one of the many threats that had circulated during Santiago's 2009 presidential campaign.

Another instance of how this fear manifested was my conversation with a police officer on election day. As I was leaving the polling station on 15 March, after the FMLN victory had been publicly announced, I ran into Laura, the only female police officer working at the Santiago police subdelegation, with whom I had chatted on several occasions. I stopped to greet her and ask when she would finish her shift. She explained that given the FMLN victory, she would probably be able to leave early. Police officers had been cautioned by their superiors that they might have to confront a troublesome situation, such as an upheaval at the national level, if ARENA were to win the elections once again: 'We were told there was a possibility of an uprising because the FMLN would not have accepted a defeat this time and had been rearming men up in the mountains.' This was the same alert that ARENA had been disseminating through its rallies and the rightwing media during the electoral campaign. The conversation underlined that fear was not just an electoral strategy but genuinely felt, to the degree that it had come to suffuse state institutions.

Although there was much talk during the 2009 presidential election that 'change defeated fear'—'change' being a key term in the FMLN's campaign rhetoric—ARENA's campaign of fear was highly persuasive in rural areas. While it is clear that the FMLN managed to instill hope in many segments of the Salvadoran population, how these segments came to vote for the FMLN cannot be explained simply by the FMLN's rhetoric of change. The intertwining of ideologies with affective economies played a major role in people's motivation to vote and participate in the electoral campaign. Their central role during the elections allowed politicians to skirt a public discussion of El Salvador's pressing economic and social problems and their respective parties' programs for dealing with them. Against this background, depending on their party allegiance, Santiagueños voted either to avoid or to facilitate political change. Even when political change was a motivation, the ultimate reason for voting for a particular party was to avoid the threat posed by the opposition party. In this sense, not only were recollections of the violent past more palpable than ever during the elections, but so was the prospect of a violent future. At the same time, FMLN constituents shared a feeling of being closer to a political shift than they had ever been, such that Santiagueñas who endorsed the FMLN remarked apocalyptically: 'If the change does not occur now, it will never occur'.

BUILDING A MIDDLE

If the reenactment of war and the 'affective economies' thereof explain the doubling of voter turnout in 2004 and again in 2009, what was different about the 2009 presidential elections that allowed for the FMLN victory? The 2009 results cannot be fully understood from within the paradigm of a rigid national political divide. During the 2009 campaign, Mauricio Funes, the FMLN presidential candidate, spoke to the economic and social concerns of ordinary Salvadorans, minimizing wartime political cleavages and appealing to Salvadorans across the political spectrum. Indeed, Funes had not participated in the FMLN until his candidacy. A charismatic leftwing journalist and human rights advocate, Funes was well known for having hosted several Salvadoran TV news and radio programs for more than 20 years. From the moment his candidacy was announced in 2007, he stressed both symbolically and literally the distinction between him and the party. Although he was representing the FMLN, he tried to maintain a certain degree of autonomy vis-à-vis the party. Funes never appeared in public dressed in FMLN red, nor did he raise his left fist or sing the party anthem at political rallies.

In contrast to the FMLN's ubiquitous identification with the Venezuelan and Cuban governments, Funes repeatedly declared his predilection for Brazilian President Luiz Inácio Lula da Silva's more moderate governance style and for Brazilian-style participatory democracy, a link reinforced by the fact that Funes's Brazilian wife had been an activist in Lula's Workers' Party (PT). Like Lula, Funes expressed a will to continue neoliberal policies while developing a social agenda to mitigate the impact of these policies on the poor. Social programs introduced by Lula in Brazil had produced substantial reductions in poverty plus a diminution of economic inequalities. In a speech delivered during a visit to Santiago on 10 March 2009, Funes stressed his commitment to stabilizing the prices of basic goods, generating jobs, facilitating access to and improvement of basic utilities such as running water, expanding the pension and healthcare systems, and providing credit and assistance to those working the land as well as social housing and other subsidies for poor families. All of these were concerns for largely rural municipalities like Santiago.

In a further attempt to distance Funes from the FMLN, the Asociación Amigos de Mauricio (Friends of Mauricio Association) was founded. This association, which included businessmen who were former rightwing advocates and high-ranking ex-military officials, attempted to build up the virtually non-existent middle in the Salvadoran political spectrum. In Santiago, a former military official belonging to this association accompanied FMLN departmental deputy Gerson Martínez on his tour of the La Paz Department municipalities. At every stop, the former military official explained to audiences that he had fought with the army during the war but that he was supporting the FMLN in 2009 because ARENA had failed to generate economic prosperity. He denied that the military was unanimously supporting ARENA, even though that party's leaders had tried to imply as much by marching with former military personnel—members of El Salvadors Veteran's Association 'General Manuel José Arce' (ASVEM)—on San Salvador streets on 7 September 2008, the day of ASVEM's fifth anniversary. This occurred after reports—part of ARENA's politics of fear—had circulated in the mass media that the FMLN would dissolve the military if it were victorious in the presidential elections.[19]

[19] 'Ávila firma convenio con veteranos militares', *Diario Colatino*, 8 September 2008.

Funes's middle position was alternatively denied by ARENA and co-opted by the FMLN. ARENA maintained that Funes's distancing of himself from the FMLN was a rhetorical ploy to trick Salvadorans into believing that it was possible to ally with that party while representing a more centralist position. Ultimately, ARENA claimed, Funes remained firmly allied with the FMLN and Hugo Chávez. While ARENA simply denied the possibility of a middle position, the FMLN asserted its embrace of this position in a rather contradictory manner. The public endorsement of Funes's candidacy by former military officials during the campaign was highly beneficial to the FMLN insofar as it demonstrated that sectors traditionally opposed to the party now supported it. On the other hand, the FMLN leadership, dominated by the orthodox wing of the party, consistently sought to minimize the distance that Funes had established between himself and the party. In this sense, both ARENA and the FMLN contributed to the increasingly polarized physiognomy of the Salvadoran political spectrum.

The immutability of the political divide that characterized the 2009 elections was thus more an *effect* of ARENA's and FMLN's mimicked reproduction of the divide than an *actual feature* of it. The relative blurriness of the divide was evidenced by the FMLN victory, which many observers believe reflected, among other things, Funes's successful building of a middle position, notwithstanding both parties' efforts to deny or co-opt this possibility. Indeed, on my visits with FMLN members to the rural northern areas of Santiago, where the population is predominantly rightwing, I encountered middle-aged men and women who declared, 'I am giving my vote to Funes but not to the FMLN.' Some went on to explain that while they did not trust the FMLN, they would vote for Funes—who seemed to them to be a decent man—owing to the country's dire economic situation. I would thus argue that Funes received massive support from the electorate by transcending the Cold War divide reenacted by ARENA and FMLN. He instead proposed concrete programs to address the pressing social and economic problems that had been sidestepped by the Peace Accords and eclipsed by ARENA's politics of fear. In so doing, he promised to satisfy ordinary Salvadorans' aspirations to an expanded vision of democracy. Indeed, his distancing himself from the FMLN attracted leftwing voters who found themselves increasingly disappointed with the party's postwar behavior.

The complexity of relationships that I have portrayed thus far reveals, as Banerjee (2007: 1561) has posited, that elections cannot be regarded as a single coherently orchestrated ritual. Indeed, elections have allowed the complexity of Salvadoran political life to surface; they have revealed the convoluted nature of the country's political divide, which contrasts sharply with the fixed and orderly depiction inherent in ARENA's politics of fear and memory. Banerjee suggests that 'we should see the ceremony of an election as a congeries of socio-cultural 'dances' emerging out of the habits, circumstances and motivations of everyday life' (2007: 1561). As demonstrated in this chapter, elections in El Salvador are events deeply imbued with the legacies of war. These war legacies have been mobilized by political elites anxious to maintain their privilege through the promotion of neoliberal policies. Yet these legacies are also persistent in Salvadorans' everyday relationships and lives partly because there has been no public discussion about the past, independent of political strategizing, in which to address the ambiguities of the wartime divide and its attached moralities.

Patronage Democracy and Internecine Factional Conflict

There is yet another layer to the complexity of El Salvador's electoral politics, as exemplified by the PCN victory in Santiago's 2009 municipal elections. In Santiago, where ARENA was victorious in the presidential elections until 2004 and the FMLN prevailed in 2009, the PCN won four consecutive municipal elections since 2000. The sharp distinction between the electoral results of the municipal and presidential elections invites one to think that there are motives beyond the ideological or war-related that influence how people position themselves and move across the FMLN/ARENA divide. The PCN was the military's official party since its founding in 1961 (Stanley 1996: 78). Elections were observed by El Salvador's military governments during the 1960s as a means to gain legitimacy but were also manipulated when necessary, as in the 1972 and 1977 elections (Stanley 1996: 78–91; Williams and Walter 1997: 63–84). After the 1979 coup d'état, the PCN increasingly became a minority party, initially displaced by reformist sectors among the military and the PDC. The latter likewise became a minority party after it lost the presidential elections to ARENA in 1989. Yet PCN and PDC support for ARENA in the Legislative Assembly has been fundamental in countervailing the increasing influence of the FMLN, as well as in passing or blocking legislation in consonance with the country's elite economic interests.

The incumbent Santiago mayor, originally an ARENA loyalist and a secretary in the municipality council during the period of ARENA rule, saw an opportunity to run for office as a member of the PCN and hence changed party loyalties in 2000. The foreign development agency present in the region, which worked hand-in-hand with the municipality council, attributed the PCN's consecutive victories to 'good governance'. Notwithstanding the public face of correctness acquired by Santiago's local government through its work with a foreign development agency, rumors suggested that PCN victories were the result of fraud. Many Santiagueños explained that in every municipal election the mayor has brought residents of Jiquilisco (in the Usulután Department), her home-town, into Santiago to vote with fake identity cards. Whether or not every detail of these rumors can be substantiated, the local FMLN leadership did realize that the 2009 electoral map of Santiago, which they had received from the country's Supreme Electoral Tribunal (TSE), included 1300 residents of four non-existent *barrios*. Indeed, as an electoral observer myself, I noted that on both 2009 election days, several citizens had tried to vote with a DUI, indicating their residence in one of those non-existent *barrios*. These citizens fled with their DUIs after FMLN members acting as polling station officials had recognized their fake identification cards but before police officers could intervene.[20]

Interestingly, some of Santiago's FMLN loyalists, who have been deeply committed to the party on ideological grounds, have voted for the PCN in postwar municipal elections. When I asked why they had cast their votes differently in municipal, legislative, and presidential elections, they explained that the mayor had invested in a number of projects in their *barrio* or *cantón* and that they would acknowledge their gratitude with a vote as long as she continued to do so. Rumors also suggested that the PCN had poured vast resources into municipal elections, hiring large numbers of people to work in party campaigns and distributing material benefits to gain loyalties. Indeed, Santiago's PCN-led government fostered the development of a network of local associations, ADESCOs,[21] in the municipality that has proved a fruitful means of fostering a political clientele. During

---

[20] The 2007 census revealed that the country's overall population, and specifically its voting age population, was substantially smaller than had been reflected in the 1992 census (Wade 2016: 77), potentially presenting a large margin of opportunity for electoral fraud.

[21] Communal Development Associations (ADESCOs) are formal organizations based in both rural and urban sectors of Salvadoran municipalities that facilitate citizens' participation in the discussion of local development needs with the municipality council.

the 2009 municipal elections, as I witnessed myself, it was in conjunction with ADESCO leaders from each sector of Santiago that the PCN organized visits to communities and the distribution of Christmas presents among them. These clientelistic practices resemble those of patronage democracies like Mexico, where the PRI has either bestowed benefits on its political clients or invested in areas where it sought to regain legitimacy (McDonald 1997: 279). Yet clientelism is neither a wholly calculative practice nor one where citizens are simply at the mercy of political leaders (Auyero 2000: 23). Calculative and affective elements merge in the formation and maintenance of political clienteles (see Chap. 7). Many Santiagueños approved of the delivery of benefits and concessions by the PCN mayor and concurred with the mayor's self-representation as 'the mom of the communities'.

Internecine disputes among FMLN's factions have also generated support, albeit subdued, for the PCN and impeded the FMLN from producing a candidate able to compete with the PCN mayor. While public discussion nationwide has focused on the FMLN national leadership division between the *ortodoxos* and *renovadores*, it is personal disputes that have led the party's departmental leadership to remove certain leaders from Santiago's FMLN, as has been the case in other La Paz municipalities. This in turn has led to major factional divisions and conflicts within the municipalities themselves and turned core constituencies against the party in municipal elections. Numerous lifelong FMLN members in Santiago acknowledged casting their votes differently in the municipal and legislative elections, both held on 18 January 2009. Meanwhile, rumors spread among the FMLN constituency about the existence of an underground alliance between the FMLN departmental leadership and Santiago's PCN mayor, which led FMLN constituents to suggest that they would perhaps abstain from voting in the 2009 municipal elections. These rumors gained credence because FMLN leaders had themselves admitted to having negotiated with the PCN mayor in previous campaigns, in which the FMLN had asked its constituents to vote for the PCN in the municipal elections in exchange for PCN's votes in the legislative elections, both these elections being held simultaneously.

Although territorial disputes and attacks on opponents' headquarters and constituencies have been especially intense between the FMLN and ARENA, the PCN has also partaken in such conflicts during municipal elections. As mentioned earlier, rumors have suggested that during electoral campaigns, the incumbent PCN municipality mayor hired her own contingent—a group of local gang members—which at times engaged in violent confrontations with members of other parties while plastering propaganda in Santiago's central streets at night. The PCN contingent most often entered into conflict with ARENA members,[22] since until 2009, the FMLN was not a significant electoral opponent in the municipality and indeed FMLN leaders admitted that subdued alliances existed between the PCN and the FMLN in municipal and legislative elections. Even though ARENA and the PCN were allied during the 2009 presidential elections, at least to the extent that the PCN withdrew its presidential candidacy two months before the elections, violence between these two parties' basic constituencies was not absent from that year's municipal elections. Given that the FMLN demonstrably increased its constituency during the campaign preceding the 2009 municipal elections, the local gang supporting the PCN also directed its aggression against FMLN constituents and loyalists, as demonstrated by the incident in Santiago's central plaza described in Chap. 3.

The persistent dominance of the PCN in Santiago shows that while the country's political divide endures, transgressions of this divide are significant enough to influence the outcome of a municipal election. The movement of people among ARENA, the PCN, and the PDC—a mobility that occurs more frequently than it does with the FMLN—along with similarities in their ideology and electoral strategizing, has favored the identification of these three parties as the Salvadoran Right. Yet patron–client relationships and the FMLN's internecine divisions have resulted in a shifting of party allegiances during municipal elections. In Santiago, people did not vote for the PCN per se, but rather for the mayor, who performed a cacique-like role. While an analysis of ritualized electoral action and the passions involved allows us to understand the motivations of basic constituencies in maintaining the country's seemingly impermeable political divide, it ignores the role of third parties as well as the movements from one party to another that are often motivated by material benefits or factional disputes, as would be the emergence of GANA out of a split of ARENA after the 2009 presidential election. Although all parties engaged in patron–client relationships, this was less so in the case of the FMLN, most likely due to a shortage of resources. Ultimately, the differences in how people cast their votes in municipal and presidential elections are symptomatic of a

[22] See, for instance, 'ARENA y PCN se enfrentan en Santiago Nonualco', *La Prensa Gráfica*, 13 December 2005.

certain degree of disjuncture between the citizenship practices that concern the polity of the municipality and those that concern the polity of the nation (cf. Stack 2003). While I observed this phenomenon first-hand in Santiago, the divergent results between municipal and presidential elections in other municipalities throughout the country indicated that the same occurs beyond Santiago. In other words, while haunting Cold War imageries and memories may patently impact national citizenship, their influence is more limited with regard to municipality-related citizenship practices, particularly in Santiago, where a third party governs and where personal and political relationships are deeply enmeshed.

THE FMLN TAKEOVER NONETHELESS

This chapter has explored the intersections between electoral politics and the politics of memory in postwar El Salvador. The 2004 and 2009 presidential elections foregrounded the persistence of war legacies and conflicts, which were expressed in anachronistic Cold War imageries and rhetoric. The resuscitation of wartime confrontations during the 2009 campaign allowed ARENA to avoid a public discussion of pressing economic issues and to counter the increasing erosion of the party's dominance—an erosion rooted in the persistence of socio-economic problems inherited from the war and perpetuated by ARENA's unpopular neoliberal agenda. Consequently, in the 2009 presidential election, both parties' core constituencies voted more out of fear than out of any real hope for substantially improving their lives. Their votes represented either a rejection of FMLN's alleged communism and abolition of private property or a rejection of ARENA's authoritarianism, corruption, and possible repression as well as this party's socio-economic policies.

This is not in contradiction with the passion and hope that core constituencies harbored. The middle position built by Funes in appealing to the disaffected portion of the electorate that did not belong to any core constituency was crucial to the FMLN's 2009 victory. Funes's charisma, along with his non-participation in the country's civil war and the massively funded FMLN campaign, allowed for a revaluation, even by Salvadorans on the Right, of the belligerent image of the FMLN generated by ARENA's politics of fear and memory and reinforced by the FMLN's own dogmatism and internecine conflicts. Yet this revaluation was also made possible by Funes's speaking directly of the social and economic problems that concerned ordinary Salvadorans and that had been consistently overlooked after the signing of the Peace Accords and through the consolidation of a liberal market democracy. In answering the broader question of why Salvadorans care to vote in postwar elections, it should also be acknowledged that patron–client relationships and internecine conflicts between party factions can at times override historical divisions, especially in municipal elections.

This chapter, like previous ones, has highlighted the relevance of wartime political cleavages in the postwar era as well as the association still made by ordinary people between ARENA and the state, which ARENA embodied for two decades. In particular, I have illustrated how the archetypal citizenship practice of voting and participating in electoral campaigns is pervaded by hostility, physical aggression, and fear. The violence that has become integral to El Salvador's electoral politics, as I have shown, is a matter of unresolved wartime conflicts as well as a political culture pervaded by violent practices. It is not just long-standing members of the FMLN and ARENA who engaged in inter-party confrontations; a large number of Salvadoran youth likewise became involved in such conflicts, even though they did not live through the war. Nevertheless, I suggest that the continuing relevance of wartime political cleavages can be attributed to the lack of any public discussion of what the war was actually about as well as to a lack of accountability with regard to wartime human rights violations. Elections, being one of the few instances in which the wartime past has been brought to the fore, have not allowed for a public discussion independent of the parties' own electoral agendas. In this sense, electoral representations of the war have only contributed to reproducing the political cleavages and moral hierarchies of wartime.

At the time I completed this book, the FMLN had already revalidated its victory in one more presidential election. In 2014, former vice-president Salvador Sánchez Cerén was elected as El Salvador's president. Not only did he represent the orthodox wing of the FMLN but he also epitomized the wartime past that has haunted the party. As mentioned earlier, as an FPL commander during the war he has been publicly suspected of being responsible for flagrant FMLN war crimes. His victory therefore carried significant symbolic weight and raised the question of whether inter-party politics might have changed with the 2009 party shift. As I traveled to El Salvador in 2014 to conduct research on the presidential election, I noted that the FMLN evoked neither the promise nor the threat it represented in 2009. Not having held executive power before, in 2009, the FMLN conjured a great sense of hope for many Salvadorans disaffected with politics after four successive periods of ARENA rule. More relevant to the discussion here, in 2014, after five years in which FMLN rule had not substantially transformed the status quo, the communist imagery so often employed by ARENA was no longer credible. Even though it was deployed during the second round of that year's elections, the focus of ARENA's discursive and symbolic construction of the FMLN as a threat focused instead on the FMLN's links with gangs as well as this party's inability to address the country's problems of economic and public insecurity (Montoya 2018). Although the FMLN won, it did so with a minimal margin, evidencing the endurance of the deep-seated and polarized FMLN/ARENA divide.[23]

In contrast to Chaps. 3, 4, and 5, which have explored how violence is built into the country's liberal market democracy, the next two chapters examine two processes related to postwar citizenship that carried the promise to potentially work to transform El Salvador's violent democracy. Chapter 6 addresses one of the few consistent efforts to deal with El Salvador's war in a manner independent of electoral strategizing. It focuses on a grassroots organization involved in the redress of the country's haunting wartime past in order to examine the role played by political cleavages in this organization's memory work. Chapter 7 investigates the political shift that brought an FMLN president to power in 2009. Whereas Chap. 6 focuses on an example of ordinary Salvadorans' sustained activism in the postwar era, Chap. 7 examines the pragmatism that has otherwise characterized many Salvadorans' postwar citizenship practices.

---

[23] The FMLN obtained only 6364 votes more than ARENA, winning with a vote share of 50.11 percent.

PART II

Toward Substantive Democracy

CHAPTER 6

Memory Work in the Aftermath of War

In 2008, the Salvadoran publisher Equipo Maíz released a map of El Salvador portraying the locations of all of the country's civil war massacres that had been documented to that date. The map was publicly unveiled on 6 September in San Salvador at a meeting with representatives of the country's organizations of war victims. The cartographic depiction of war violence, created with information collected by members of these grassroots organizations, offered some unexpected revelations. After the northern Chalatenango Department, La Paz was the region with the most war massacres depicted on the map—47 in all—a number surpassing even that of a former war zone such as the northern Morazán Department. This was striking for a department that has barely appeared in conventional accounts of the country's civil war, aside from references to guerrilla encampments on the slopes of the Chichontepec Volcano, located on the border between the La Paz and San Vicente departments. The implications of this map of war violence are twofold. First, it underscored the fact that, as I have shown in Chap. 2, the violence perpetrated by the state against 'subversives' during the war severely affected the populations of departments like La Paz whose unorthodox war histories have been ignored. Second, and more pertinently for this chapter, the map suggested that important, albeit non-official, memory work has been taking place in departments such as La Paz during the postwar era. I borrow the term 'memory work' from Ferrándiz (2010), who employs it in his research on exhumations of civil

© The Author(s) 2018
A. Montoya, *The Violence of Democracy*, Studies of the Americas,
https://doi.org/10.1007/978-3-319-76330-9_6

war victims in Spain to refer to activities and actions performed for the purpose of recovering and reconstructing the past.

In this chapter I examine what constitutes the memory work performed by ordinary Salvadorans and how this work contributes to postwar El Salvador's contentious politics of memory. As described in the previous chapter, in the postwar era, the country's two main political parties, representative of the opposing sides during the civil war, have largely maintained a code of silence on the subject of the war. This silence has amounted to an avoidance of critical reflection about the war and wartime human rights violations, aside from the 'militant memories' (Sprenkels 2011) put forth by the two parties for their core constituencies. It has been mainly during presidential elections, notably in 2004 and 2009, that political elites within ARENA have explicitly invoked the war. These references to wartime El Salvador have, however, been expressed in a stereotypical manner that has served a particular politics of memory but done little to reconcile the ongoing divisions between ordinary people who continue to identify with one or the other wartime sides.

Meanwhile, public silence about the war has not translated into silence in more private domains. Since my first visit to Santiago in 2001, many ordinary Salvadorans have told me their war stories, recounting them as personal or collective experiences. On subsequent visits, I learned about the peripheral work being done by NGOs and grassroots organizations whose double aim has been to publicly explain the war and demand accountability for wartime human rights violations. As explained in Chap. 2, the Father Cosme Spessotto Committee, a grassroots organization, has been conducting this kind of memory work in La Paz since 2005. My participation in the committee's activities during 2008 and 2009 provided me with insights into the memory-building processes taking place in the aftermath of war. These processes have been conducted by ordinary people without any support from political parties or authorities, but with the collaboration of professional human rights NGOs that specialize in the technologies of memory. Many committee members are relatives of war victims who experienced the war themselves; a few fought as guerrillas, others participated in political organizations and suffered prosecution and torture, and most of them lost relatives. Their relationship to war victims, I argue, inevitably has implications for their design of a politics of victimhood.

Ordinary Salvadorans who participate in NGOs and grassroots organizations like the Father Cosme Spessotto Committee have a very different purpose in mind when they invoke the war than does ARENA during presidential elections. The memory work performed by these organizations, I argue, has aimed to retrieve a past with which Salvadoran society has not yet come to terms in order to resolve this past and enable a different future. Specifically, the committee has sought reconciliation predicated upon retributive and restorative justice. The affective manipulation of dead bodies has served as the basis for both their excavation of memory and their evaluation of a postwar scenario with which they have felt highly disillusioned. Roots in 1970s liberation theology have significantly influenced the postwar memory work, specifically with regard to its praxis and the nature of the changes sought. Given the motivations underlying the memory work that has been taking place in postwar El Salvador, this chapter shows that memory-building processes can be seen not just as an interpretation of the past in light of present concerns, as memory studies have generally postulated (see, for example, Lowenthal 1985; Connerton 1989; Halbwachs 1992; Assmann 1995), but also as an orientation toward the future. The goal, ultimately, is to give future generations an opportunity to overcome the fragmentation that has characterized postwar Salvadoran society. As I will show, the committee's orientation toward the future is nonetheless rooted in the political cleavages of the past.

MUTED REMEMBRANCE

On 2 September, during the 2008 electoral campaign, an interview on El Salvador's leftwing Channel 33 with the then-FMLN presidential candidate Mauricio Funes triggered a public discussion on the opportunities that existed in the postwar era for seeking retributive justice vis-à-vis war crimes and human rights violations. Funes was asked by the interviewer whether—assuming he were victorious in the 2009 presidential elections—he planned on repealing the 1993 amnesty law passed by Cristiani's ARENA government with the support of PCN and the abstention of PDC immediately after the publication of the report by the Commission on the Truth for El Salvador. The candidate replied that a repeal of the amnesty law would create a climate of ungovernability in the country that would not allow a future to be built. His stand on an issue that both major political parties had avoided sparked reactions from both the Left and the Right. Editorials and articles were published in the country's main rightwing newspapers *El Diario de Hoy* and *La Prensa Gráfica*, and interpretations by ARENA members of Funes's statements were broadcast on rightwing television channels 2, 4, and 6.

In a politically self-serving gesture, ARENA—along with the aforementioned media outlets—asserted that the FMLN resisted a repeal of the amnesty law because of the high number of assassinations for which the FMLN's own members, including its vice-presidential candidate Salvador Sánchez Cerén, would be accountable. The country's rightwing media stressed that Sánchez Cerén, as a commander of the FPL during the war, must have been aware—even an intellectual author—of this guerrilla organization's internal purge, confirmed by eye witnesses, which entailed the assassination of hundreds of combatants who had deserted the guerrillas or were deemed guilty of collaborating with the army (see Galeas and Ayala 2008). Indeed, while there is a paucity of available information of FMLN-inflicted violence during the war, there does exist evidence that the FMLN's involvement in human rights violations might be deeper than has been acknowledged (Sprenkels 2005: 71–74).

In impugning the FMLN's motives for resisting a repeal of the amnesty law, ARENA made no reference to the fact that the truth commission report had attributed 85 percent of the war's assassinations to the army, related police forces, paramilitary groups, and death squads, while only 5 percent were attributed to the FMLN guerrillas (United Nations 1993: 58). The rightwing party made declarations thereof in a way that would benefit its own electoral campaign for the 2009 presidential election, aiming to thwart the possibility that the Left could occupy the moral high ground, in contrast to a party like ARENA that had been associated with wartime death squads. Meanwhile, the FMLN, whose charter[1] superficially declared a commitment to the recovery of historical memory, has made only half-hearted efforts toward a public discussion of the war. The Historical Memory Secretaryship within the party, for example, has had no public impact beyond remembering and honoring former commander-turned-FMLN political leader Schafik Handal since he passed away in 2006 (see Sprenkels 2011). The party has indeed not been particularly outspoken about the amnesty law or interested in revisiting wartime human rights violations out of fear of prosecution of its own members (Collins 2006: 727; Sprenkels 2005, 2012).

Leftwing Salvadorans participating in NGOs and grassroots organizations like the Father Cosme Spessotto Committee also spoke out against Funes's declining to repeal the amnesty law. At the unveiling of the war

---

[1] Article 5 of the 2006 reform of the FMLN charter, published in *Diario Oficial 239, Tomo 373, 21 December 2006* (see FMLN 2006).

massacres map by Equipo Maíz described at the beginning of this chapter, two young members of organizations devoted to memory work—invigorated by the presence of the former guerrilla commander and then-FMLN deputy Nidia Díaz—voiced their discomfort with Funes's declarations and the FMLN leadership's silence. They excoriated FMLN for betraying its origins and its commitment to those who had died during the war. After their contributions, Nidia Díaz explained to the audience that during the electoral campaign, the FMLN and its presidential candidate Mauricio Funes had had to take a strategic approach to issues, such as wartime human rights violations, that could potentially alienate voters inasmuch as they stirred public controversy. Díaz then reaffirmed the FMLN's wholehearted commitment to working with war victims should its presidential candidate win the elections. However, despite her attempts to persuade the audience, members of these organizations remained keenly aware of the FMLN's lack of participation in postwar memory-building processes, from its absence in mourning and commemorative activities to its failure to raise public awareness in the municipalities that it has governed or from the seats that it has held in the Legislative Assembly. The disillusionment with, and abandonment by, the FMLN has been felt even by the human rights organizations, whether involved in memory work or other endeavors, that were linked to the various FMLN factions since their inception in the 1970s and 1980s (Sprenkels 2005).

Public silence with regard to the war, reinforced by the amnesty law, has thus reigned throughout El Salvador's democratization process. Yet public silence has not necessarily entailed oblivion. Ordinary Salvadorans have, for years, shared their stories of the country's 1980s civil war, albeit almost exclusively with friends and relatives. In addition, notwithstanding the paucity of thorough historical accounts published by Salvadorans, war-related literature—including testimonial accounts and memoirs by ex-guerrillas and survivors of war violence[2]—has proliferated in the postwar era. Such testimonial accounts and memoirs have their value; they have indisputably provided insights into the singularity of personal war experiences while depicting these as representative of the experiences of particular social categories. It is also in the repertoire of testimonies that troubling memories, such as the assassination or disappearance of relatives during

---

[2] See, for instance, Metzi (1988), López Vigil (1991), Stephen (1995), Amaya et al. (1996), Henríquez Consalvi (2005), Díaz (2006), Sánchez Cerén (2008), Bichkova de Hándal (2009), and Peña (2009).

the war or experiences of torture, can be addressed. Meanwhile, a few works have been released that contest the views described in the extensive testimonial literature and memoirs by ex-guerrillas, offering a completely different interpretation of the war.[3] Yet the aforementioned testimonies, memoirs, and conservative revisions of historical events or figures have neither contributed to breaking the national public silence about the war nor promoted discussion of it.

In El Salvador, it is difficult to speak of an official memory of wartime given that neither ARENA nor the FMLN has made any systematic attempts to produce or disseminate a hegemonic historical account of it. Nor did this substantially change with the FMLN victory in the 2009 presidential elections, even as this party's governments undertook some undeniable symbolic steps to revisit the war. One such step was the public forgiveness issued by President Funes on behalf of the state to the victims of wartime state-sponsored violence on the 2010 anniversary of the signing of Peace Accords.[4] This apology would be reiterated over the years, most notably two years later, at a ceremony at El Mozote commemorating the twentieth anniversary of Peace Accords, which symbolically placed the controversial massacre that occurred there in the public eye. In postwar El Salvador, therefore, the past has not been taken away through the writing of history by one side—as had occurred, for instance, in Francoist Spain where there was a clear victor—but simply ignored by both sides.[5] By evading a revision of the war's history and events, the FMLN has indirectly handed over to ARENA a primacy over the representation of wartime in public discourse, which ARENA has reduced to electorally motivated stereotypical accounts and imageries. The Right's control of the main media has of course been key in securing the wide dissemination of ARENA's war-related imageries and narratives during elections. For committee members, then, the 'recovery' of memory, given a context in which an official history that acknowledges the structural foundations of

---

[3] See, for instance, Escobar Galindo (2002), Galeas (2004), Panamá Sandoval (2005), Galeas and Ayala (2008), and Valdivieso Oriani (2008).

[4] A complete version of Funes's speech at this event can be read at http://www.contrapunto.com.sv/documentos/discurso-presidente-mauricio-funes-xviii-aniversario-de-la-firma-de-los-acuerdos-de-paz.

[5] Perhaps hindering the development of the historiography on the country's war is the fact that in El Salvador, history courses do not exist in secondary educational curricula and the subject of history has been subsumed under the social sciences. The only existing history department at the university level was founded as late as 2001 at Universidad El Salvador.

the civil war and violence is lacking, has entailed a retrieval of the wartime past from the public silence to which it has hitherto been relegated and an acknowledgment of the denial and distortion to which it has been subject.

THE RELIGIOUS ROOTS OF MEMORY WORK

A salient feature of the memory work being performed in postwar El Salvador is its intimate relationship with the Catholic Church, specifically the progressive wing rooted in 1970s liberation theology, which is today quite marginal. One of the organizations leading the memory work at the end of the 2000s, Oficina de Tutela Legal (Legal Guardianship Office), was part of the Archbishopric of San Salvador until its closure in 2013. Its predecessor, Socorro Jurídico, had been founded by Jesuit priest Segundo Montes in 1975 and then taken on by Archbishop Óscar Arnulfo Romero in 1977 to provide a means by which to denounce the assassination, abduction, torture, and incarceration of ordinary Salvadorans during the years leading up to the civil war (Sprenkels 2005: 41). In a context of systematic state repression, Socorro Jurídico became the place where Salvadorans would dare to lodge a report and receive the legal assistance they lacked the means to afford. After Romero's assassination by death squads on 24 March 1980, the task of denouncing human rights violations became institutionalized under the leadership of Archbishop Arturo Rivera y Damas. In 1982, Tutela Legal was founded with the twofold goal of providing an opportunity for the relatives of victims of human rights violations to report these violations and promoting a dialogue between the war's opposing sides in order to facilitate an end to the conflict. Tutela Legal's archives—filled with reports and evidence of wartime human rights violations that served as a basis for investigations by the truth commission on El Salvador—testified to the work that this organization conducted during the 1980s. Following the cessation of the conflict, Tutela Legal continued conducting independent investigations on human rights violations that occurred both during and after the war.

The Catholic Church's role in the political life of the country is not unique to El Salvador but is a general feature of the Latin American region (Kirk 1979; Levine 1986; Planas 1986; Peterson et al. 2001).[6] Following

---

[6] Although liberation theology is specific to Latin America, revolutionary theologies also gestated in Western and Eastern Europe, North America, Africa, and Asia (Kirk 1980; Rowland 1999).

the Second Vatican Council in the first half of the 1960s and the 1968 Medellín Conference of Latin American Bishops that built upon the former, a large number of priests in different areas of Latin America disseminated a progressive Christian hermeneutics that, by incorporating Marxist categories of analysis and a critique of capitalism, sought to mobilize underprivileged populations to seek social justice and ameliorate their life conditions. This progressive rereading of the Bible, which came to be known as 'liberation theology', was propagated in El Salvador during the 1970s via the work of local priests and laypeople with grassroots and Christian communities (Berryman 1986; Cáceres Prendes 1989; Presswood 1996; Peterson 1997). Most members of the Father Cosme Spessotto Committee have recounted to me that their wartime participation in political and revolutionary organizations stemmed from their relationships with local priests, who in the 1970s encouraged them to acknowledge the political roots of poverty and actively pursue transformation rather than resigning themselves to deprivation and inequality, as Catholic priests had heretofore encouraged. It was the active political role taken on by so many of El Salvador's priests and laypeople that, from the late 1970s onward, led to their repression and assassination by death squads and police forces, including the assassination of Father Rutilio Grande on 12 March 1977 and Father Octavio Ortiz on 20 January 1979.

Romero, who in 1977 was nominated Archbishop of San Salvador owing in part to his seemingly innocuous attitudes vis-à-vis contemporary political events and his generally good rapport with the Salvadoran elite, gradually changed his views (Martín-Baró 1985). The Archbishop responded to the increasing repression of the late 1970s by embracing the 'preferential option for the poor' and denouncing the excesses and violence perpetrated by the army with the backing of political elites. Following Rutilio Grande's assassination, Romero denounced army violence and emphatically demanded an end to repression in his eloquent Sunday sermons at San Salvador's cathedral.[7] On 24 March 1980, Archbishop Romero was gunned down by a sniper while celebrating mass at the chapel of the Divine Providence Hospital in San Salvador—an assassination allegedly orchestrated by ARENA-founder Major Roberto D'Aubuisson. Over the next week approximately 150,000 Salvadorans paid their respects at

---

[7] A complete version of his last sermon, wherein he begged the military to end its repression and disobey all orders to kill, is available in Romero (1987).

Metropolitan Cathedral, where Romero's body lay in state, and attended his funeral on 30 March. During the funeral in Gerardo Barrios Square, which faces the cathedral, the army launched an attack on the crowd that resulted in 30 deaths and countless injuries (Martín-Baró 1985: 18–19). Romero's assassination is, for many Salvadorans, the landmark event that signals the beginning of the 12-year civil war (see also Americas Watch 1991). Salvadorans' respect of his memory and legacy turned his declaration that 'si me matan, resucitaré en el pueblo salvadoreño' (If they kill me, I will rise again in the Salvadoran people) into prophecy.

Archbishop Romero's persona is hypostatized not just in the memory work that seeks moral reparation for victims and their relatives but also in an ongoing division within the Catholic Church. Romero's remains are buried in the San Salvador Cathedral constructed after the earlier building was destroyed by a fire in 1951. The cathedral is notable for the ostentatious decor of its main floor, a sharp contrast with the deterioration and decay in the vicinity of the building. When I last visited it in 2009, a wing on the main floor housed a portrait of Jose María Escrivá de Balaguer, the Opus Dei[8] founder; no trace of Archbishop Romero was visible. Romero's remains were instead to be found in the crypt beneath the cathedral's main floor. An empty and sober space, simply decorated with a portrait of Romero and floral motifs on the columns surrounding a central altar, the crypt was open to the public only during working hours. During these hours, it was often empty, aside from a few people visiting Romero's grave. At the bottom of the crypt, behind the altar, was a bronze sculpture by the Italian Paolo Borghi under which Romero's remains rest. The sculpture portrayed Romero's body lying flat; on his chest was a red ball symbolizing the shot that ended his life. His body was covered with a cloak, each corner held by one of the four Evangelists, also sculpted in bronze. Behind his grave, the bottom wall was covered with tombstones, most empty but some containing the remains of members of the clergy or individuals who stood up in defense of human rights, such as María Julia Hernández, Tutela Legal's director from its inception until her death in 2007.

---

[8] Opus Dei is an ultra-conservative Catholic movement founded in Spain in 1928 and now disseminated worldwide. It has played an important political role in Spain, with members participating as technocrats who embraced economic liberalization during the Francoist dictatorship (Cazorla Sánchez 2010: 5) and afterward as part of the judiciary that has blocked initiatives to redress the nation's civil war past.

The division of the cathedral's space and the relegation of Romero's remains to the crypt speak not just to the conservatism of today's Catholic Church but, more specifically, to an ongoing division between conservative church leaders and the smaller number of priests who maintain Romero's legacy and persevere in working with the Salvadoran population to transform an unjust social order. In the late 2000s, the cathedral's Sunday mass epitomized this division. While many Salvadorans attended the mass celebrated at 10 am by the high clergy on the main floor of the cathedral, hundreds of others congregated in the crypt half an hour later to attend a mass delivered by one of various priests with a progressive stance on contemporary political issues. Masses in the crypt were accompanied by popular songs formerly played at the peasant-like masses of the 1970s and 1980s, some in honor of Romero. These present-day masses were organized by the *Comunidad de la Cripta* (Crypt Community), a group composed predominantly of women who participated in various social movements. A number of them were deeply involved in human rights organizations devoted to memory work, such as the Center for the Promotion of Human Rights 'Madeleine Lagadec' (CPDH).[9] They met a few times a week to prepare interpretations of scripture that were read at each Sunday mass before the homily. In a conversation with the women of the Comunidad de la Cripta, they explained to me that this material was subject to censorship by the cathedral's head priest, who struck out every word or phrase deemed 'too progressive'. Sermons, by contrast, escaped censorship and were unusually progressive.

Other instances in 2009 when the division within El Salvador's Catholic Church was very much in evidence were the anniversary of Romero's death and the anniversary of his birth on 24 March and 15 August, respectively. On both these dates, as had occurred annually, thousands of people peregrinated to San Salvador to commemorate Romero and his legacy, crowding into the crypt while the main floor of the cathedral remained unaffected. Leaders of Evangelical Protestant churches that had aligned themselves on the Left of the political spectrum also attended these

---

[9] The CPDH was named after a French nurse, Madeleine Lagadec, killed during the war. Founded in 1992 to collect testimonies of wartime human rights violations for the Commission on the Truth, it has since devoted itself to memory work, for instance, assisting victims in the preparation of compensation claims or leading and funding various exhumations throughout the country.

commemorations, from which the Catholic Church elite had been conspicuously absent. The participation of Evangelical leaders contradicted the predominant assumption that Protestant churches are inherently conservative because of their rejection of participation in worldly issues and promotion of compliance with the status quo (see Peterson et al. 2001: 7). Romero has come to be seen not just as a political symbol for the majority of left-leaning Salvadorans—some of whom consider themselves primarily *romeristas* rather than FMLN adherents—but also as the exemplary figure for those devoted to memory work in postwar El Salvador.

While a petition from the progressive wing of the Salvadoran Catholic Church to canonize Romero was submitted in March 1993, it was only in November 2014 under Pope Francis that the Vatican issued a positive response by declaring Romero a martyr—a step in the beatification process prior to canonization. Romero's legacy—a matter of contention and division within the Salvadoran Catholic Church—had been consistently invoked by conservative church sectors over the years so as to hamper his beatification. As this book goes to press, however, it is expected that, under Pope Francis, Romero's and Father Rutilio Grande's canonization will occur imminently.

Meanwhile, judicial actions to bring to trial the material and intellectual authors of his assassination have remained slow and limited. In 1993, a brother of Archbishop Romero, along with Tutela Legal, took the case before the Inter-American Commission on Human Rights (IACHR), which in 2000 deemed the Salvadoran state responsible for the violation of the Archbishop's right to life and for having eschewed any investigation into the episode, prosecution, or sanction of those responsible, and recommended that an investigation be carried out.[10] Given the unfeasibility of judicial action in El Salvador back then, two of Romero's brothers filed a civil lawsuit in Fresno, California, against Álvaro Rafael Saravia, a former Salvadoran military officer and one of the intellectual authors of Romero's assassination, who had moved to California. This action was possible through two pieces of United States domestic legislation, the 1789 Alien Tort Claims Act and the 1991 Torture Victim Protection Act, that allow foreign citizens to sue anyone based in the United States who might have been responsible for human rights offenses or torture. In 2004 Fresno's federal court ruled Saravia liable in absentia. To date, however, there has been no penal

---

[10] To read the IACHR report on the case, visit http://cidh.org/annualrep/99eng/Merits/ElSalvador11.481.htm.

prosecution or arrest for the prelate's assassination. It was not until May 2017, almost a year after the repeal of El Salvador's amnesty law, that a criminal case for his murder has been reopened in El Salvador, thereby finally, belatedly, following the IACHR's recommendations.[11]

Perhaps the most evident sign of the postwar control of El Salvador's Catholic Church by the conservative wing and its lack of interest in pursuing justice for wartime and human rights violations was the dismantling of Tutela Legal in 2013. In an interview in February 2014, one of Tutela Legal's former employees explained that on arriving at the organization's offices in El Salvador's Archbishopric on 30 September 2013 to start their working day, employees found Tutela Legal's entrance doors barricaded with metal sheets. Later that morning they learned about the Archbishop José Luis Escobar Alas's decision to shut down Tutela Legal with no prior notice and no explanation. Its employees were compelled to sign their resignations and given just one opportunity to recover a few items from the offices. Tutela Legal's unique archive containing evidence of more than 50,000 cases of wartime human rights violations, however, remained at the Archbishopric.

In the months that followed, the Archbishop received innumerable complaints from national and international NGOs, as well as victims whose cases were archived at Tutela Legal's offices or under investigation by its employees. Protests were organized by social organizations in front of the cathedral to pressure the Archbishop and publicly denounce his decision. To these public denunciations, the Archbishop responded with different explanations. After initially suggesting that Tutela Legal no longer had a purpose, the Archbishop subsequently argued it needed some reorganization, and then made allegations that its employees had incurred irregularities in legal, administrative, and accounting-related matters.[12] Tutela Legal and other human rights NGOs put forth their own hypothesis for the closure: in light of the possibility that the Supreme Court's reconsideration of the amnesty law might lead to its repeal,[13] the Archbishop had

---

[11] While in 1987 Salvadoran public prosecutors requested Saravia's extradition from the United States, El Salvador's Supreme Court finally withdrew this request and judicial action was thenceforth blocked.

[12] See 'Arzobispado cambia por tercera vez el argumento que lo llevó a cerrar Tutela Legal', *El Faro*, 7 October 2013.

[13] Just ten days earlier, El Salvador's Supreme Court had admitted a lawsuit from two human rights organizations, the UCA Institute of Human Rights (IDHUCA) and the Foundation for Studies on the Application of Law (FESPAD), that challenged the constitu-

become concerned that the Catholic Church might become involved in judicialization processes given Tutela Legal's archives and extensive work on wartime human rights crimes.

The existence of two churches and two antagonistic attitudes toward memory work within Catholicism has been evident not only in San Salvador but also in municipalities like Santiago. The persistent postwar division within the Catholic Church in this municipality found expression in the late 2000s in central Santiago's two parish churches. The Church Santiago Apostol has by and large had the largest number of parishioners in the municipality. Located on the left side of the city council building, its newly erected structure—the original was demolished in 1978 after decades of deterioration, with only a half-ruined tower remaining—is notable for its distinctive round shape. For many years, Father Luis, who was widely believed to align himself with the municipality's PCN mayor, administered this church.

In 2005, another priest, Father Óscar, arrived in Santiago, having been transferred from a parish in a Chalatenango municipality because, he suspected, its local ARENA candidate considered him a threat to his success in the 2006 municipal elections. Father Óscar worked at the Church Santiago Apostol with Father Luis for a few months. Eventually, the latter and his parishioners became uncomfortable with Father Óscar's criticisms of the work of the PCN mayor. At this point, Father Óscar moved to the abandoned El Calvario Church at the entrance to Santiago, on a street that links the center with the Coastal Road. With the help of the parishioners who followed him to El Calvario, this church was repainted in white and red and adorned with a mural of Romero's image and a quote by Romero on the frontal façade that read: 'It is sad to be forced to leave the homeland because it has no just order within which to find a job'. The interior of the church was decorated very simply, with portraits of Romero hanging on some of its pillars.

Just as there have been two churches in San Salvador coexisting within the cathedral—with those following liberation theology and Romero's legacy relegated to the basement and thus to relative invisibility—during the years that Father Óscar was posted in Santiago, there were two municipal parishes emblematic of the Catholic Church's fundamental division: a large central one supported by the mayor and attended by the majority of

tional character of the amnesty law. See 'Sala admite demanda para declarar inconstitucional ley de amnistía', *La Prensa Gráfica*, 20 September 2013.

Catholic Santiagueñas, and a smaller one attended by a leftwing minority. As mentioned in the previous chapter, Father Óscar's overt manifestations of his political beliefs, including the annual celebration of a mass and vigil to commemorate Romero's assassination and a mass during the 2008 municipal campaign to bless the FMLN candidate, led rightwing Santiagueños to dub him 'the guerrilla priest'. He also demonstrated a commitment to the memory-building processes led by the Father Cosme Spessotto Committee. Whenever he was available, he accepted invitations to celebrate mass at the committee's regular, often monthly, commemorations in the municipalities of La Paz where war massacres and repression occurred. Yet his role in regional memory-building processes was limited to occasional participation in the committee's public events and his reading of the Bible as per Romero's legacy. Priests from neighboring municipalities supportive of the committee's activities likewise had a limited role in memory work; they were more concerned with the day-to-day running of their own parishes.

In sum, a progressive faction within the Catholic Church has persisted in postwar El Salvador despite all the prewar and wartime repression experienced by those who advocated liberation theology within the clergy and Salvadoran society at large. The Church's progressive wing has survived even in the face of the conservative turn signified by the nomination of Fernando Sáenz Lacalle, an Opus Dei member, as San Salvador's Archbishop in 1995 and his replacement in 2009 by José Luis Escobar Alas, also an adherent of mainstream Catholicism and under whose tenure Tutela Legal was closed down. However, in present-day El Salvador, the transformative quality of liberation theology that informed progressive positions within the Catholic Church has gradually waned, with many local progressive priests like Father Óscar remaining critical of rightwing national and local governments yet chiefly concerned with spiritual and family issues (cf. Gómez 2001: 124; Peterson et al. 2001: 4). Their sermons scarcely touch on the structural issues discussed by priests and laypeople during the 1970s and 1980s. In this sense, although the progressive factions within the Catholic Church are supportive of memory-building processes, they are no longer the driving force they once were. In postwar El Salvador, it is ordinary people who have taken on this role. Yet liberation theology has been an undeniable source of inspiration for their postwar memory work.

THE COMMITTEE

The Father Cosme Spessotto Committee is emblematic of the nexus that exists in El Salvador between memory work and the Catholic Church, as are other human rights and grassroots organizations (e.g. IDHUCA, Tutela Legal, CO-MADRES,[14] or Asociación Pro-Búsqueda) that constitute part of the national alliance called Comisión Pro-Memoria Histórica. Not only does the committee name attest to that nexus, but its practices are largely rooted in liberation theology. It owes its name to the priest assassinated by death squads in the San Juan Nonualco Church, in La Paz, on 14 June 1980. Likewise, many committee members participated in peasant cooperatives, organizations, and Christian base communities promoted by progressive priests during the 1960s and 1970s. Like some of his fellow committee members, Hernán, the committee's main leader and founder, went on to join revolutionary organizations during the 1970s and 1980s. He never took up weapons, instead dedicating himself to logistical work. In line with so many other Salvadorans who embraced liberation theology, he considered the violence of the guerrillas legitimate given that it was rooted in a Christian notion of justice and a profound sense of solidarity with the poor. Yet in the postwar era, he has worked strenuously to promote a future free of the kind of violence experienced by Salvadorans during the war.

In the aftermath of war, Hernán joined a committee of war victims based in Tecoluca, a municipality in the neighboring San Vicente Department, many of whose residents supported or had links with the FMLN. It was at a meeting of the Tecoluca-based committee that Hernán met Isaías, also from La Paz. Realizing that this organization had no interest in the human rights violations that had occurred in La Paz during the war, the two men went on to found the Father Cosme Spessotto Committee in 2005. Gradually, other residents of La Paz joined the new committee's meetings and activities. By the time I conducted my research in 2008, it was being led by a small group of mostly middle-aged men, including Hernán and Isaías, some of whom had a university education. Some of the leaders were employed in the educational or cultural sectors, while others did either agricultural work or occasional small jobs in the informal economy. Committee leadership aside, the large majority of committee

---

[14] Committee of Mothers and Relatives of the Political Prisoners, Disappeared and Assassinated of El Salvador 'Monseñor Óscar Arnulfo Romero' (CO-MADRES).

members were illiterate elderly women working in the informal economy, mostly as street or market vendors, to compensate for their lack of a pension and deteriorating economic status. Although some of them had actively participated as guerrillas during the war, the majority were widows who mourned husbands and youth lost in the war and had raised their orphaned children and grandchildren on their own.

Before the committee was founded, some of its members had already initiated memory work in their communities. Isaías, who lost his father in a massacre in the Cantón Los Platanares in Zacatecoluca on 2 June 1980, had created a record about the episode along with three other men who had survived the massacre or were, like Isaías, relatives of victims. The handwritten document included detailed information on the military operation that began that day at 6 am in the south of Santiago Nonualco and finished in the afternoon in the south of Zacatecoluca, having decimated the southern parts of the San Rafael Obrajuelo and San Juan Nonualco municipalities that separate Santiago from Zacatecoluca (see Figure 2).[15] Nearly 200 people, including men, women, children, and elders, were killed in this operation, which was jointly led by the army and police forces. A list of the 39 victims assassinated in Los Platanares and their ages was included at the end of the document. The purpose of the document was stated at the outset:

> so that the people of the 'Truth' Commission are able to conduct all necessary investigations regarding these serious human rights violations, as well as judge and punish the military that participated in the massacre, whether intellectually or materially.

The document was signed on 15 August 1992, and a copy handed over to researchers involved in the investigations of the Commission on the Truth for El Salvador. There was no substantive response from the truth commission, focused as it was on a few high-profile cases. The authors of the document waited until 2008 to request Tutela Legal and CPDH that they conduct an exhumation of their relatives' bodies, an endeavor for which CPDH finally had the funds in 2011.

Others, like Esperancita, had begun a relentless search for abducted relatives long before the war's end. Two of her sisters—one of whom was

---

[15] An UCA-produced short film about the massacre is available at https://www.youtube.com/watch?v=J5FL_pGL7ss.

pregnant—along with the husband of one of these sisters had been abducted at the beginning of the war. Witnesses provided evidence that this had occurred during a visit to relatives in San Salvador. Even as this book goes to press, Esperancita has not found out what happened to them or to the child presumed to have been born after the abduction. Although there are no records indicating that the child was born, the Salvadoran NGO Asociación Pro-Búsqueda has found that the disappearing of Salvadoran children belonging to those abducted, assassinated, or imprisoned during the war and subsequent adoption by other families, very often among the military, was a systematic practice during the country's war. The members of the committee are, in short, relatives of people assassinated or abducted during the war in La Paz. They came together with the common goal of finding out what happened to their relatives—whether they were abducted or, like so many nameless bodies, buried in unmarked graves.

The committee's memory work is built upon a 'dead-body politics'. Recovering the bones of relatives through exhumations, honoring them, and providing them with a proper burial are the primary objectives of committee members. The question then is why members devote themselves to these activities and how the bones are significant to the committee's memory work. Dead bodies or bones have a highly symbolic value for various reasons. They are the remains of relatives who disappeared in a tragic manner—either assassinated or abducted—and in the context of the traumatic historical episode of war. Given the close relationship between the people involved in memory work and the bodies or bones, exhumations—especially of those who did not receive a proper burial—may elicit emotions in a way that other records of war violence cannot. For instance, a 60-year-old woman who was gravely ill in 2009 confessed to me that she was afraid of dying without having unearthed her sons' and husband's bones. 'Who else will do it if I am not here?' she wondered with anguish. Committee members also believed that exhumations would help assuage haunting war memories and give closure to processes of grief and mourning. Being reunited with the osteal remains of kin would help put an end to the uncertainty that has characterized the relationship between the dead and the living in the aftermath of war. However, especially for the committee leadership, memory work did not end with the fulfillment of people's pressing need to find their relatives and give them a proper burial. Beyond the intimate link that existed between the committee members and the dead bodies, there was another way in which bodies were symbolically relevant, one that concerned the wider public: the relationship between the bodies and the history of their country's war.

Dead bodies and bones have played a significant role in the work of the Father Cosme Spessotto Committee, as well as the work of other similar groups, because of their very concreteness and materiality. The physical quality of the bones helps to make the historical past immediately visible and public. The technical process following their exhumation turns the bones into the 'scientific evidence' needed to challenge denials of massacres or accounts that function as apologetics for their perpetrators.[16] By analyzing the osteal remains and the objects found in close proximity to them, archaeologists and forensic anthropologists can reconstruct many details about the person to whom they belonged and how that person was killed. This level of precision contributes, as Verdery (1999: 20) suggests for postsocialist countries, to a rethinking and repositioning of the social categories, such as 'communists' or 'guerrillas', by which the peasant population was often defined by the Salvadoran army. For instance, Sanford (2003: 43) describes how an exhumation in 1994 of the remains of alleged guerrillas at a mass grave in the Guatemalan village Plan de Sánchez, in Baja Verapaz, revealed that the majority of the victims were unarmed women, children, and elderly people. Similar is the case of the El Mozote massacre waged by El Salvador's Atlacatl Battalion from 11 to 13 December 1981, in the northern Morazán Department (see United Nations 1993: 155–165; Danner 1994; Binford 1996, 2016). Exhumations conducted in late 1992 and early 1993 confirmed that this army operation was launched against civilians, the majority of whom were, once again, women, children, and elderly people. In contrast to ARENA's discursive politics of memory, the committee and similar organizations that perform memory work have used the concrete and relatively indisputable evidence of bones to document and reconstruct violent war episodes. The exhumations help to fulfill two main objectives: the relatives' desire to concretize their emotional relationship with the victims, and the committee leadership's ethical and political commitment to writing the history of the war in La Paz.

Crucially, in contrast to other forms of record, bones and bodies are speechless and hence subject to manipulation. As Verdery (1999: 28) has stated 'remains are concrete, yet protean; they do not have a single

---

[16]For an account on the role of the scientific technologies at work in memory-building processes, see Wagner (2008).

meaning but are open to many different readings'. The ambiguity of bones is why, despite their 'reading' by archaeologists and forensic anthropologists, much memory work does not limit itself to excavating bones but also carries out a commensurate 'excavation' of memory through testimony (Ferrándiz 2008; Sanford 2003: 17–18). In this sense, a dialogical relationship is established between bones and testimony that synergistically emphasizes the evidentiary value of each. Testimony is the personal account that attests to the lived experience of a particular episode. While it is difficult to define testimony as wholly personal or social, its designation as a juridical category obfuscates its otherwise ambiguous relationship to 'the truth' (Binford 2000). Aware that testimony can be strongly contested, groups like the Father Cosme Spessotto Committee have emphasized in their memory work the relevance of bones, and their dialogical relationship to testimony, as indelible evidence of war episodes.

As of my last interview with Hernán in April 2017, the number of exhumations the committee had seen conducted in La Paz territories was seven. All of the massacres had been perpetrated by the army, sometimes backed by local civil defense units, in the *cantones* of various La Paz municipalities. Given the lack of funding available to the organizations that conduct exhumations and the small number of judges that have admitted the exhumation requests once the funds have been secured, the committee's memory work has been limited largely to the recording of testimonies and their integration into a historical narrative, as well as the organization of mourning activities at the sites of unmarked graves. Since their committee's founding, its leaders have collected numerous first-hand testimonies of war crimes committed in the region. This has allowed the committee to identify and investigate 82 massacres that occurred in eight La Paz municipalities; only 47 had been documented at the time Equipo Maíz designed the massacres map to which I referred at the outset. In the committee's work, testimony has inevitably preceded bones, the latter standing merely as a physical validation of testimony rather than benefiting from the full synergies of a dialogical relationship. The indefinite deferral of exhumations until organizations like Tutela Legal or the CPDH are able to secure the funding and judicial permits to conduct them has frustrated many committee members, who seek above all to be reunited with their relatives' remains.

THE RECONFIGURATION AND RESIGNIFICATION OF TIME AND SPACE

The aforementioned limitations notwithstanding, the committee's postwar memory work, based on both a dead-body politics and testimony, has the potential to contribute to both the reconfiguration (endowing with a new shape) and resignification (imbuing with new meaning) of time and space, in ways similar to those described by Verdery (1999) in her discussion of postsocialist reburials. The exhumation and reburial of countless nameless bodies in post-Yugoslavia, she explains, contributed to the creation of new nation-states, the rewriting and reshaping of national histories, and the reconceptualization of time (Verdery 1999: 95–127). In El Salvador, time has been reconfigured and resignified in at least two notable ways. As explained in Chap. 2, the collection of war testimonies in La Paz, and their corroboration by the few exhumations conducted so far, has yielded a war chronography that diverges from the standard national one. In other words, the landmark events employed to indicate the beginning and end of the war nationwide do not coincide with those of the La Paz municipalities, revealing that the periodization of national history has concealed or denied regional variations of war violence. This actual exercise of writing the history of the war has been conducted by the committee leadership, since the large majority of committee members are illiterate. The future-oriented nature of this memory work has also been clear: the writing of history has been aimed at future generations rather than the victims themselves.

In addition, the memory work performed by groups like the committee has the potential to yield a resignification of the present, resulting in part from the compression of time provoked by the public and visible immediacy of the past that bones and testimony alike evoke. In the late 2000s, the pervasiveness of past legacies in present-day El Salvador was often inadvertently brought to light by Salvadorans as they morally assessed the present in private by comparing it to a past whose enduring qualities—violence, political division, and inequality—had received scant public acknowledgment. Meanwhile, memory work forcibly reintroduced the past into the public domain through the materiality and symbolic efficacy of bones and the documentary quality of testimony, although it has done so in a limited manner given the marginality of memory work in El Salvador. The bones and testimony have contributed to disseminating a heightened awareness of the past in postwar El Salvador—albeit a past actualized through change and reinterpretation—that does not in and of itself enable ordinary Salvadorans to conceive of the present as located within a trajectory toward a substantially different future. Yet in trying to bring closure and resolution by making the past visible and public, the committee has been providing the tools for reorienting a future that might otherwise be inevitably shaped by a troublesome past. This point becomes clearer through an exploration of the ways in which the committee's memory work has the potential to resignify space.

Memory work has the potential to resignify physical space, particularly the country's geography of war and quotidian spaces pervaded by wartime memories, and also to reconfigure Salvadoran political space.[17] The bones and especially testimony collected by the Father Cosme Spessotto Committee have contributed not only to providing a divergent war chronography but also to revealing an unexpected war cartography as reflected in the massacres map printed and distributed by Equipo Maíz. Since 2005, the leaders of the committee have interviewed anyone willing to provide testimony on his or her own war experience as well as details about violent episodes that occurred in the region. Not only have these interviews allowed the committee to document the 82 massacres that, to date, are known to have occurred in La Paz, but they have also helped further the committee members' goal of writing the war history of La Paz. Their efforts have resulted in a book manuscript still awaiting a publisher as this book goes to press. As noted at the beginning of this chapter, La Paz, a region considered to lie outside the former war zones, appeared on the Equipo Maíz map as one of the regions where the most war massacres had been identified—an undeniable result of the committee's active documentative work.

Memory work can also yield a resignification of quotidian spaces, which can then be transformed into sacralized sites of mourning or memorialization. The Father Cosme Spessotto Committee has conducted investigations to determine the sites of unmarked graves or massacres and then designated these locations for mourning events. For instance, the commemoration held for the first time in the Cantón Las Ánimas on 25 July 2009, to which I referred in Chap. 2, took place on the plot where four men and one woman, all relatives assassinated at the beginning of the war, were covertly buried by local residents who found their bodies. The book

---

[17] 'Political space' seems an appropriate metaphor given the spatialization of politics that exists in El Salvador, and in Latin America by and large, which is largely defined by the Left/Right divide.

cover offers an image of this plot. The unmarked graves would be unnoticeable but for four parallel ridges (two of the bodies were buried in the same grave) sticking out of the ground. The relatives of these deceased left the area during the war or were likewise assassinated. Rosa, the wife of Gaudencio Galán, the first person buried there, decided to return to Las Ánimas in the 2000s. She has since requested that the plot be cared for, but her wishes have been ignored by other residents, who regularly let their livestock trample the graves when crossing the plot. The Galán family, Rosa and her five daughters, have attempted to buy the plot. Although left-leaning, the local parishioners in charge of the current Las Ánimas chapel have refused the Galán family's requests, claiming that because the old chapel was located on that plot, it belongs to Santiago's Parish church and hence cannot be sold. The Father Cosme Spessotto Committee, unaware of this contention, held a commemoration on that plot, with the ultimate aim of repositioning the dead in the community both morally and physically, that is, publicly honoring them while resignifying the space in which they are buried. The mourning event assembled the local population of Las Ánimas on this previously disregarded plot, at least temporarily imbuing that space with emotive meaning and sacralizing it for the participants. Although the resignification of space may not be immediate, this commemoration served to resuscitate the community's debate over the plot and the significance of the unmarked graves that lie within it and of so many other unmarked graves scattered around Las Ánimas.

The activity of the Father Cosme Spessotto Committee has had the potential to resignify regional political space in four ways. First, the celebration of mourning activities in many La Paz municipalities, as well as the seven exhumations carried out in Zacatecoluca, have elicited residents' war memories. As shown in Chap. 2, the first commemoration of the war victims, held in Las Ánimas on 25 July 2009 at the plot containing four unmarked graves, elicited general discussion about the war as well as the wartime experiences of attendees and their relatives. The limited impact of its memory work notwithstanding, the committee has managed to bring into public debate in some areas of La Paz relatively nuanced readings of wartime events that sharply contrast with ARENA's Manichaean war rhetoric. In organizing mourning events, the committee has also fostered a therapeutic and cathartic space in which an intimate community of mourners have been able to address and share their grief. Second, the memory work performed by groups like the committee has sought to resignify Salvadoran political space by repositioning the dead—hitherto ignored, silenced, or defamed—and honoring them. I discuss this in further detail in the next section, since repositioning the dead has the potential not only to reconfigure political space but also to imbue it with a new morality.

Third, postwar political space has also been at least outwardly reconfigured by the introduction of a standardized language of human rights into memory work. The human rights approach has provided a political language for what would otherwise remain intimate and unspeakable, a language with which to speak about past atrocities but also to press claims on the state on the basis of these atrocities. As in the case of indigenous movements throughout Latin America, the memory work in El Salvador has also benefited from the international support provided by the transnational language and mechanisms of human rights.[18] Alongside regional grassroots organizations like the committee, there have been a number of NGOs like Tutela Legal whose memory work has become professionalized and linked to larger networks of human rights organizations. These links were evident in Tutela Legal's language of denunciation and restitution in the late 2000s. Members of Tutela Legal participated in the Father Cosme Spessotto Committee meetings and trained committee members in the human rights approach and its relevance for claim-making by war victims. Since then, the committee leadership publicly voiced the right of the relatives of victims to 'truth, justice and reparation'. The adoption of professionalized and standardized human rights language does not, however, mean that committee members have had the same voice as their professional counterparts. Material reparation and accountability, which have been strong components in the agenda of professional human rights organizations like Tutela Legal, and no doubt important for the committee, have not been the major matter of concern for many of its members. The majority have been fundamentally concerned with finding out what happened to their relatives, reuniting themselves with their remains, and giving them a proper burial. However, while some professional NGOs have made attempts to judicialize a few war crimes, their agenda has not prioritized

[18] Until the amnesty law was repealed in 2016, the few cases of judicialized wartime human rights violations benefited not only from United States domestic legislation, as had Romero's, but also from international human rights systems and the universal jurisdiction principle that enables legal action in third-country courts. For instance, the abduction of two minors, the Serrano Cruz sisters, during a military operative in 1982 and the El Mozote massacre were taken to the Inter-American Court of Human Rights in 2003 and 2012, respectively, while a lawsuit was lodged in Spain in November 2008 for the 1989 assassination of six Jesuit Fathers, their housekeeper, and the housekeeper's daughter at the UCA (Collins 2006; Binford 2016: 238–251).

accountability or claim-making, at least when compared to equivalent organizations in other countries (Collins 2010). Nor have accountability efforts by individuals flourished either.

Fourth, the Father Cosme Spessotto Committee, like other organizations that conduct memory work, had the potential to resignify El Salvador's postwar political space by presenting itself as a political actor during and after the country's elections. Although aligned with the Left—since many committee members or their relatives fought as FMLN guerrillas or participated in FMLN-linked popular organizations during the war or have been affiliated with this party in the postwar era—the committee and like-minded organizations have remained independent from the FMLN and had their own agendas, to which FMLN politicians have paid little more than electorally motivated lip service. During the 2009 elections, committee leaders met with the FMLN municipal candidate from Zacatecoluca and sent a written petition to this party's presidential candidate, Mauricio Funes, urging both men to commit themselves to memory work and take seriously the demands of the relatives of war victims should they win the elections. Given the effective lobbying efforts by Father Cosme Spessotto Committee leaders on behalf of the relatives of war victims, the FMLN's municipal candidate for Zacatecoluca, Francisco Hirezi, felt impelled to receive the committee leadership and listen to their demands. During the electoral campaign, Hirezi, a doctor at the Rosales National Hospital in San Salvador, emphatically declared his commitment to the committee's work and promised his support after the elections. To compel him to publicly demonstrate his commitment to memory work, he was invited to committee meetings. He participated, knowing that doing so would be fruitful for his political campaign. Once he won the elections, however, his attitude toward committee leaders changed, and he hedged on the issue of fulfilling his preelectoral promises. His behavior confirmed once again the limited support that the FMLN as a political party has provided to memory work.

After El Salvador's 2009 party shift, organizations like the committee involved in memory work intensified their lobbying and moral pressure vis-à-vis the newly formed government, assuming it would be more responsive to war victims' claims and needs than any prior administration. They attended countless meetings with First Lady Vanda Pignato—appointed Social Inclusion Secretary once the FMLN took office—to discuss their proposals for truth, justice, and reparation. Their strenuous efforts did eventually see some results, albeit limited. In 2010, the FMLN administration founded the National Commission for the Reparation of Victims of Human Rights Offenses and, in 2013, approved a reparation program for wartime victims.[19] This program has fallen short of expectations, being only a thin version of the reparation demands propounded by human rights and victims' organizations such as the committee and, moreover, very poorly endowed. Indeed, the justice component claimed by human rights NGOs and grassroots organizations such as the committee was excluded, thereby inhibiting victims' access to comprehensive reparation.

The resignification of time and space that memory work by organizations like the Father Cosme Spessotto Committee has achieved or has the potential to achieve is not just an expression of the intimate aspirations of relatives of war victims, but also a moral commentary on the postwar era and the roles allotted to the war and the deceased. Significantly, while many committee members have been victims of postwar violence themselves—subject to extortion, beaten up by gang members, or having suffered the violent death of a young son—they have dealt with these grievances privately. The work of the committee has thus been strictly limited to collectively dealing with the traumas of the wartime past and has not encouraged a similar treatment of postwar traumas. I would suggest that there are at least two reasons for this disjuncture between wartime and postwar victimhood. First, the sense of 'not-knowing' exactly what constitutes postwar violence—a 'not-knowing' emanating largely from the ambiguity and grayness characterizing this violence—has made it difficult to determine the subjects upon whom to place demands. Second, the multiplicity of violent actors and forms of violence in the postwar era has further complicated ordinary people's ability to take a collective approach to the mourning of postwar victims.

Part of the difficulty in collective organizing with regard to postwar traumas is related to the resignification of violence and changing value of death in the aftermath of war (Moodie 2006: 72–73). In the new value regime, disseminated largely via the triumphalism of the architects of transition, the state has faded away as an agent bearing any responsibility for the high postwar levels of violence. In a context of unintelligible and

---

[19] Programa de Reparaciones a las Víctimas de Graves Violaciones a los Derechos Humanos Ocurridas en el Contexto del Conflicto Armado Interno, Decreto Ejecutivo No. 204, *Diario Oficial*, 23 October 2013.

random violence, postwar fatalities—whether as a result of a bus accident or a homicide—and grievances are represented as unfortunate accidents, thus dissolving the pertinence of a language of political rights (Moodie 2006: 76). Memory work has therefore remained limited to wartime human rights violations even in the face of the increasing postwar victimhood experienced by committee members themselves. In sum, while memory work has been concerned with creating the conditions of possibility for a qualitatively different future—one in which the dead and their morality have been repositioned—it has not had reverberations for recent human rights violations and grievances.

A New Moral Universe Rooted in the Past

Ever since their organization was founded and until 2014, members of the Father Cosme Spessotto Committee conducted monthly mourning activities in the rural areas of La Paz where residents were massacred during the war. At these events, which were attended by the relatives of those assassinated, photographs of the dead were displayed, often flanked by large portraits of Archbishop Romero and Father Cosme Spessotto. The names of those assassinated at the site were read aloud one by one. If known, the victim's age and date of death were noted, along with a mention of whether they had been abducted. The reading of names was always followed by testimonies from one or two relatives of war victims from the area, testimonies to which everyone listened to attentively yet pensively, as though reliving their own wartime experiences through those of the testimony bearers. The central part of the event was a mass. A local priest supportive of the committee's work was invited to deliver a sermon honoring the war victims and offer prayers for the bodies, most of which had never received a Christian burial. During the war, relatives or neighbors of the deceased had usually buried the bodies hastily, hoping to evade the repression that might ensue if they were caught in the act by military or local civil defense units. Sometimes bodies were carelessly buried by the murderers themselves in order to obliterate evidence of the assassination, although this occurred infrequently given that a terrorizing and deterrent effect was sought by the army and police forces through the display of dead bodies in public places. The ceremony would conclude with a floral tribute to the dead, one of its most emotional moments; an image of the flower-bedecked graves following one such event in Las Ánimas appears on the cover of this book.

With its ritualized mourning events, the Father Cosme Spessotto Committee has sought to reposition the dead by bringing them into the light of postwar political space and restoring their honor and moral virtue. As a committee leader explained in a 2017 interview, these events became less frequent after the 2009 party shift due to the chikungunya (a mosquito-transmitted disease) affecting many committee members and the escalation of homicides and gang control of the rural areas where wartime massacres were commemorated. From 2014, the committee has commemorated all of the La Paz massacres and other human rights violations at a single mourning event held annually in a Zacatecoluca parish on the third Saturday of December, christened by the committee as 'the Day of the Martyrs'.

The approach to victimhood exhibited at such mourning events, and throughout the committee's research, deserves careful attention since it denotes a particular proposition for the terms of reconciliation in El Salvador. 'Today the only people you can trust are the dead', I was once told resolutely by a leader of the Father Cosme Spessotto Committee. His assertion, I suggest, captures the essence of the memory work performed by the committee, which is a moral judgment about the present that also informs future-oriented action. On the one hand, the assertion was a critique of postwar politics. Those FMLN guerrillas who survived the war and now participate in formal politics as members of the legalized FMLN party have not lived up to the expectations of many leftwing Salvadorans. Criticisms are often leveled against the FMLN political leadership for having sold out and thus betrayed those who died during the war, whether they were fighting to transform an unjust social order or were accidentally caught in the crossfire. A significant number of Salvadorans involved in memory work have voted for FMLN candidates in postwar elections but are nonetheless cynical about the motivations of FMLN leaders (see also Sprenkels 2005: 79–98). Committee members' cynicism is partly rooted in the apparent disinterest that FMLN leaders have demonstrated in discussing the war and its roots, in recognizing the war's futility given the persistence of public and economic insecurity, and in recalling and honoring its victims.

Yet the assertion that only the dead can be trusted is not just a critique of the present, but it also highlights the righteousness that committee members attribute to those who died in pursuit of justice. Committee members believe that their morality must be celebrated in order to bring about a new moral universe, that is, in order to create the conditions of possibility for national reconciliation. The dead-body politics underpinning the committee's memory work thus pursues the resignification of postwar political space by restoring the morality of the dead.

Underlying the resignification of political space sought by the committee has been the notion of 'martyrdom'. At every mourning event, committee members have reminded the audience of the need to restore the dignity and honor of war martyrs. According to Christian doctrine, those who freely accept their own death as a demonstration of their faith in Christ can be considered martyrs. Initially, this was a minimalist notion of Christian martyrdom, restricted to the clergy and focused strictly on spiritual witness to Christ as demonstrated through liturgy. This notion was revised during the twentieth century, notably by the Second Vatican Council, such that martyrs now include not just those who die for their faith in Christ but also those who die for Christ's teachings, including peace and justice (Peterson 1997: 94–95). Given the persecution to which those who promote 'a just life' have been subjected in most of Latin America, the notion of Christian martyrdom has been expanded to include not just priests and laypeople killed by state-sponsored paramilitary groups, but also ordinary people who died for any Christian precept (Peterson 1997: 105–107; Sobrino 1984: 178–181).

The committee leadership believes that anyone who died without fighting but as a result of the war qualifies posthumously as a 'martyr'. Their designation as martyrs is thus not necessarily determined by their affiliation with the church, but rather by the nature of their participation in the conflict. The committee has thus distinguished between 'martyrs' and 'heroes'. 'Heroes' died as a result of fighting against inequality and injustice.[20] 'They died holding a rifle', as the same committee leader explained to me to make the distinction more graphic. In an answer to my question about where those who died fighting with the military would fit in this moral taxonomy, I was told categorically, 'in limbo'. According to committee members, those who died as a result of fighting with the army, army-controlled police forces, and death squads were not fighting for 'the right reasons' and are victims worthy of compassion but not honor. In

---

[20] Committee members, like liberation theologians, believed that the violence resulting from an insurrection does not necessarily clash with any of Christianity's teachings if the violence is inevitable and stems from a profound solidarity with the poor, that is, a public and unconditional testimony of love for the masses and a concomitant promotion of justice (see Sobrino 1984: 181).

segregating 'good victims' (martyrs and heroes) from those deemed unworthy of honor, the committee has maintained an implicit distinction between 'good' and 'bad' wartime violence. In this sense, committee members have maintained and reproduced the moral hierarchies and dichotomies of war. This is not surprising, since committee members are themselves relatives of the martyrs and heroes assassinated and abducted by the military, police officers, and members of paramilitary groups. Interestingly, however, committee members have asserted that 'all Salvadorans are war victims, even those who tortured or killed as members of the military'. This deployment of an all-embracing notion of victimhood contrasts with the committee's parallel differentiation of the entire category of Salvadorans who died as part of the military and paramilitary groups and are symbolically relegated to a 'limbo'.

A pertinent question, then, is what politics of victimhood the committee has promoted and what its implications are. On the one hand, in acknowledging war victims of both sides, committee members have underscored 'the ontological primacy of victimhood or suffering' (Jeffery and Candea 2006: 289). Although all committee members have aligned themselves with the Left, they declare that it is their aim to document all war violent episodes in La Paz, whether state-sponsored or perpetrated by guerrillas. Out of the 82 massacres they have investigated as of 2017 in which at least 2232 Salvadorans were killed, 9 of those massacres affecting 92 people were FMLN-perpetrated. In this sense, the committee's designation of victims has not discriminated on the basis of religious affiliation (e.g. priest /laypeople /ordinary people) or people's side during the war (e.g. military /rightwing mayor /trade-unionist /guerrilla). Victims, the committee has maintained, were not necessarily non-agentive or even non-violent during the war. As a committee member explained to me, young Salvadorans in their early teens were conscripted during the war, indoctrinated against the dangers of communism and the need to defend democracy, and trained to kill savagely. Yet, to committee members, those who fought with the army need to be distinguished from guerrillas who died fighting injustice and inequality, inspired by a notion of divine justice. Committee members thus make a distinction between the victims of the opposing sides of the war—partly a necessary result of the prospect of future accountability that would require a distinction between the juridical categories of 'victims' and 'perpetrators'.

On the other hand, the committee's foregrounding of 'martyrs' over all other victims speaks to the country's ongoing tensions between politics and victimhood (cf. Jeffery and Candea 2006). Committee members have suggested that there was indeed a non-agentive victim, one that did not resort to violence, 'the martyr'. On the one hand, this may have been a means to underline that the majority of war victims were civilians uninvolved in armed combat. On the other, within a persistently polarized context, their rhetorical foregrounding of the 'martyrs' as 'innocent victims' might have sought to render their demands on the state more persuasive, even as, in fact, committee members are relatives of both 'martyrs' and 'heroes' alike. By symbolically placing army combatants in limbo, committee members have implied that their memory work is concerned with a particular set of victims. It is the work of other organizations, such as those composed of veterans, to voice the interests of other kinds of victims. The moral vocabulary of martyrdom and victimhood, along with the standardized language of human rights learned through training sessions with professional NGOs, has been deployed with the ultimate aim of legitimizing moral and material reparation, which includes repositioning 'the honorable dead'. In the committee's formulation of victimhood, human rights are subordinated to the committee's own moral taxonomies rooted in a religious ethic. Even as they acknowledge the existence of victims on both sides of the war, not all victims are regarded as bearers of the right to truth, justice, and reparation on equal terms.

Despite a nominally all-encompassing notion of victimhood deeply rooted in Christian compassion, the committee leadership has practiced a politics of victimhood through the kind of differentiation that has typified other contexts characterized by a divided memory (see Ballinger 2004). Of course, the fact that the memory work conducted in this context is carried out mostly by relatives of war victims who lived through the war themselves may be a central reason that their work, and its attendant politics of victimhood, has differentiated between categories of victims. However, I surmise that this differentiation may also stem from the importance that the committee leadership has placed on the historical and structural dynamics that enabled the war and the fact that state-sponsored assassinations far outnumbered those by guerrillas. Even though they have professed a universal ethics against violence that considers the fratricidal war in the 1980s a futile event given its outcome, they have deemed the war inevitable in light of the prewar economic and political conjuncture. In this sense, they have decisively established victimhood as indissociable from politics. Yet, as I have noted earlier, it should be underlined that demanding accountability for wartime human rights violations necessarily entails drawing a distinction between the juridical categories of 'victims' and 'perpetrators'. While mostly concerned with reuniting with their loved ones and restoring their dignity, the committee has not discarded future investigations to identify and prosecute criminal responsibility. Committee members have been willing to locate victims on both sides of the war, yet their ultimate aim of future justice-as-accountability has led them to predicate their politics of victimhood upon a rather restrictive notion of who constitutes a victim and who, as a relative of the victim, is entitled to moral and material reparations.[21] Their notion of reconciliation has thus necessarily built upon differentiation rather than dissolving the differences rooted in the war.

The dilemma of how to deal with wartime human rights violations is one faced by many postconflict societies. The notion of 'reconciliation' that pervades political transitions to democracy tends to be predicated upon amnesty, national public silence, and lack of accountability (Grandin 2005). Reconciliation is generally equated with the attainment of future national unity through forgiveness, which usually amounts to impunity.[22] The South African Truth and Reconciliation Comission is perhaps the best example of a transition in which amnesty was not predicated upon public silence (Wilson 2001). Yet, in postapartheid South Africa, the amnesty granted to perpetrators of violence willing to offer their testimony in public hearings negated the possibility of both criminal and civil prosecution and in turn limited victims' prospects for material reparation (Wilson 2001: 23–25). It was assumed in the South African transition that the mere act of 'truth-telling' would lead naturally to forgiveness and reconciliation.

In El Salvador, the Commission on the Truth's report suggested that reconciliation amounts to 'a new relationship of solidarity, coexistence, and tolerance', one that would be predicated on 'the fraternal unity of the Salvadoran people' following a process in which perpetrators were prosecuted and victims compensated (United Nations 1993: 175). It thus propounded that restoration would follow the judicialization of wartime human rights violations, although reform of the judiciary was recom-

---

[21] In this regard, it is worth noting that in promoting criminal prosecution and public accountability, truth commissions impose their own kind of silence by building upon clear-cut categories of 'victims' and 'perpetrators' that obliterate the messiness of war (see Theidon 2008: 11–13).

[22] However, in some cases, such as Argentina and Chile, the demand for accountability could not be suppressed in the long term and, eventually, retribution through human rights trials was enforced (Sikkink and Walling 2007).

mended as a prior step. However, the findings and nominally binding recommendations produced by the commission were undermined. The reform of the country's judiciary remains incomplete, while the amnesty law forestalled both accountability and retributive justice. When a case was opened or the alleged victimizers convicted, either the judiciary hindered the process or the amnesty law served to dismiss the sentence (Collins 2010: 156–158, 173–175; see also Binford 2016: 138–153 for the El Mozote massacre). Perhaps more importantly, even though avenues existed to circumvent the amnesty in cases where crimes had violated constitutional rights, the hurdles to pursue them meant that accountability was not a priority for Salvadoran human rights organizations (Collins 2010: 183–186). For postwar pursuits of retribution and restoration, therefore, the language of religious morality has come to fill the vacuum left by the absence of legal processes. Even as professional NGOs performing memory work have increasingly adopted the language of human rights, grassroots organizations like the committee have subordinated human rights to their own moral taxonomies,which are defined by the hierarchies of the war and strongly influenced by progressive Christian theology.

In short, the 'memory work' conducted in postwar El Salvador by organizations consisting of relatives of war victims differs substantially from the 'politics of memory' practiced by ARENA during elections. While both have political and moral purposes and reveal the invocation of memory as a highly mediated act, the former is predicated upon a laborious process of documentation and analysis that entails exhumations and testimony, whereas the latter resorts exclusively to stereotypical depictions and rhetoric. Yet 'memory work' does something more than merely bring back the past; it also aims to reassess the past in order to orient action toward future change. In being effected in the present, memory-building processes operate through mechanisms that both 'actualize' the past and 'potentialize' a different future. The haunting wartime past is purposefully actualized, along with its inexorable transformation through time, with the ultimate aim of allowing it to settle and create the conditions of possibility for a future that builds upon the past yet diverges from this past insofar as it is based on retributive and restorative justice. Whereas in the 1970s it was the progressive wing of the Catholic Church that was the driving force behind work by rural Salvadorans aiming at qualitative social change and the catalyst of hope, in postwar El Salvador it is the marginal organizations leading memory work that have taken on this role, albeit still influenced by the reverberations of liberation theology.

The memory work by the Father Cosme Spessotto Committee in the second half of the 2000s is one example of how poor Salvadorans are experiencing and building citizenship in the postwar era. Their recent incorporation of a rights-based language notwithstanding, committee members have, for years, endeavored to define who is entitled to moral and material reparation by the state as well as to place claims on the state concerning their self-referential victimhood. The committee believes that a dead-body politics would serve to reassess the past and ultimately to mark change, as Verdery (1999: 19–20) has shown vis-à-vis the manipulation of bodies in postsocialist countries. The literal and figurative manipulation of bodies in postwar El Salvador has corresponded to an as-yet-marginal volition to qualitatively transform El Salvador's violent democracy by resignifying and remoralizing Salvadorans' relationship to time and space, especially those realms haunted by war ghosts. Memory work in El Salvador, based as it has been on a dead-body politics, is, in short, a means of making political statements that are not being made in the domain of party politics and that could not be so powerfully expressed by merely discursive means.

The work of the Father Cosme Spessotto Committee, performed with the aim of transforming the nation's psyche and political life, has put forth a politics of victimhood and a process of reconciliation predicated upon wartime cleavages and dichotomies rather than on their dissolution. Even if all Salvadorans were victims during the conflict, the committee has emphasized the need to distinguish between categories of victims in order to attain future reconciliation. From this vantage point, unity and reconciliation are necessarily premised on difference. In an ironic twist, as much as committee members are concerned with precluding the possibility of the resurrection of armed conflict or the resumption of past forms of extrajudicial violence, they have been unable to extend their scope of action to the human rights violations of the postwar era, violations of which many members have been themselves victims. Nor have organizations of victims of postwar violence emerged that would advance claim-making with regard to current predicaments.

CHAPTER 7

The 2009 Shift

On 16 March 2009, a day after the FMLN had been declared the victor in El Salvador's presidential election, Mauricio Funes addressed the massive audience of FMLN loyalists celebrating their party's victory in San Salvador with the following declaration: 'Ahora es el turno del ofendido, ahora es la oportunidad de los excluidos, ahora es la oportunidad de los marginados, ahora es la oportunidad de los auténticos demócratas' (Now it's the turn of the offended, now it's the opportunity of the excluded, now it's the opportunity of the marginalized, now it's the opportunity of the authentic democrats).[1] His paraphrasing of Salvadoran poet Roque Dalton (1962) was consistent with the rhetoric of change that had typified the FMLN 2009 electoral campaign. During the campaign, Funes and the FMLN had criticized the deepening of economic and public insecurity that had occurred during the 20 years of ARENA governments. Rather than proclaiming a transition to socialism or the reversal of ARENA's neoliberal agenda, Funes had promised a greater inclusiveness if the FMLN was victorious. Funes and the FMLN had presented themselves as *'el partido del pueblo'* [the party of the people] in direct opposition to the elitist governing party ARENA. In this sense, Funes's declaration the day after the election emphasized that the FMLN victory was more than the replacement of one party by another; the FMLN victory marked an opportunity for the inclusion of those who had been excluded by elitist governments, both

---

[1] 'Funes: "llegó el turno del ofendido,"' *Faro de Vigo*, 16 March 2009.

© The Author(s) 2018
A. Montoya, *The Violence of Democracy*, Studies of the Americas,
https://doi.org/10.1007/978-3-319-76330-9_7

historically and during ARENA rule. It is in this context of proclaimed regime shift, characterized by the promise of change and hope that accompanied the FMLN victory, that I explore ordinary Salvadorans' citizenship practices.

Aside from the marginal work by the Father Cosme Spessotto Committee and other grassroots movements, the attitudes toward the state that I have most often encountered among Salvadorans include distrust, fear, an unwillingness to report human rights violations, and defeatism in the event of ill-treatment by state actors (see Chaps. 3 and 4). All these attitudes amount to an avoidance of engagement with the state. However, given that 'civil society' exists empirically as an independent entity and denotes instead deeply imbricated domains and practices, I surmise that the seeming disengagement of Salvadorans is actually the effect of a complex series of relationships. In this chapter, I thus draw connections between citizenship and transformations of the state in postwar El Salvador. I begin by asking how the 2009 party shift impacted citizenship. This leads me to the further question of why, given their consistent distrust and fear of the state, ordinary people simultaneously request that they be cared for by the state. In answering these questions, I seek to understand how poor Salvadorans who do not participate in grassroots movements experience, craft, and practice citizenship in the postwar era.

In his seminal essay, Marshall (1992) defined 'citizenship' as a legal status that endows members of society—territorially equated with the nation-state—with a set of civil, political, and social rights and duties. Recent ethnographic research has, however, moved away from this normative definition and underscored instead the processual nature of citizenship. Rather than being an end point, the condition of 'citizenship' is constantly being remade through people's practices and experiences vis-à-vis the state (Sassen 2003; Holston 2008; Lazar 2008). Along similar lines, I aim to animate the otherwise dead and abstract category of 'citizenship' (Berlant 2009: 292) by exploring how feelings of fear, distrust, and disillusionment pervade and impact state-citizenry relationships. This entails a concomitant exploration of how Salvadorans imagine the state. I argue that El Salvador's poor craft their own exclusions/inclusions vis-à-vis the state in addition to those exclusions to which they are automatically subjected. Paradoxically, the poor have high expectations of the state even as they avoid engagement with certain state institutions and actors. I thus aim to show how citizenship is not only an unfinished condition, but also one that is highly contradictory in nature. In El Salvador, the contradictions of citizenship are predicated on seemingly antithetical and irreconcilable notions of, or ways of imagining, the state that in turn spark both a fear of and longing for the state. The conditions of citizenship and stateness, I suggest, have to be studied as one and the same process of crafting. Doing so allows for an understanding of the ways in which post-war citizenship practices have contributed to advancing neoliberalization in El Salvador.

I examine these issues through glimpses of Santiagueñas' encounters with the state, as well as through their rumors and conversations about the state, which are akin to those I observed among Salvadorans from other municipalities. Recently, the primacy of the nation-state as a domain that circumscribes citizenship has been questioned. Gordon and Stack (2007: 120) have argued that while appropriating citizenship is a state project, the state may not be successful at it. Instead, citizenship has been studied as the condition and practices of those inhabiting the city, the latter understood as a site of connection and intersection of differently scaled phenomena (see Sassen 2003; Holston 2008). Yet, while citizenship is irreducible to a relationship to the state, I surmise that the relationship to the state is nevertheless an important component of citizenship—even if by omission or elusion. In light of Santiagueños' and other Salvadorans' sudden engagement with the state immediately after the 2009 party shift, this chapter examines practices of citizenship that involved an investment of affect in the national government and its institutions.[2]

The Turn of the Offended

One Sunday morning before the 2009 presidential election, a 60-year-old man entered the FMLN headquarters in Santiago, which were temporarily located on the central Avenida Anastasio Aquino. Both headquarters and avenue were noisy and crammed with people, as Sunday is the main market day, and central Santiago attracts a multitude from rural areas as well as neighboring municipalities. The 60-year-old man timorously approached

---

[2] A full understanding of citizenship, however, should consider its multiscaled nature and explore the distribution of affect in loci other than the nation-state, such as El Salvador's relations with the United States and transnational processes of various kinds. Indeed, critics of 'methodological nationalism'—the assumption, pervasive in social analysis, that the state is a natural entity—have underlined its rootedness in specific Western processes of state formation (see Wimmer and Glick Schiller 2002).

a local FMLN member, who was seated behind a desk and wearing the party's official red T-shirt, and explained in a soft voice that he would like to find his brother, of whom he had had no knowledge since the war. The 60-year-old man was referred to Marcos, a middle-aged Santiagueño and member of the Father Cosme Spessotto Committee, who had come to the FMLN headquarters to help print red T-shirts with the white FMLN logo for the campaign. The two men sat down together in a corner of the head-quarters, and both agreed to let me join them. The 60-year-old explained to the committee member that his brother had been conscripted into the armed forces at the beginning of the war and then disappeared. He hoped to learn his brother's whereabouts, whether he had died, and, if so, where his remains might be. They made an appointment for a week later, at which point the 60-year-old man would bring in all the information he could about his brother, including a photograph, and the committee member would conduct a formal interview. The FMLN member asked the man for his name, but he refused to provide it—a predictable response given Salvadorans' persistent fear of discussing war-related issues in public, especially in rural areas. The man never returned. However, once the FMLN had won the March 2009 presidential election, a number of similar requests were channeled through the FMLN in Santiago and ultimately referred to the Father Cosme Spessotto Committee.

Don Antonio's search for a brother of his is an instance of how Santiagueños initiated a search for their relatives after the FMLN victory. After the FMLN had taken office in June 2009, 50-year-old Don Antonio spoke to several FMLN members, with whom he had campaigned during the electoral season, about his interest in finding out what had happened to his youngest brother during the war. Marcos, the same Father Cosme Spessotto Committee member who had met with the 60-year-old man, arranged to meet with Don Antonio at his house to collect the details of his brother's disappearance. Curious as to why Don Antonio and others like him would begin searching for their relatives at this point in time, I accompanied Marcos. Don Antonio had never before related details of his brother's disappearance to anyone outside the family, so he nervously ram-bled on about the war before talking about his own brother. First he told us the story of a second brother who had lived in a Zacatecoluca *cantón* and was killed there in 1989. This brother, originally a participant in the ORDEN death squad, had informed the army about any guerrilla activity occurring in the Cantón El Recuerdo where he lived. After the guerrillas took hold of the Hacienda El Nilo, where he worked, and found his

ORDEN identification card, they gave him the option to defect and join the guerrilla forces. He did so, and began sleeping in the mountainous areas of Zacatecoluca after the army came to his house in search of him. He then fled to Guatemala to avoid persecution; unhappy there, he decided to return home a few months later. Fifteen days after his return, Don Antonio lamented, his brother was killed by the army at his own home.

Don Antonio then told us about his youngest brother, the one about whom he was seeking information. His youngest brother had from the beginning willingly joined the FPL guerrilla organization. He was studying in Zacatecoluca, or so the family believed; actually he had been an FPL member since he was 15. The last time Don Antonio saw his brother was before the last guerrilla occupation of the Zacatecoluca Cathedral, in which his brother took part. As Don Antonio was told by a mutual acquaintance, his brother later fought on the slopes of the Apopa Volcano, located in the San Salvador Department. A month before the 1989 guerrilla offensive in San Salvador was the last time he was seen. The family stopped receiving news about him after this point and assumed he was dead. However, years later, the family learned through one of his guerrilla colleagues that 'El Caballo' (his war pseudonym) was still alive. With his arms and legs mutilated, he did not want to return to his family, and by the war's end he had requested exile in Australia, where he presumably still lived. Don Antonio recounted a conversation with Father David, an FMLN departmental representative in parliament, in which Father David declared that it was time to begin asking questions about the abducted and the dead, now that the FMLN was taking office. It was then that Don Antonio decided to begin the search for his youngest brother.

The initiatives of Don Antonio and others like him led me to enquire how the FMLN victory in the 2009 March presidential election, an event widely characterized as 'historic', impacted practices of citizenship and the extent to which the victory acted as a catalyst for hope. In addition to several personal initiatives by Santiagueños to find out about relatives who had gone missing during the war, the FMLN victory triggered reports of police extortion and of corruption and nepotism within state institutions such as schools and hospitals, as described in Chap. 3. This was striking given the generalized underreporting of both wartime and postwar crimes and the avoidance of state institutions described so far. As I have shown in earlier chapters, the Salvadoran state is largely understood to be defined along party lines—an effect of the level of state capture performed by

ARENA through peacebuilding and 20 years of rule (cf. Wade 2016). It thus makes sense to ask how the party shift that brought the FMLN to power may have influenced the ways in which Santiagueñas perceive and relate to the state. More specifically, I ask what led people like Don Antonio to initiate engagements with the new governing party soon after the 2009 election. Those eager attempts to effect change or resolve haunting wartime problems seem to suggest the emergence of new horizons of hope in a postwar context where citizenship had been heretofore characterized chiefly by survival and adaptation. The question, then, is whether the country's party shift changed disaffected Salvadorans' aspirations and their imagination of possible futures. Answers, I suggest, revolve around the transient nature of citizens' attempts at transformation and their channeling of these attempts through a political party, in this case the FMLN, rather than state institutions.

The Persistence of Economic and Public Insecurity

Marta sat at her dining table clutching a wad of worn, sweaty dollars and surveying the bills from the water company that lay strewn across the table top. She had been saving, she explained to me, to pay the more than US$200 she owed the water company for a second plot of land she owned. Although the house built on that plot had collapsed in the 2001 earthquakes and the family, unable to rebuild, no longer consumed water there, monthly water bills had been arriving since early 2010, each amounting to more than US$100. Marta—a woman then in her 70s who lacked a state pension and was piecing together an income from the informal sale of homemade meals, bread, and pastries as well as occasionally clothes—had been unable to pay the bills. Her failure to pay one bill in particular in early 2010 led the Intercommunal Administrator of Los Nonualcos and Masahuat Drinkable Water and Sewage Systems (AISAPANM), the private company that administered the local water system back then, to add monthly interest arrears to the bill, which by this point exceeded US$200. The same problem had occurred with the water bills for the house in which I lived with Marta's family. Until the beginning of 2008, the monthly water bills for each of the family houses had amounted to a mere US$4.56. In April 2009, the water bills suddenly increased to about US$30. Then, in March 2010, the bills increased once again, this time verging on US$100. While Marta and the remaining adult members of the family living in the house managed to keep up with the payment of the bills for the main house, they were unable to do the same with the water bills for the other property. Marta had complained to company employees about the high bills for water the family had not even consumed, but her complaints had been ignored. Although she had requested that the company turn off the service for the abandoned plot, no one from AISAPANM ever arrived to do so. By the end of 2010, Marta decided to save up enough money to pay a bill that would otherwise have kept escalating. This was not an isolated case in Santiago; the leftwing newspaper *Diario Colatino* reported that, according to Santiagueñas' complaints, water bills had undergone a 700 percent increase from January to March 2010.[3] The populations of the neighboring municipalities experienced the same problem.[4]

In 2007, water distribution and the administration of water systems had been privatized in Santiago, as had gradually occurred throughout the country. While the National Administration of Aqueducts and Drains (ANDA)—the state company that until 2007 had administered water systems and distributed water throughout the country—remained a public institution, local administration of water systems had been 'decentralized', that is, delegated to municipal administrations that subsequently outsourced it to private companies that differed from one region to another.[5] AISAPANM was the company distributing water in Santiago and its neighboring municipalities at the time I was doing research. This company outsourced the reading of meters and issuing of bills to SERVINTA. Contrary to other regions where the population had protested against water privatization from the start, Santiagueños did not initially perceive a change aside from the fact that the bills were now being issued under the name of

---

[3] 'Santiagueños preocupados por excesivos cobros de agua potable', *Diario Colatino*, 17 March 2010.

[4] 'Cobros excesivos por el agua potable', *La Prensa Gráfica*, 31 May 2010.

[5] The *Política Nacional de Descentralización* (National Policy of Decentralization) was approved in 2007 by Saca's ARENA government, although the decentralization of water services had already begun in 1998 with a loan contract between ANDA and the IDB (FUNDE 2009: 54). Claims citing the inefficiency and underfunding of ANDA water systems as well as the country's low tariffs for water use were raised to legitimize the strategy of 'decentralization' of the management of the country's water resources (see PNUD 2006: 14–15; Dimas 2007). Although technically water administration had been 'delegated', this was indeed a covert form of privatization (via outsourcing) where municipality councils could not administer it themselves. Meanwhile, El Salvador's drinkable water coverage has been one of the lowest in Latin America, covering only 58 percent of the population in 2004 (PNUD 2006: 12).

AISAPANM. In 2008, major work was undertaken by AISAPANM to replace the old water pipes and meters of Santiago's *barrios*. It was in April 2009, shortly after the work had been completed, that bills registered a dramatic rise of approximately US$25 per month. By mid-2010, many dwellings' water bills were exceeding US$100, thus surpassing the country's monthly minimum wage in the realm of agriculture, in which many Santiagueños were employed.[6] Like Marta, many Santiagueños began to leave their bills unpaid. Interest arrears were added to unpaid bills, such that Santiagueños were receiving monthly bills ranging between US$200 and US$500 by the end of 2010. This occurred without a concomitant amelioration of water quality or a lifting of restrictions limiting water supply from late in the evening until 8 am or even to two days a week, depending on the season.

Given that in some areas of Santiago water is supplied by community water systems independent of ANDA, people were knowledgeable enough about water systems to venture an explanation for the vast increase in the municipality's water bills. They suggested that the new pipes installed by AISAPANM had been left with so much pressure that the meters were moving even when water was not running. When Santiagueños began complaining about the situation to the AISAPANM office in the municipality El Rosario, the company's employees settled the claims by insisting that bills were based on what the meters had registered. Neither Santiagueñas nor the consumer protection associations to which they resorted were able to take their complaints any further up in the AISAPANM administration. The majority of their complaints were voiced not just against the company AISAPANM but against the Salvadoran state, which had left Santiagueños feeling unprotected. The Peace Accords had failed to address their economic predicaments, and now the postwar governments were only exacerbating them.[7] As already explained in previous chapters, given El Salvador's long history of economic insecurity and inequality, poor Salvadorans have tended to imagine the state as an independent and self-interested group of people—'the fourteen families', as the Salvadoran elite is popularly described. In a similar vein, the

---

[6] El Salvador's official minimum wage is dependent on the economic sector. Someone working in the agricultural sector, the main source of employment in Santiago, would have earned US$3.24 per day in 2009 and 2010. See Decreto Ejecutivo No. 133, *Diario Oficial*, 19 December 2008.

[7] This was especially the case in the country's rural areas after the collapse of the rural economy in the 1990s (Segovia 2002: 256).

privatizations of the postwar era are understood by poor Salvadorans as yet another means by which the country's elite has furthered its own interests.

Crucially, while the privatization of El Salvador's water administration had been undertaken by an ARENA government, the escalation of bills in Santiago began after the FMLN victory in the 2009 presidential election, with amounts verging on US$100 during the second year of FMLN rule. The FMLN government thus proved to be engaging in a mere continuation of the ARENA governments' economic policies, with the persistence of the privatization and deregulation of public utilities like water being only one case in point. It is true that the FMLN government has, from the moment it took office in June 2009, implemented welfare programs targeting the poor, such as the *Programa de Apoyo al Plan de Agricultura Familiar* (Family Agriculture Plan Support Program, PAAF) which offers technical and financial support to the agricultural sector; expanded access to primary healthcare in both urban and rural areas through the newly created *Equipos Comunitarios de Salud* (Health Community Teams, ECOS); the distribution of uniforms, shoes, supplies, and food at public schools in order to increase attendance; and, in municipalities suffering from poverty and extreme poverty, the introduction of a basic universal, non-contributory monthly pension of US$50 for Salvadorans aged over 70 who have no other income (see Perla and Cruz-Feliciano 2013). These programs were particularly appreciated in rural areas like Santiago's *cantones* where poverty has concentrated in the postwar era and where the population subsists largely on agriculture and many families had stopped sending their children to school to avoid the associated costs.

Admittedly, the first FMLN government did not veer away from the country's previous macroeconomic policy but instead maneuvered within its margins. Funes had, after all, declared during the presidential campaign that, were he victorious, his government would not reverse the unpopular policy of dollarization, withdraw from trade agreements, default on external debt obligations, or renationalize specific economic sectors. This was not just an attempt to calm fears disseminated by ARENA in the run-up to the election, suggesting that an FMLN government would negatively affect the country's economy and discourage foreign investment; it was also a steadfast declaration, and implicit gesture to members of the business community who had supported his candidacy, that a Funes-led administration would not seek to transform the essence of previous economic policies or undermine the foreign and national interests that had benefited most from those policies. Nor did his reforms introducing progressive taxation achieve higher levels of tax revenues or redistribution, partly because of the recession affecting El Salvador when Funes took office (Menkos 2013). In maintaining neoliberal policies and simultaneously developing a piecemeal and social policy targeting the poor, the FMLN government was mimicking Lula's Brazilian government, for which Funes had publicly expressed admiration during the campaign.[8] While not even leftwing Santiagueñas expected the FMLN government to undertake radical economic measures such as reversing dollarization, they had nevertheless expected the new government's social policies to be broader in scope and more immediate and profound in their impact.

The postwar Salvadoran state has widely been considered uncaring not just due to increasing economic insecurity but also due to the persistence of public insecurity, which many ordinary Salvadorans believe in turn stems from state corruption and impunity. This way of imagining the state did not significantly change with the 2009 party shift. During my one-month visit to Santiago in December 2010, Santiagueñas from different areas of the municipality told me of recent robberies and ongoing extortion. Even after the FMLN victory, Santiagueñas have tended to avoid engagement with police officers, given their frequent appearance in rumors and stories of violence and impunity. Part of my motivation for returning to El Salvador in December 2010 was to continue my research collaboration with the Father Cosme Spessotto Committee on Las Ánimas residents' wartime experiences. It was through interviews with residents of Las Ánimas that I learned about the violent episodes that had recently occurred in the area.

In one of these interviews, a female ex-guerrilla combatant who was recounting her family's wartime experiences switched abruptly to an account of the recent robberies to which a number of Las Ánimas residents had been subject in the second half of 2010. Several families, she explained, had been assaulted at night by a few men who had arrived at their homes shortly before midnight. Identifying themselves as police officers, carrying badges and weapons, and dressed in uniforms, they barged

---

[8] Indeed, Latin American governments who self-recognized as Center-Left or Left, the so-called Pink Tide governments, have shied away from structural transformations. Instead they were only able to expand their country's poverty alleviation programs via massive revenues from extractive industries, at least until the slowdown of China's economy from 2012 (Webber 2017).

into the house as soon as the door was opened. They threatened and beat up residents to obtain everything that was valuable. These robberies had occurred on a monthly basis since June 2010. Other Las Ánimas residents with whom I spoke confirmed having suffered them. Most of the assaulted families opted not to report the episodes. Involving as they did police elements such as uniforms and badges, the episodes left such an imprint on Las Ánimas residents that they had come to distrust the police. They feared that police might be complicit in the robberies or that those responsible might learn about their reports through corrupt police officers and retaliate. They also remarked that, unless explicitly called, police rarely came to Las Ánimas due to its remoteness from central Santiago. Even when summoned, they took a long time to arrive and were often unhelpful. The female ex-guerrilla's shift from wartime to postwar violence in mid-conversation suggests that the image of abusive police barging into a house at night revived haunting memories of wartime police repression and harassment. The robbery episodes epitomize how past and present, licit and illicit have comingled and conjured a gray zone of politics in postwar El Salvador.

In the postwar era, the state has increasingly gained a phantasmatic quality through episodes of organized crime and homicidal violence involving state actors. One of the episodes widely discussed at the end of 2010 was Spanish-French journalist Christian Poveda's assassination in September 2009. The circumstances of his assassination, allegedly by the gang members featured in his documentary film *La Vida Loca*, were interpreted by Santiagueños and the country's media as highly obscure.[9] A Zacatecoluca-based priest supportive of Funes—albeit not the FMLN—suggested in a conversation with me that Poveda was assassinated because he was about to film a documentary on the country's state-drug trafficking connection. Other explanations by Salvadorans for this and other violent episodes occurring after the FMLN had taken office likewise hinted at the grayness of El Salvador's political life and the existence of backstage links that might apply to actors in the FMLN as well as ARENA. During my fieldwork in 2008 and 2009, poor Salvadorans had consistently made references to ARENA politicians' involvement in election fraud, outsourcing of homicides through gangs, active suppression of leftwing activism, and profiting from privatizations (as in the case of the private security

---

[9] See 'En el aire los motivos de la muerte de Christian Poveda', *ContraPunto*, 10 March 2011.

industry). While rumors of state corruption and involvement in organized crime were commonplace, drug trafficking was not a particularly salient topic of conversation until I returned to El Salvador at the end of 2010. In numerous conversations with Salvadorans across the political spectrum, I noted that linkages between drug trafficking and the state had now become a significant explanation for some of El Salvador's postwar ills.[10] Given the persistence of economic and public insecurity throughout FMLN government's first year, the question arose as to whether there had been a sustained shift in citizenship practices along the lines of what seemed to occur immediately after the FMLN victory.

An Uncaring State

In El Salvador, ordinary people have historically othered the state as a result of the concentration of power in the hands of the elite and the military. As described in the Introduction, since 1931, and throughout most of the twentieth century, the Salvadoran state consisted of an enduring alliance between the military governments and the economic elite that permitted the maintenance of political power by the former and economic accumulation by the latter (Stanley 1996; Wade 2016). The cohesiveness of Salvadorans' notion of the state can thus be attributed to the concentration of economic capital, along with the effective means of violence, in the hands of a small elite.[11] During the 2009 municipal and legislative elections, FMLN leaders visiting the rural and urban areas of Santiago alluded in their speeches to the historical accumulation by the elite. Father David, a former priest who fought with the FPL, and Gerson Martínez, a former FPL commander, occasionally joined FMLN rallies since both were running as FMLN members of parliament representing La Paz. Their speeches

---

[10] This may be related to the Funes government's increasing recognition of El Salvador's state institutions' involvement in drug trafficking. An example of this was Funes's explicit reference to the corruption within the PNC during the 64th UN General Assembly in September 2009 (Meléndez Reyes 2016: 82).

[11] Bourdieu (1999: 57) suggests that 'the state is the culmination of a process of concentration of different species of capital: capital of physical force or instruments of coercion (army, police), economic capital, cultural or (better) informational capital, and symbolic capital'. However, I would suggest that in El Salvador, concentration of economic capital by the elite and securing its reproduction over time has historically motivated the concentration of other kinds of capital, notably a monopoly on the effective means of violence through an alliance with the military.

consistently revolved around the need for 'the change' epitomized by the FMLN, given that the ARENA governments had succeeded in consolidating a century-old elite only by exacerbating deprivation among the rest of the population. References to the country's elite as 'the fourteen families' were never absent. In this sense, the state has been othered not just as a result of practices of concentration but also as an effect of representation.

While the term 'the state' is absent from Santiagueñas' everyday vocabulary, they allude to stateness through a range of terms. The vocabulary of stateness deployed by Salvadorans attests to the imagining of the state as independent from the poor masses. The popular currency of 'the fourteen families' metaphor, along with terms like 'the oligarchy' and 'the elite', reinforces and reflects Santiagueños' imaginary of the state as the instrument of a small portion of the population. The 'fourteen families' metaphor, I observed, was used not just in formal political discourse but was also deployed by the poor across the political spectrum to express their disillusionment with the Peace Accords and to point to the source of their economic woes. This vocabulary of stateness has been mobilized largely by Marxist–Leninist analyses—popularized among the rural poor during the 1970s through political schools led by the PCS and political-military organizations or, especially in rural areas, through the progressive readings of the Bible and political conjuncture of the CEBs—that conceived of the state as an instrument by which the elite wields power.

Santiagueños' references to the state are not abstract; the state has been endowed with material substance through either personification or identification with the elite political party. From his election in 2004 until 2009, ARENA President Elías Antonio Saca was blamed by leftwing and disaffected Santiagueños for all the country's economic ills. So was ARENA, even though members of other parties also had seats in the parliament. Indeed, notorious corruption by, for instance, state institutions of order was ultimately blamed by left-leaning and disaffected Santiagueñas on ARENA. The strong identification between the state and the governing party was partly based on the implicit idea, especially among left-leaning Salvadorans, that ARENA has deployed state institutions to serve its own economic and political interests. In light of this, neoliberal policies with a strong impact on ordinary people—such as the privatization of several sectors, including public utilities, and dollarization—have, as noted earlier, been interpreted as a means by which the elite has consolidated power rather than as an economic measure undertaken for the common good. An acquaintance of mine summed up a widespread public sentiment from the late 2000s when he suggested: 'The dollarization was only for the benefit of the elites, like everything else ARENA has done'.

Interestingly, the personification of the state apparatus, and its identification with the governing party, has played out differently since the shift that brought the FMLN to power. While Funes became the new face of the government after the FMLN took office in June 2009, I observed by the end of 2010 that the identification of the state with the FMLN had become much more complex. At this point, Santiagueños, including those on the Left, were grumbling constantly about Funes's and the FMLN's inability to change anything and the worsening of public and economic insecurity. While some suggested that the FMLN had become an elite and thus behaved no differently than ARENA, others suggested that ARENA was so deeply entrenched in state institutions due to patronage-based recruitment and backstage power that Funes and the FMLN had been unable to accomplish anything. Many Santiagueños implied with their comments that the Salvadoran postwar state is captive to ARENA to such an extent that a party shift could not by itself trigger any substantial transformation. The implicit suggestion was that the country's problems of economic and public insecurity had no easy and short-term solution. This is a sentiment that has endured, especially after cases of corruption by both ARENA and the FMLN were reported in the following years.[12]

Against a background of persistent economic and public insecurity, and despite the party shift enabled by the 2009 presidential election, Santiagueñas have continued to regard the state as fundamentally uncaring. Despite the initial postelection euphoria that led so many Santiagueñas to attempt to resolve their most pressing problems, citizenship practices had not varied substantially a year after the election. Santiagueñas continued to circumvent state institutions insofar as possible and to resolve their problems privately. With regard to public insecurity, a large number of poor Salvadorans continued to assume that

---

[12] The last three former presidents, Francisco Flores, Tony Saca, and Mauricio Funes, have been accused of corruption, illicit enrichment, and money laundering. Francisco Flores died before the end of his trial, Tony Saca was imprisoned, and Mauricio Funes sought asylum in Nicaragua. See 'Muere Francisco Flores, el expresidente de El Salvador en el centro del escándalo por una millonaria donación taiwanesa', *BBC*, 31 January 2016; 'Tony Saca, el segundo expresidente a juicio por enriquecimiento ilícito', *El Faro*, 23 February 2016; 'Nicaragua da asilo político al expresidente Funes, investigado por cinco delitos de corrupción', *El Faro*, 6 September 2016.

reporting to or engaging with the institutions of order was not an option. As noted in Chap. 4, the majority opted to transform their routines and, if they could afford it, relocate their homes. The imagined—yet practically meaningful—gulf between the state and the citizenry resulting from the latter's exclusion on the basis of economic insecurity was thus reinforced by Santiagueños' active disengagement from the state. In other words, many Santiagueños not only perceived the state as uncaring, but eschewed engagement with state institutions because of the perceived corruption and involvement of state actors in 'shadow networks of power' (Gledhill 1999) pervaded by violence. This view of the state persisted a year after the 2009 election, perhaps because of the country's ongoing economic insecurity—exemplified in this chapter by the lack of regulation and state intervention in the provision of and excessive charge for water to Santiagueñas—and the persistence of a popular perception that state institutions of order might themselves be part of the problem of public insecurity. Ordinary people's everyday experiences and practices have thus contributed to engendering and reproducing the state as an independent entity.

Yet the state is inescapable. Salvadorans interact with an ensemble of state institutions and state actors in their everyday lives through quotidian practices, operations, and encounters, such as the renewal of their identity cards or the attendance of their children at local public schools. Salvadorans do not generally reflect upon these everyday encounters with the state unless they represent a source of fear, abandonment, or dissatisfaction. Instances in which everyday state-citizenry encounters are reflected upon include corruption, sectarian redistribution of public resources, and inadequate state investment in services such as public healthcare or education. Interestingly, while people have not engaged with certain branches of the state, most notably its institutions of order, they have invoked the rhetoric of citizens' rights, critiqued the state's uncaring attitude, and, more recently, participated in postwar electoral campaigns. Indeed, not only is the state inescapable for Salvadorans, but the idea of the state is at times longed for. I thus suggest that Salvadorans do not fully avoid the state but only circumvent certain state institutions and actors. In the face of economic and public insecurity, the practice of clientelism has gained salience as a means by which to engage with the state.

ENGAGING THE STATE

One Wednesday morning in October 2008, when the electoral campaign that would bring Funes and the FMLN into office had not yet officially begun, the ARENA headquarters were packed with old men and women from the *cantones*—even though there was no party meeting underway. As I went in, I realized why. In the middle of the headquarters, piled high, were hundreds of two-pound bags of beans. The crowd of men and women from the *cantones* awaited their turn to receive them. A few disoriented men and women in peasant garb were informed by an ARENA leader about the procedure for obtaining the beans. 'You need to have signed up as a member of ARENA and then be shortlisted by a leader in your community. You can sign in now to be eligible for the next distribution', the ARENA leader explained. Some of the men and women queued to join the party. Shortly thereafter, the same ARENA leader called out the names of those who were on the list to receive the bags of beans. While I myself did not witness any other comparable distribution, I heard constant talk during the 2008 and 2009 campaign of ARENA's regular distribution of primary need goods. Beans, seeds, fertilizer, corn, and other goods, ranging from soap to shoes, were often distributed by municipal ARENA leaders among people who had agreed to formally join this party, many of them impoverished Santiagueños from the *cantones*. Indeed, some Santiagueños enthusiastically awaited electoral campaigns, keenly aware that these were a source of informal employment and concessions by political parties for a number of months. Until 2009, the then-ruling ARENA party was the one most able to deploy resources nationwide, though the PCN and PDC have emulated these practices when the municipal or regional candidate was a wealthy person willing to invest in the electoral campaign or had access to public resources.

During the 2009 electoral campaign, which unofficially commenced in 2007, a high number of Santiagueñas were informally employed by ARENA and placed on a weekly 'pay-roll' to advocate for this party in their *barrio* or *cantón*, to work as a secretary, to inform ARENA leaders about other parties' electoral strategies, or to run as a candidate for the municipal council. Apart from those enrolled by ARENA, a number of Santiagueños also advocated for this party in exchange for specific concessions or promises. Men frequently arrived at the ARENA headquarters to request that a municipal candidate sponsor the football team in their *cantón* with, for instance, a contribution of uniforms. Women would also visit the party headquarters, requesting a job for a son or a daughter or expounding their housing needs. Some of these requests were satisfied; others remained as promises to be fulfilled should ARENA win the election. This was the case for María, a young single mother who volunteered on behalf of ARENA by attending to logistics at Santiago's polling station on election day in March 2009. After the FMLN victory had been confirmed, she looked greatly disheartened while tidying up the high school that had served as a polling station. In a conversation with me, she lamented that the promise of a house for her and her daughter by the local ARENA leader had been contingent on ARENA's ability to retain the presidency. It has indeed been a common practice to channel job, housing, and other such requests through political parties rather than state institutions, especially during elections.

Patronage-based alliances, whether based on clientelist or other bonds, already existed in El Salvador's electoral politics during the nineteenth and early twentieth century as means through which to influence electoral outcomes (Ching 2014). In contemporary El Salvador, clientelism is not unique to electoral periods. Nor is it unique to rightwing political parties. It is a deeply established vehicle and network of state-citizenry relationships. While I have no evidence that patron–client relationships developed within Santiago's wing of the FMLN to the same degree that they were evident in ARENA, I surmise that this was due in part to the local FMLN's limited resources, at least comparatively, throughout the 2009 electoral campaign. There were nonetheless instances, both during and after the campaign, in which FMLN clientelistic practices surfaced, either as a party strategy or as recourse for specific local leaders. This was partly due to resources received from the Cuban and Venezuelan governments. For a number of years, the FMLN has operated a program of fully funded university grants that have allowed Salvadoran youth to pursue an undergraduate medical degree in Cuba. The program *Misión Milagro* (Miracle Mission) likewise has offered needy Salvadorans all-expenses-paid trips to Cuba and Venezuela to receive eye surgery for their cataracts. The benefits of these two programs were largely advertised during the 2009 electoral season. During the months preceding the election, the FMLN hired party loyalists for a program called *Fábrica de Empleos* (Jobs' Factory); those hired for a few months conducted door-to-door surveys regarding people's work status. Not only did this program provide temporary jobs to unemployed FMLN loyalists, but it also sparked employment expectations among those surveyed. Job concessions, which have been an FMLN practice both in and outside of electoral periods, have allowed a number of FMLN loyalists in Santiago to obtain permanent jobs as public health promoters. After elections, many FMLN loyalists from Santiago who had actively participated in the party's campaign paid visits to Father David, elected deputy for La Paz in January 2009, who willingly wrote reference letters and helped with networking so that they could obtain at least temporary jobs.

An example illustrative of the commensurability of ARENA and FMLN clientelistic practices concerns the distribution of agricultural consumables like seeds and fertilizer among Santiago's peasant population. In 2006, the ARENA government implemented the *Semilla Mejorada* (Improved Seed) program, dedicated to alleviating the debts incurred in acquiring consumables by small-scale peasants practicing subsistence agriculture. Although theoretically a public program targeting small-scale peasants at large, the distribution of seeds and fertilizers turned into a local patronage practice. As admitted by several ARENA loyalists, consumables were distributed among the population by local ARENA party leaders rather than state institutions. ARENA's municipal candidate in Santiago boasted about having managed to negotiate with his party to allow a number of Santiagueños to benefit from the *Semilla Mejorada* program. What he did not mention was that the seeds and fertilizer were given only to ARENA loyalists, thus serving as a means of both attracting and rewarding political constituents to his 2009 campaign.

While such practices were criticized by many FMLN leaders, both nationally and at the municipal level, they were also mimicked by leaders of this party right after the new government took office. In Santiago, in compiling lists of small-scale peasants who would potentially benefit from the *Semilla Mejorada* program, the local FMLN leadership discriminated against ARENA and other rightwing parties' loyalists as well as voices internal to the FMLN that were critical of their own party's resort to partisan practices. Indeed, depending on the sector of Santiago, seeds were distributed among FMLN loyalists who did not cultivate the land at all, sold among the population instead of distributed, or retained by a handful of FMLN loyalists. Delivery of agricultural consumables through the FMLN instead of state institutions occurred nationwide, judging from accounts by FMLN members who received the seeds and fertilizer in other departments. Explicitly as well as implicitly, FMLN loyalists suggested that, after their party's success in the presidential election, it was now 'their turn' to engage in, and benefit from, the programs from which they had hitherto been excluded on the basis of their party allegiance. In this sense, Funes's assertion—paraphrasing Salvadoran poet Roque Dalton—that his government would represent 'the turn of the offended' turned out to express a generalized sentiment of entitlement among a large segment of FMLN loyalists.

As I have suggested earlier, clientelistic and partisan practices are not unique to electoral periods; they also work as a rather efficient and personalized form of everyday interaction for a range of purposes. I have frequently seen Santiagueñas turn to acquaintances to be released from a payment for a medical test, to obtain a timely appointment with the doctor, or simply to receive personalized and quality treatment for a health problem. Political parties and networks of relatives and acquaintances have proven their ability to allocate resources and resolve citizens' problems in a more efficient manner than state institutions. The magnitude of these clientelistic practices is such that Santiagueñas often say that the ability to access certain resources, services, and jobs is only the result of *tener cuello* (having connections, literally 'having neck'). Political parties and personal networks have also been deemed a safer channel for dealing with problems of public security than state institutions of order. Indeed, as I will describe in the next section, a report of a case of police extortion that Santiagueños made soon after the FMLN took office was channeled through acquaintances in the FMLN rather than through the institutions of order.

Clientelism has often been treated as premodern, anti-democratic, and dysfunctional (for critiques of this view, see Gupta 1995; Auyero 2000; Gledhill 2004a; Lazar 2008: 21). Lazar (2008: 116), however, has made a case for the contrary. She argues that in Bolivia's local electoral politics of the late 1990s, participation in electoral campaigns in exchange for jobs practically worked as if ordinary Bolivians stood for election themselves, where clientelism could be regarded as constituting an efficient form of representative democracy rather than an anomaly. In other words, far from undermining liberal precepts of citizenship, Lazar argues, clientelism may in fact advance the values and principles embraced by a liberal democracy with greater efficiency. A different perspective, however, asserts that clientelism is tantamount to charity since it contributes to dissolving the idea of citizens as equal rights-bearers (Boltvinik and Hernández cited in Gledhill 2005: 81). For the case of El Salvador, I suggest that both perspectives are useful. As I have illustrated through the examples, patron–client relationships are a means by which political parties attract constituents. Yet clientelism also constitutes a valuable and creative form of interaction with state actors for the purpose of dealing with ongoing and increasing economic and public insecurities. Santiagueños have frequently embraced clientelism in order to avoid the inefficiencies and irregularities of state institutions. As Auyero (2000: 26) has observed about Peronist politics in Argentina, the analysis of 'clientelism' sheds light on the ways in which the problem-solving of ordinary people in deteriorating circumstances is inextricably linked with the political life of the country. Yet the language frequently deployed in the analysis of clientelism assumes and imposes relationships that are alien to ordinary people's networks of problem-solving (Auyero 2000: 23): 'the very terms that govern the analysis—*flows, exchange, rational choice*—… are foreign to the logic of problem-solving enacted through the "clientelist network."'

Although publicly disapproved of by ordinary Salvadorans through rumor and gossip, clientelism may at times be a consensual mechanism—rather than one simply imposed by the state—for efficiently obtaining what ordinary people consider to be their entitlements vis-à-vis the state. In El Salvador, clientelism is clearly a form of redistribution or problem-solving, albeit one not free of its own inefficiencies and problems. Although it retains an aura of illegitimacy and illegality, clientelism is widely practiced and morally accepted, depending on the circumstances and the vantage point. Avoiding institutional inefficiencies or grievances and helping out kin are positively self-assessed by those engaging in clientelistic practices yet defined as corruption when practiced by others. The practice of clientelism implies a notion of the state as a distinct group of actors with which citizens nonetheless engage through political parties and personal networks. While I observed certain Santiagueñas circumventing state institutions and officials, many did engage with them through participation in clientelistic practices with more personalized and trustworthy state actors. In the next section, I explain how Santiagueños' circumvention of certain state institutions and actors and their engagement with others shows that a certain type of state has been sought even as the existing one has been feared or distrusted.

FUNDAMENTAL TENSIONS IN THE RELATIONSHIP TO THE STATE

Fear of, and longing for, the state were simultaneously harbored by the population of the Hacienda La Pastera, in the lowlands of Santiago, where, by serendipity, I ended up teaching adults to read and write for several months in 2009 as part of a literacy program run jointly by a Spanish

NGO and the Salvadoran government. While initially convinced that my role there had nothing to do with my fieldwork research, my daily visits to the area and the relationships I built with residents soon allowed me to learn about their predicaments. Subject to robberies, extortion, and harassment from police for over a year, residents of this area decided to report these incidents after the FMLN had taken office in June of that same year. Two residents told me about their problems with the police officer who led the *Grupo de Tarea Conjunta* that patrolled the area and asked me to write a letter on their behalf explaining the situation and requesting that an investigation be opened. They asked me to address the letter to Father David, by then an elected deputy for La Paz. Carlos, a resi-dent of La Pastera, traveled to Zacatecoluca to deliver the letter at the *Tribuna Abierta* (Open Platform), an event held every Sunday in this municipality. At the *Tribuna Abierta*, FMLN leaders in public positions sought to demonstrate their commitment to transparency and public accountability as well as their willingness to entertain people's views and pressing needs. Although serving more as FMLN electoral propaganda than as an actual means of popular participation, the weekly *Tribuna Abierta* had a permanent audience. After the 2009 presidential election, a number of people would queue at the end of the event to approach Father David with requests for jobs or other needs. This was the moment at which Carlos was able to deliver the letter. Father David read it with atten-tion, then lauded Carlos for his initiative and promised to get in touch immediately with the head officer at the departmental police subdelega-tion in Zacatecoluca. A few weeks later, per the letter's request, the *Grupo de Tarea Conjunta* had been removed from La Pastera.

Although La Pastera's population had engaged with the FMLN instead of filing a formal report, their ultimate aim was to receive state interven-tion. As noted earlier, a broad range of claim-making on the state is often indirectly channeled through political parties and networks of acquain-tances and kin. This, I suggest, is symptomatic of the contradictions inher-ent in citizenship practices vis-à-vis the state. Clientelism both utilizes and consolidates the networks through which Salvadorans find that a variety of insecurities and problems can be resolved with relative safety. This is not to imply that clientelism is an utterly calculatory and rational practice; it is largely motivated by sentiments of fear and distrust of the state that encourage a diversion of direct engagement with state institutions. It is through networks populated by political parties as much as those made up of acquaintances and relatives that people implicitly express their longing for the state. An indirect form of engagement with the state, patron–client relationships simultaneously constitute an active search for the state by citizens, be this motivated by a search for protection or any other outright entitlement. A relevant question is why people in postwar El Salvador have sought to relate, albeit indirectly, to a state they fear and sometimes avoid.

Navaro-Yashin (2002) has analyzed a similar situation in 1990s Turkey through the notion of 'cynicism'. During the 1990s, Turkish citizens criticized state corruption through jokes and gossip yet seemed to behave as though they were unaware of it. Navaro-Yashin (2002: 159–171) has explained their attitude as a form of cynicism: despite their awareness of fraud and corruption, Turkish people carried on as though they did not know about it, thereby contributing to the reproduction of the status quo as well as the idea of the state. Cynicism, Navaro-Yashin has observed, was ultimately rooted in a pragmatic concern with survival. Lazar (2008: 92) offers a different interpretation of a similar contradiction in her description of El Alto, a Bolivian town, in the late 1990s. There, people willingly related to the state through clientelism despite their disillusionment with the state and criticism of its corruption. Rather than viewing their approach as cynical, Lazar interprets Bolivian citizens' indirect engagement with the state not just as a survival strategy but as a public manifestation of their expectations vis-à-vis the state and a way to make the state accountable.[13] I would suggest that Santiagueños' simultaneous disengagement and indirect engagement with the state is equally rooted in survival strategies, these understood as ways of dealing with and adapting to ongoing economic and public insecurities. However, the coexistence of seemingly antithetical notions of the state and contradictory feelings toward state institutions and actors that has motivated practices of both exclusion and inclusion in El Salvador correspond to different motives.

Salvadorans have recognized the inevitability of their relationship to the state in one way or another. The state is hence not avoided altogether; indeed, the state is actively sought, even if only indirectly, through personal networks. Despite their fear or distrust of the existing state, Salvadorans have also aspired to a certain type of state, a state that provides and protects. Cynicism thus cannot explain how they have engaged with state actors, and survival explains only why they have circumvented certain state institutions and sought indirect ways of engaging with them.

---

[13] Herein clientelism was, however, not free of cynicism, since it was publicly criticized as corrupt yet widely engaged in.

Longing, in addition to survival, sheds light on Salvadorans' complex and contradictory relationship to the state. The state, conceived as an all-powerful agent, is an object longed for as well as feared.[14] Although the state can take on a phantasmatic quality that engenders widespread fear, the state has also been invested with the power to counteract the very source of this fear, as La Pastera's episode demonstrates. Ultimately, Salvadorans' longing for the state amounts to an aspiration for enhanced or expanded inclusion, above and beyond the ability to participate in formal politics through the archetypical citizenship right of voting.

Through conversations and rumors, Salvadorans have depicted the state as a separate and powerful elite that has resulted from practices of concentration. This imaginary stems from a perception that the state is disinterested in the problems of the poor, as well as from an inhibition about relating to a state that they have come to associate with feelings of fear and distrust. In depicting the state as a small and discrete group of actors, Salvadorans have effectively complained about its failure to redistribute wealth, its withdrawal from security functions, and its contribution to public insecurity, as conveyed through allusions to the grayness of postwar politics, as much as they have asserted their aspiration to enhanced inclusion. In other words, Salvadorans desire that the state deploy its power to redistribute and protect,[15] thereby operationalizing a notion of citizenship with an important social and material component. This notion of citizenship, which includes social and civil as well as political rights, resonates with Marshall's (1992). It is indeed predicated upon the notion of the welfare state—a Western post-Second World War development minimally developed in El Salvador and then increasingly dismantled by the ascendance of neoliberal reform. Insofar as the notion of the welfare state is relatively foreign to El Salvador, it is pertinent to enquire as to the basis of Salvadorans' sense of rights and their longing for a protective state.[16]

---

[14] Aretxaga (2003: 394) explains these kinds of contradictory investments in the state precisely as a result of the power with which the idea of the state is imbued.

[15] Moodie (2010: 139–168) has found similar aspirations for expanded inclusion among San Salvadorans in the post-Accords decade. Their crime stories indicated that they yearned for a state that would protect them, foster a community of belonging, and promote socioeconomic development.

[16] Yet regional models of this kind of state exist in other Latin American countries, such as Mexico and Brazil, where populist regimes have promised a sort of welfare state but failed to deliver it.

I suggest that the desires, aspirations, and expectations that Salvadorans have invested in the state—fear, distrust, and disillusionment notwithstanding—may stem partly from the liberal traditions of Latin America and their increasing coalescence throughout the twentieth century, with emancipatory and socialist ideologies. As Baud (2007) has observed with regard to indigenous groups' quest for citizenship in the Andean countries, the republican tradition of these countries increasingly led throughout the twentieth century to the nation-state's becoming a legitimate interlocutor and hence the basis for definition and entitlement of citizenship rights and responsibilities. In El Salvador, this liberal tradition manifested in the early twentieth century in intellectual Alberto Masferrer's definition of a 'minimum vital' that would guarantee a decent life, both morally and materially, to any human being; this definition went on to influence the Christian Democratic agenda in the 1960s (Racine 1997: 211).

Meanwhile, the reverberations of liberation theology as well as the later dissemination throughout the transition to democracy of an international human rights rhetoric—although of limited penetration—should likewise not be underestimated. A rhetoric that emphasizes rights over duties percolated through to the mass of the Salvadoran population via the analyses and practices of liberation theologians and grassroots organizations such as the CEBs during the 1970s and 1980s. Despite the tensions that developed between the Catholic Church and those who embraced prior liberal ideologies advancing the secularization of the state,[17] the syncretism of Latin American liberation theology redefined the relationship of the Catholic Church to both the state and civil society (Dussel 1996: 275). In so doing, it also, I suggest, redefined citizenship by publicly denouncing the exclusion of 'the nonpersons', 'the poor', or 'the people' by local elites and power structures and by proclaiming this population's right to the socio-economic entitlements and political subjectivity that had hitherto been denied to them:

> These times, therefore, bear the imprint of a new presence of the poor, the marginalized and the oppressed. Those who were for so long 'absent' in our society and in the Church have made themselves—and are continuing to

---

[17] The church's increasingly open attitude toward liberal positions during the twentieth century paved the way for, among other things, the foundation of Christian Democratic parties throughout Latin America (Dussel 1996: 278).

make themselves—present. It is not a matter of physical absence: we are talking of those who have had scant or no significance, and who therefore have not felt (and in many cases still do not feel) in a position to make plain their suffering, their aspirations and their hopes. But this is what has started to change. (Gutierrez 1999: 20)

As observed by Gutierrez (1999: 21), the empowerment of the poor led to struggles for social justice throughout Latin America, from the raising of public awareness of the marginalization of the poor to the formation of guerrilla insurgencies. The accommodation of a Marxist analysis of poverty and exploitation and the foregrounding of the socio-economic rights of the poor may have influenced how Salvadorans articulate their aspirations and their right to a state that provides.[18] The language of rights and increasing expectations as to what the state should ultimately be and do, even if there is no hope that it will transform in the short term, I argue, has been accentuated by the increasing relevance of an international human rights rhetoric, which has been partially embraced by certain Salvadoran grassroots movements (e.g. the Father Cosme Spessotto Committee) that network with international or professionalized organizations.

Holston (2008) and Sassen (2003) have underlined the tension that exists between formalized definitions of citizenship as a legal status and informal practices and formulations of citizenship, which are necessarily conjoined. Building upon this distinction, I argue that Salvadorans' practices of citizenship, largely informed by their experiences in the 1970s and 1980s, are directed toward enhancing the social and material aspects of their condition of citizenship beyond their ability to exercise archetypal political rights such as voting. Their resort to practices of citizenship in which they extricate themselves from the state (e.g. underreporting) is not a product of apathy or acquiescence but, instead, a search for creative responses and adaptations in the face of their country's postwar corruption, violence, and impunity. In other words, while Salvadorans are subject to certain exclusions, they also have an important role in crafting citizenship. By suggesting that the 'presence' of political subjectivity may mani-

---

[18] It is nonetheless analytically relevant to note that the notion of the 'welfare state' differs—both in origin and substance—from the definition of citizens' political and economic entitlements introduced by eighteenth- and nineteenth-century liberal ideologies. So does the liberal notion of citizen greatly differ from the collective notion, deployed by liberation theologians, of 'the poor' as rights-bearers.

fest in domains transcending formal politics, Sassen (2003: 62) has similarly argued that powerlessness and invisibility do not negate political subjectivity or citizenship. Practices of citizenship are indeed embedded in 'very specific conditions, opportunities, constraints, needs, interactions, contestations, interests' (Sassen 2003: 61) that define their contradictory and changing nature.

Rather than an 'insurgent citizenship' that destabilizes and crafts entrenched formulations of citizenship, as has been the case in Brazil since the 1970s (Holston 2008), I would suggest that Salvadorans' contradictory practices conform an 'adaptive citizenship' not necessarily oriented toward the subversion or erosion of structural or entrenched exclusions that reproduce inequality but certainly toward a search for creative ways to manage those exclusions. While Holston (2008: 4) has suggested that formalized and non-formalized definitions of citizenship remain deeply entangled—both limiting and enabling each other—I would instead argue that citizenship consists of a synthesis of formalized/non-formalized and structural/conjunctural exclusions and inclusions that give it a highly contradictory nature. In short, citizenship is not just 'a mechanism to distribute inequality' (Holston 2008: 7) but also a vehicle by which ordinary people can make decisions about their own inclusions and exclusions for themselves. The agentive possibilities of citizenship are perhaps better expressed by Gordon and Stack's (2007: 127) definition of citizenship as a 'room for maneuver', that is, 'the freedom to pursue livelihood'. This is a practice of citizenship beyond the state in contexts where people are not only ignored by the state but also ignore the state themselves.

Gordon and Stack (2007: 127) suggest, like Holston, that this search for autonomy is necessarily 'insurgent', given the state's project of appropriating citizenship. I am, however, reluctant to describe it as such for the case of El Salvador given the longing that Salvadorans have expressed for the state—their complaints about, and circumvention of, state institutions and actors notwithstanding. In other words, Salvadorans have not renounced the state even as they have often autonomously pursued their livelihood in the face of persistent public and economic insecurity and the state's fearsome or inefficient nature. The influence of the regional context in this aspiration to a state that provides and protects should also be taken into account. New Left and Center–Left governments that came to power from the late 1990s in various Latin American countries enacted a 'return of the state' through their challenge of previous neoliberal tendencies, but especially their expansion of social agendas and welfare spending with the revenues from export-led growth models alongside their responsiveness to citizens' demands more generally (Grugel and Riggirozzi 2012). As explained earlier, Venezuela and Cuba had, for years, subsidized university studies and eye surgeries for Salvadorans. I thus surmise that these and other Latin American governments must have embodied the imaginary upon which the longing for a state that delivers took root among segments of left-leaning and disaffected Salvadorans in the late 2000s. In the next section, I return to an analysis of the relationship between hope and poor people's practices of citizenship in El Salvador, specifically in the aftermath of the 2009 election.

An Ephemeral Space of Hope

The many initiatives undertaken by ordinary Santiagueñas shortly after the FMLN victory in the 2009 presidential election waned a few months after Funes had taken office, thus attesting to the ephemeral nature of the hope that had inspired them. The 2009 electoral campaign had instilled hope in the population through rhetorical elements such as the FMLN motto 'nace la esperanza, viene el cambio' (hope is born, change is coming). Funes's public embrace of 'the preferential option for the poor' while visiting Romero's grave after officially taking office on 1 June, along with his assertion that it was 'the turn of the offended', did communicate to ordinary Salvadorans that the time for 'change' had arrived, however belatedly. Yet, given the deep disillusionment stemming from both the waning of the utopian revolutionary project of the 1970s and the perceived failure of the Peace Accords to address transformations other than institutional reform, many Santiagueños have scarcely invested hope in the postwar era; whatever hope they have invested has been driven by urgency and characterized by short-term horizons.

Santiagueños made constant references during the electoral season to how little faith they had in an FMLN government's ability to introduce substantive change, given the structural transformations that would be required. Indeed, so skeptical were many of them that they began negatively assessing Funes and the FMLN almost immediately after they had taken office. This leads me to suggest that hope has become exceedingly difficult to grow and maintain in El Salvador, given its people's history of disillusionment and their awareness of the magnitude of the transformations required. When the FMLN won the election, many Santiagueños suddenly actively sought or engaged with the state, deciding that they would attempt to fulfill their pressing needs on their own initiative. Yet while many ordinary people, especially those on the Left, believed the FMLN government provided a more friendly milieu in which to engage with the state than the ARENA governments that had preceded it, they remained skeptical that their fundamental problems of economic and public insecurity would be addressed.

The perception that the FMLN government fostered an appropriate milieu for problem-solving was achieved partly through the personalized attention that FMLN governmental leaders gave to ordinary people. After the FMLN victory, the *Tribuna Abierta* already functioning in Zacatecoluca was brought to Santiago, and FMLN leaders such as deputy Father David began visiting different sectors of the municipality. His visits gave a personal face to the national government and excited expectations that the new administration would be responsive to people's demands and needs. In Las Ánimas, where there was still no potable water system, the population was encouraged by local FMLN leaders to elaborate a census and a map with the locations of residents' homes and present it to the FMLN government as part of a formal request for a water system. In central Santiago, the leadership of a local association met with Father David to request funding for a water system whose construction had commenced in 2003 and subsequently been abandoned due to a lack of funds. In other sectors, Santiagueñas listed the needs of their communities and visited Public Works Minister Gerson Martínez in his office in San Salvador. While people were warmly received in these meetings, they never heard back from government representatives about the concerns they had shared.

Part of the hope that Santiagueños invested in the party shift stemmed from the workings of political clienteles in El Salvador. Among some Santiagueños, the party shift was perceived as an opportunity for those hitherto excluded to benefit, whether from economic prerogatives or from unprecedented opportunities to report human rights violations. Given the FMLN's self-definition as 'the government of the people', reinforced by its characterization of the former ARENA governments as elitist, this party's victory engendered high expectations as to how Santiagueñas, especially those who had demonstrated support for this party during the 2008 and 2009 electoral campaign, would benefit. Anticipated benefits included jobs for FMLN loyalists or their relatives, the replacement of ARENA's bureaucrats with FMLN loyalists, and public works and deliveries of seeds to the areas where party loyalists lived. Yet the FMLN victory also elicited fear and distress among those on the Right, given that

ARENA's electoral politics of fear had drawn firm associations between the FMLN ex-guerrillas, communists, and terrorists, and that ordinary people had widely assimilated the state with the governing party. I was, for instance, told of a number of old women who became physically ill following the FMLN victory; as noted in Chap. 5, they did not want to leave their homes for fear of what the new FMLN government would see fit to do with them. In this sense, the 2009 elections distributed and mobilized hope unevenly across the political spectrum, a pattern consistent with the wartime political cleavages that have persisted in the postwar era.

Nuijten (2004) has described how the Mexican state has, like El Salvador's, been a source of disillusionment as well as a 'hope-generating machine'. Her study of land disputes in a Mexican peasant community in the first half of the 1990s has demonstrated that state bureaucracies—while pervaded by conflict, distrust, and opacity—have contributed to reproducing the idea of the state and to maintaining hope by never settling cases of land disputes and only sporadically offering signs of their continuation. In the late 2000s in El Salvador, by contrast, the stagnation, or even exhaustion, of hope led the poor either to resign themselves in the face of certain exclusions or to attempt to deal with these exclusions through political parties, acquaintances, and relatives with personal contacts within the state bureaucracy rather than through the state institutions themselves. Salvadorans felt simultaneously entitled to and deprived of a state that cared and provided. Given that they could not envision its materializing in the short- or medium-term, a protective state or a state that cared was for them an abstract ideal rather than something they hoped would materialize in the near future; in practice, therefore, hope has been stripped of any utopian connotations and invested instead with a pragmatism that has limited both its focus (to certain events or periods) and its temporal horizon (the short term). Even in areas that were FMLN strongholds during the war or were repopulated by the end of it and have in general maintained better-organized and more proactive populations, Salvadorans' hopes have waned (see for instance Silber 2011).

In a context in which hope is informed not by what is desired but by what is deemed obtainable, citizenship is directed less at transformation than at adaptation. This development hinders the prospects of a hope that is enduring and action-oriented. Indeed, Appadurai (2007) has argued that hope emerges precisely in the space that is left between utopia, on the one hand, and pragmatism and policy on the other. In contrast to the sense of urgency that characterizes the hopes of El Salvador's disenfranchised and poor, Appadurai (2002) identifies the logic of patience as crucial for the maintenance of hope in the long term. The postwar disjunction between desire or aspiration (utopia) on the one hand, and pragmatism on the other, has eliminated the intermediate realm of hope (a potentially realizable future, a sense of possibility). The suppression of this intermediate realm has had paradoxical consequences, for while Salvadorans seem to have longed for more state intervention, their avoidance of or indirect engagement with state institutions and actors quite inadvertently has served the uncritical advancement of neoliberalization (cf. Gledhill 2005: 82). Let me return to water privatization to illustrate this point.

In Santiago, demands for potable water in sectors where this was not provided, or for the amelioration of existing water systems, went unaddressed by the ARENA governments throughout the 2000s. In the face of unmet water needs, populations of various sectors of Santiago worked throughout the decade to privately procure a water system. When water service was subsequently 'decentralized' (i.e. privatized), public allegations that water tariffs would rise led people to concentrate on developing the water systems in their communities (e.g. buying a new water source or continuing the building of an unfinished water system) rather than placing claims on the state with regard to the quality of public water systems.

On my visit to Santiago in 2010, I attended the meetings of a group of neighbors in a sector with a private water system. Immediately after the 2009 presidential election, residents had asked the FMLN government and ANDA to supply them with new reasonably priced pipes, but their requests had gone unanswered. They had requested credit from several banks, but, due to the incipient economic crisis, it had been denied. A participant at the meeting suggested an alternative solution: 'There's a man living near the Coastal Road who people say needs to launder drug-trafficking money; a friend of mine got him to supply her with uniforms for her entire school. I can ask my friend where his mansion is, and we can go ask him for the pipes.' Even after the FMLN had taken office, Santiagueñas seemed to have given up on the state and be seeking their own pragmatic ways to move beyond its limitations, rather than pressing claims on the state to improve water distribution or regulate tariffs. It is in this sense that citizenship as 'room for maneuver' resonates with neoliberal notions of self-help citizenship, even as the state keeps disciplining and policing its citizens (cf. Gordon and Stack 2007: 130).

In postwar El Salvador, the consolidation of neoliberalization has partially relocated the state. Non-state actors—such as the drug-trafficking lord mentioned by Santiagueños in the aforementioned case—may occasionally be involved in provisions ordinarily expected from the state, but I suggest that the most commonplace form of state relocation has occurred within political parties. Whether ruling or not, political parties have become major actors and channels of what were theoretically public functions of provision; this development has consolidated an identification of the state with the governing political party, which is able to mobilize a great many resources, both public and private, through circuits that blur the public/private divide and turn what ought to be a public entitlement into a private gift. This is especially so in areas like Santiago, where war memories and the persistence of different expressions of violence in peacetime have fragmented sociality and diminished the power of social movements and personalized networks other than those capable of mobilizing resources such as political parties, or relying on trusted networks of relatives and close acquaintances. An argument can be raised here regarding the applicability of Klein's (2008) 'shock doctrine'. The traumatic episode of El Salvador's 12-year war, preceded by a decade of escalating police repression, especially in the country's rural areas, and the persistence of homicidal violence and public insecurity during peacetime, I suggest, have enhanced the capacity of neoliberalization to develop well beyond its dimension of economic reform without significant contestation.

Under the ARENA governments, many Santiagueños and residents from neighboring municipalities opted to circumvent the state. Their practices of self-exclusion cannot be fully explained by the country's rampant violence, corruption, and impunity, or by economic insecurity aggravated by neoliberal economic policies. Haunting war memories of police and military involvement in war atrocities and the conjuring of a postwar gray zone of politics also led Santiagueños to avoid the state. Yet, rather than completely detaching themselves from state institutions and actors, Santiagueñas have privately managed their own problems of public and economic insecurity, often reverting to more personalized self-help networks, such as political parties, acquaintances, and kin, through which to engage with the state in a safer and more productive way. Not only have these intermediaries been more trustworthy than standard governmental channels, but they have often proved more efficient. I thus suggest that the citizenship practices of Santiagueños, especially those concerning their relationship to state institutions and actors, have been characterized by a management of their own inclusions and exclusions. This is a pragmatic form of citizenship; it is citizenship as 'room for manoeuver' as much as it is citizenship based on survival. In this sense, I suggest that in the late 2000s, Santiagueñas practiced a sort of 'adaptive citizenship'. Even as they have circumvented the state, Santiagueñas have yearned for a state that provides and protects; they have, in other words, imagined themselves as citizens through their relationship to the state (Montoya 2015). Funes's government did not seem to have contributed to any substantial alteration of Salvadorans' citizenship practices despite initially suggesting otherwise. Although initially the FMLN seemed to be promising to tackle ordinary people's needs via the wide consultation process it runs before elections to design the party program, this approach led to disappointment a year after the party's victory. In this context, not only have Salvadorans' postwar citizenship practices stemmed from increasing insecurities due in part to escalating violence and the impact of neoliberal reforms, but they themselves have also enabled neoliberalization by consolidating networks that have allowed for a relocation of state functions.

Many Salvadorans who were initially thrilled at the prospects of the FMLN victory became deeply disillusioned soon thereafter. Perhaps this was inevitable given that the country's problems of economic and public insecurity are so deeply entrenched that little transformation was possible in the short term. What was initially deemed 'the turn of the offended'—whether interpreted as an appropriate milieu in which to bring about transformations or as an opportunity to reap the benefits of a relationship with a new political clientele—soon gave way to a continuation of previous citizenship practices. While this does not mean that the FMLN has completely lost its popularity as proved by its reelection in 2014,[19] Salvadorans have once again become skeptical about the possibility of short-term change. Insecurities have continued, as well as a relationship to state institutions and actors that is fraught with fear and distrust. Far from constituting a historic turning point, the FMLN victory and this party's assumption of power have thus far simply represented a continuation of Salvadorans' political subjectivities. In the post-2009 election context, Salvadorans have frequently expressed not only their disillusionment with the FMLN government but also their lack of options, given that neither ARENA during its 20 years in power nor the two elected FMLN governments since

---

[19] Indeed, in 2010, the year in which most of the events in this chapter occurred, 50.3 percent of Salvadorans stated in surveys that they approved of Funes's government, even though the majority believed that the country's situation was the same as, or worse than, before (IUDOP 2011: 40, 42–43).

2009 have managed to resolve their problems and insecurities. Nevertheless, the rapid disillusionment of Salvadorans a year after the FMLN's victory is consistent with the exceedingly high initial expectations and the urgency and finitude that characterized their hope in the aftermath of the 2009 FMLN victory.

CHAPTER 8

Conclusion

Throughout the book, the examination of the relationship between violence and political life in postwar El Salvador has served as the groundwork on which to nuance official representations of El Salvador's
democracy. Even as El Salvador has been lauded internationally, ordinary
Salvadorans have made rather critical assessments of their country's postwar era. Fieldwork conducted in 2008 and 2009, 16 years after the war's
end, as well as during several follow-up trips, allowed me to shed light on
how ordinary Salvadorans have made sense of violence and maneuvered
their way through the insecurity of the postwar era. Through their stories
and practices, it has become clear that violence and El Salvador's political
life are deeply enmeshed in ways that resonate with wartime even as they
differ from it. This book has thus shown that the official tale of the country's transition from war to peace does not adequately convey the transformations that have unfolded after the signing of the Peace Accords in 1992.
The transition in El Salvador must be understood as a process that has
enabled the consolidation of a violent democracy—one in which wartime
memories and unresolved social and political problems of the war persist
and in which various forms of violence have consolidated as everyday features of political life.

In drawing comparisons with wartime that portray the postwar era in a
rather negative light, Salvadorans have implicitly acknowledged that the
war came to an end. Yet they have also articulated that, in the face of
ongoing public and economic insecurity, their experiences of the postwar

© The Author(s) 2018
A. Montoya, *The Violence of Democracy*, Studies of the Americas,
https://doi.org/10.1007/978-3-319-76330-9_8

era do not radically differ from those of wartime and in fact may be 'worse than the war.' Of course, these utterances cannot be taken at face value since the evocation of the past in the present is always an act mediated by hindsight and current concerns. I found evidence of this blurring together of wartime and postwar experience not just in their utterances but also in how they practiced democracy, for instance by reenacting wartime frictions and conflicts or by reinstating political cleavages. In this book, I have suggested that both Salvadorans' stories and practices be taken seriously as evidence challenging the triumphalism of El Salvador's government and members of the international community with regard to the unfolding of the country's transition from war to peace. This is particularly so in light of the evidence—specifically the clandestine connections that exist between political actors and violent actors and the resemblance between licit and illicit economies of violence—suggesting that violence has become intrinsic to how democracy operates.

A Critique of El Salvador's Model Transition

My ethnography has shown that a complex interplay of processes, both historical and emergent, has marked how ordinary Salvadorans have experienced and made sense of the postwar moment and the violence that has persisted throughout. Legacies inherited from the past have manifested in the postwar era materially—as in the persistence of the country's elite and entrenched socio-economic inequalities—as well as in the form of haunting war memories. Acknowledgment of these legacies permits an understanding of why wartime frictions and political cleavages, including fears by the Left of ongoing repression by a newly elected ARENA government and fears by the Right of a new guerrilla uprising and the specter of communism, suffused the 2009 presidential election. Legacies of the past have also pervaded El Salvador's political and everyday life outside electoral events, albeit in more subdued or even imperceptible ways that nevertheless became evident during my ethnographic research in Santiago. Santiagueños—especially those who were left-leaning or critical of the ARENA governments and had lived through the war—consistently made sense of violence by resorting to their knowledge of the wartime past. Violence in the postwar era was, to them, more than simply a gang problem. While gangs were frequently invoked in their explanations of postwar violence, these explanations coexisted with the suggestion that much of this violence was similar to the kind of state-sponsored 'political violence' that had characterized the war.

Explanations informed by haunting war memories notwithstanding, ordinary Salvadorans on neither the Left nor the Right have regarded the persistence of violence in El Salvador's postwar era as a mere continuation of wartime violence; rather, they have shared the view that postwar violence is at least partly related to the new opportunities opened up by the political and economic transformations experienced by the country at the end of the twentieth century. This is exemplified in the views of Santiagueños aligned with the Left, who constituted the majority of the people with whom I developed close relationships during my research. A widespread assumption among left-leaning and disaffected Santiagueñas is that political and state actors belonging to ARENA have benefited from escalating public insecurity in the postwar era via their participation in the flourishing private security industry. Leftwing and disaffected Santiagueños' view that ARENA members' vested interests in the persistence of public insecurity are illegitimate implicitly draws an analogy between the Salvadoran state and the postwar criminal. This serves to illustrate how leftwing Santiagueñas in particular have considered postwar violence to be politically connected, albeit in this case in ways that go beyond the restrictive definition of 'political violence' employed to describe the ideologically driven violence of wartime. They believe that political actors partake of activities, whether licit or illicit, that contribute to and benefit from the persistence of homicidal violence. This belief effectively expands the notion of 'the political' to refer to the country's political life rather than merely a set of underlying ideological motivations. It also sheds light on how violence has become built into the ways that El Salvador's liberal market democracy operates. Although I did encounter allusions to postwar corruption and economies of violence from rightwing Santiagueños as well, they did not refer to ARENA members specifically but rather to a vague array of political and state actors.

The aforementioned explanations notwithstanding, postwar violence has been far from clear-cut for ordinary Salvadorans. In conducting my research, I realized that ordinary people of all political persuasions in Santiago and neighboring municipalities found homicidal violence and death threats highly ambiguous and often unintelligible, even as they tried to fix their meaning by resorting to wartime experiences and suggestions of political corruption. The perpetrators of violence and their motives were the subject of rampant rumors and constant conjecture. These rumors, while communicating particular analyses of postwar El Salvador, evidenced the difficulty that ordinary people have experienced in attempting to make sense of postwar violence. Rumors, as an object of enquiry in and of themselves, provided me with information regarding how ordinary people in Santiago speculated about postwar violence. Rumors regarding specific episodes occurring in the municipality, along with high-profile episodes occurring elsewhere in the country but commented upon locally, shed light on the ambiguous features of postwar violence: clandestine connections, shadowy political links, state's backstage domains, the merger of the licit and the illicit, the phenomenon of 'doble cara' (two-faced), and the coalescence of political actors and violent entrepreneurs—all features that have been confirmed by investigative journalism and reports by human rights organizations.

In light of the ambiguity that rumors have underscored, I have suggested that ordinary people in Santiago have made sense of postwar violence through their conjuring of a gray zone of politics. In this gray zone, ambiguity stems from the coalescence and merging of a multiplicity of forms of violence and violent actors as well as from the attempts of political actors to render illegible certain connections and activities. A distinction prevails nonetheless in the emphasis placed by leftwing and disaffected Santiagueñas on the wartime roots of this gray zone, which they consider to be populated mainly—but not only—by ARENA actors. Crucially, not only do rumors point to what ordinary people consider plausible explanations for the postwar violence, but the rumors also serve as a heuristic device for them. Rumors thus have consequences. Confronted by fear-inflected rumors, people have increasingly distrusted and circumvented state institutions of order, such as the police, and opted not to report episodes of postwar human rights violations.

The conjuring of a 'gray zone' of politics via the rumors circulating among ordinary people in postwar El Salvador, as well as additional interview and media evidence, has led me to suggest that postwar violence is neither external nor a threat to the country's political life, as the official and media emphasis on the trope of gangs implies, but is instead intrinsic to it. Rumors and citizenship practices suggest that violence is deeply built into how the country's democracy operates, both its political life and its procedural elements. Perhaps nowhere was this so clear as during the electoral campaigns leading up to the 2009 municipal, legislative, and presidential elections. During these campaigns, symbolic, ritualized, and affective components of the country's political culture, which had become common currency among ordinary people, were pervaded by fear and violence. Most Santiagueños who belonged to a political constituency and actively partook in electoral events contributed in some way to a reenactment of the country's civil war. Reports by the country's media outlets and rumors alike confirmed the occurrence of this reenactment throughout the country. Meanwhile, through rallies, propaganda, and rightwing mass media, ARENA disseminated a formulaic version of the wartime past so as to enact a politics of fear that benefited its electoral campaign. The nationwide reenactment of the war and ARENA's politics of fear, as well as the passions and animosities these stirred, stemmed, I suggest, from an avoidance by chief political actors of a public critical discussion about what the country's civil war had really been about and about the prospect of redress for wartime human rights violations.

Elections—a crucial element of normative definitions of democracy underpinning democratization processes and a criterion by which the quality of a democracy is oftentimes assessed—evidenced how the triumphalist tale of transition could hold even as various forms of violence became increasingly entrenched in El Salvador's democratic practices and procedures. In postwar El Salvador, elections conducted with apparent fairness in the eyes of international observers have been for ordinary Salvadorans a moment of heightened fervor and hostility. More importantly, the emphasis placed by the international community on the quality of El Salvador's elections ignores the pervasiveness of fear and public insecurity, both during and outside the country's electoral campaigns. Indeed, my ethnographic observations of the 2009 electoral campaign revealed, both symbolically and literally, violent aspects of the electoral process that were far from trivial insofar as they represented, to some extent, a reenactment of the wartime conflict.

There are thus grounds on which to suggest that postwar violence is deeply constitutive of El Salvador's liberal market democracy. The persistence of violence, homicidal and otherwise, has correlated with contemporary processes of statecraft (such as the country's neoliberalization) as much as with legacies of the past. Long-standing structural inequalities and the wartime past partly explain why ordinary people, especially left-leaning Salvadorans, have regarded the successive ARENA governments as uncaring and indeed as a major source of their public and economic insecurities. Against this background, ordinary people have also voiced a belief that unpopular measures such as the privatization of public utilities and the country's dollarization, both of which were part of ARENA's project of neoliberal restructuring, have served as a means by which the country's elites have reproduced their wealth. The continual conjuring of a gray zone via rumors suggests that the reproduction of wealth by elites happens not only through licit means and domains but also through the illicit. The involvement of political actors in drug trafficking and money laundering has become an ubiquitous subject of rumors circulating among ordinary people of all political orientations as well as a subject of media scandal. This book has drawn on implicit, on-the-ground critiques of democracy as a political regime that has enabled routine homicidal violence to persist rather than advancing its eradication as heralded by the Peace Accords. Crucially, ordinary people in Santiago, neighboring municipalities, and the capital have attributed this situation to the accommodation of various forms of violence by the actors, institutions, and mechanisms of democracy. My observations of Santiago's political life during and outside the 2009 electoral campaign came to confirm this interpretation.

By focusing on how ordinary people make sense of violence, draw connections between violence and democracy, and engage in citizenship practices, this book has explored a main tenet of the transition paradigm underpinning post-Cold War peacebuilding operations: the assumption that transitions out of authoritarianism, accompanied by certain institutional reforms, evolve inevitably into peaceful democracy. Expounding on a premise of critical political theory that asserts that violence may be as intrinsic to elements of democracy as to authoritarianism, this book has ethnographically examined the ways in which violence can become built into democracy's political life and procedural aspects. My goal was not to propound an alternative definition of democracy but rather to underscore the often neglected or misrepresented relationship between violence and polyarchal forms of democracy within the transition paradigm, particularly when political and economic liberalizations have been engineered in parallel. In so doing, I have exposed the inadequacy of the teleology implied by democratization and peacebuilding processes.

I have thus illustrated throughout the book that in postwar El Salvador, violence and democracy, rather than existing in tension, are deeply intertwined: 'Rather than viewing violence as simply an indicator of democracy's "failure" (as the democratization paradigm does), an anthropological perspective on democratic discourse reveals the ways in which democracy and violence are intimately entangled in both the establishment of democratic regimes and their ongoing maintenance' (Arias and Goldstein 2010b: 18). The on-the-ground unearthing of the relationship between violence and democracy that this book has undertaken shows that in El Salvador violence is part and parcel of political life, albeit in ways that may not be as straightforward and identifiable as during previous authoritarian regimes. The difficulty in pinpointing the problem of violence in postwar El Salvador stems from its multiplex forms, sources, actors, and activities. Compounding the difficulty is a politics of (in)visibility, partly enacted by the former ARENA governments (see Moodie 2009), that renders obscure the deep relationship between El Salvador's postwar violence and the institutions and mechanisms of democracy.

This entanglement of violence and democracy is not unique to El Salvador. As shown by related theoretical and comparative endeavors (see Arias and Goldstein 2010a), the examination of this fundamental relationship is crucial to understanding how violence has become pervasive and routine in much of contemporary Latin America. Countries such as Mexico, Brazil, Argentina, or those in the Northern Triangle, all of which enjoy democratic regimes, have seen their levels of public insecurity, corruption, and impunity rise consistently and consolidate at high levels in the new millennium even as they have displayed democratic state functioning. Arias (2010: 245) has suggested that 'systems of governance exist in Latin America today that tolerate the activities of multiple armed groups and dramatically high levels of crime. While this may involve certain particular institutional failures, it in no way reflects a broad failure of the state'. This trend throughout the region calls into question the tenets of democratization scholarship that have informed post-Cold War peacebuilding operations, and it invites further explorations of, first, the relationship between violence and democracy in a context of concurrent political and economic liberalization, and, second, the role of historical legacies in the consolidation of this relationship.

MANUFACTURING LEGITIMACY

How can El Salvador represent both a model political transition and one of the world's most violent democracies? As I have suggested in this book, the answer to this question is twofold. On the one hand, as explained in the previous section, a violent democracy is not a paradox once we admit the capacity for certain forms of democracy to accommodate violence. On the other hand, from the perspective of the transition paradigm underpinning the 'technical' interventions that aimed to democratize conflict-ridden El Salvador, the country's postwar violence is considered to be perpetrated mainly by deviant youth and hence external to its democratic regime. This book argues that while members of the international community and some social scientists have lauded El Salvador's political transition and democratic regime, the ways in which ordinary Salvadorans of various political orientations regard and experience it is a different matter. Even as the transition may have contributed to manufacturing the legitimacy of government, it cannot be assumed that legitimacy is accomplished wholesale or uncontested given Santiagueños' and other Salvadorans' consistent criticisms—albeit differing by political alignment—of the country's postwar political life.

By the end of the 1980s, the ARENA government headed by President Alfredo Cristiani came to terms with the idea that the country's armed forces could not defeat the FMLN guerrillas and that the continuation of conflict would have profoundly negative consequences for business. It was this pragmatic consideration, as well as the leading elite faction's reduced dependence on land—redistribution of land among the peasant population being one of the FMLN's demands on the negotiating table—that led the leadership of the then-governing party ARENA to willingly engage in peace negotiations with the leadership of the FMLN guerrilla organization. In the immediate aftermath of war, as the government enacted the Peace Accords mandate, it advanced a process of rapid economic liberalization with the twofold goal of attracting foreign direct investment and convincing international financial organizations that El Salvador deserved their loans and support. In this process, the sanitizing of El Salvador's public face was as necessary as demonstrating a commitment to a global neoliberal agenda, the so-called Washington Consensus. El Salvador's transition to democracy was thus a priority for a governing elite seeking to activate business and relocate its economic interests following the collapse of prior sources and circuits of accumulation rooted in the country's 1990s' agricultural crisis, as well as for an international community critical of counterinsurgency actions but also convinced that certain 'technical' interventions—consisting of parallel political and economic liberalization—would lay the foundation for and lead toward a peaceful and democratic future.

El Salvador's transition thus worked to forge the legitimacy of its democratic government and the interventions thereof. As both this book and previous research have demonstrated (see also Moodie 2010), the ways in which El Salvador's democratic governments have manufactured the legitimacy of the postwar political regime—albeit not fully intentionally—have been twofold: first, marking a rupture with the past, and, second, depicting democracy as a panacea. This book has ethnographically shown, however, that this legitimacy is relatively unsettled vis-à-vis ordinary Salvadorans of all political orientations in Santiago and, as evidenced by the media, throughout El Salvador. Their rumors, gossip, and stories—which occasionally found confirmation in police leaks, the reports of human rights organizations, and media scandals or investigative journalism—hinted at a politics of (in)visibility that allowed a constellation of forms of violence and violent actors, and the connections between them and the country's political life, to remain relatively clandestine. The emergence of a gray zone points to the existence of attempts to keep this constellation ambiguous and illegible. A politics of (in)visibility does not imply that everything about violence remains unacknowledged and hidden. On the contrary, it is the very hyper-visibility of actors like gangs and their violence that permits other kinds of actors and their actions and connections—such as the hiring of gangs by political actors—to remain clandestine.

The pervasiveness of haunting war memories and the persistence of wartime political cleavages themselves challenge the rupture between war and peace claimed by the official tale of the transition. Meanwhile, in criticizing state institutions and actors in the postwar era, ordinary Salvadorans have effectively questioned and discredited the country's existing democracy. Given the persistence of homicidal violence and economic predicaments, as well as the government's perceived unwillingness or inability to resolve them, I found widespread disaffection among ordinary Santiagueñas on both the Left and the Right. An intermittent symptom of this disaffection has been the substantial degree of abstention in postwar elections. An additional, and more systematic, symptom has been ordinary people's circumvention of state institutions and actors and their reliance instead on self-help networks—whether of political parties or kin and acquaintances—that have in turn allowed aspects of the country's neoliberalization to go largely uncontested in a rural area like Santiago. While ordinary people's comments regarding the state and their citizenship practices can be seen as indicative of a disbelief in democracy, my research shows that Santiagueños likewise maintain a vision of democracy as a panacea, thereby shedding light on democracy's multivalent nature, that is, how democracy works as a signifier for various political forms. Yet the democracy left-leaning Salvadorans yearn for, which seems unattainable in the short-term, has been evacuated from the present and relegated to an abstract future—a future made vividly present during the 2009 electoral season.

The Panacea of Democracy

While ordinary Salvadorans have experienced deep disaffection and questioned the legitimacy of their liberal market democracy, voter turnout doubled in the 2004 presidential elections and again in 2009. As explained in the book, in the 2009 elections, members of both ARENA's and FMLN's basic constituencies voted largely according to their fears. Depending on their position on the political spectrum, ordinary Salvadorans' votes were either a rejection of a feared totalitarian FMLN regime or a rejection of a potentially repressive ARENA regime that would also exacerbate their economic predicaments. Yet Funes's victory in 2009 was rooted in his ability to attract the votes of those members of the disaffected electorate less distraught over the dire scenarios that representatives of both political parties had predicted would play out in the event of a victory by the opposing party. Funes addressed ordinary people's pressing economic and social problems, which ARENA in particular had ignored and even eclipsed in deploying its politics of fear. With his speech auguring change and the addressing of socio-economic inequalities, Funes managed, if only temporarily, to rekindle hope in the panacea of democracy among large numbers of disaffected Salvadorans. I thus suggest that, at the time, even as the majority of ordinary people criticized the ARENA democratic governments, they maintained their aspiration for a democracy in which a state that provides and protects plays a central role. This was the case even though ordinary people have associated democracy as much with the disillusionment triggered by the transition as with the panacea originally promised by the Peace Accords.

Interestingly, the memory work performed by the Father Cosme Spessotto Committee in the municipalities of La Paz has both articulated a critique of El Salvador's contemporary democracy and sought to create the conditions of possibility for an alternative democracy. They consider the country's current democracy to be built upon unresolved wartime problems, among them a failure to redress wartime human rights violations. Their quest for retributive and restorative justice is not merely an expression of disaffection; more fundamentally, it is an assertion of their belief in substantive democracy as a solution to the country's social ills. They have articulated this belief prioritizing the lexicon of religious morality over the lexicon of international human rights typically deployed in interventions related to the advancement and legitimization of democracy. Through their memory work, Committee members have implicitly put forth a notion of democracy that is largely rooted in the wartime past, that is, in the redress of wartime human rights violations, the honoring of wartime victims, and the public discussion and thorough documentation of the history of the country's civil war.

The memory work by Committee members and the spontaneous initiatives undertaken by left-leaning Santiagueños after the 2009 FMLN presidential victory demonstrated that not only do these Salvadorans believe in democracy, but they embrace a deeper vision of democracy than the one deployed by members of the international community involved in peacebuilding operations, who have focused on such outward criteria as the maintenance of formal institutions, the celebration of fair multiparty elections, and freedoms of press and public expression. Left-leaning people in Santiago believe that the panacea to their pressing social and economic problems does not lie in 'democracy' per se, but rather on a deepening of 'democratic relations and practices' such that democracy encompasses an addressing of their public and economic insecurities by state institutions and, increasingly, a redress of the wartime past rather than its erasure. Theirs is a notion of 'deep democracy' that differs from the 'liberal market' version existing in El Salvador and resonates with the broader definition of democracy disseminated in the aftermath of the Second World War, when the democratic value of equality was expanded to include human development and the address of poverty (see Appadurai 2007: 31), and with the radical ideologies that underpinned political struggle throughout Latin America in the second half of the twentieth century (see Lievesley 1999; Grandin 2004; Moodie 2013). The participation of Latin Americans in mass politics during the aftermath of the Second World War yielded a particular regional interpretation of democracy; there was 'a commonsensical understanding of democracy not as procedural constitutionalism but as the felt experience of individual sovereignty and social solidarity' (Grandin 2004: 4).

CONCLUDING REMARKS

As noted in the piece of ethnography with which this book began, on 15 March 2009, after El Salvador's electoral results had been publicly released, Funes stated that the FMLN victory in the presidential elections represented 'a new peace accord'. His expression stressed the historic importance of the former guerrilla and leftwing opposition's accession to office via the displacement of ARENA, the rightwing party that had represented the interests of the country's long-standing political and economic elite for two decades. In so doing, he depicted the FMLN victory as a 'critical event', one that would not just entail a party replacement but that—grounded as it was in the government's adoption of 'the preferential option for the poor' and the constitution of the presidential handover as 'the turn of the offended'—would institute new modes of action and being.[1] He implied that his government would address the pressing social and economic problems of ordinary people, including homicidal violence and public insecurity, which had been neglected by the successive postwar ARENA governments. However, a few years into FMLN rule, when I traveled to El Salvador to conduct additional fieldwork, I noted that the hope embraced by ordinary people immediately following the 2009 election had devolved into the pragmatism and short-term orientation that had characterized their practices during ARENA rule. On these grounds, I suggest that the 2009 FMLN victory was not the critical event that Funes claimed it would be.

Postwar disillusionment among ordinary Salvadorans, especially those on the Left who had supported or engaged in the armed conflict of the 1980s, is certainly related to the notion of democracy they had held prior to that struggle. As Grandin (2004: 191) has put it, 'Throughout Latin America, the majority of nations now enjoy constitutional rule. Yet for those throughout the continent who gave their lives, the current state of affairs cannot be what they meant for democracy.' In addition to their disillusionment with the existing form of democracy, it is possible that ordinary people's disillusionment and short-term horizons of hope are reinforced by the consolidation of public and economic insecurity and the perceived futility of the historic party shift that brought to office a guerrilla-turned-party to transform the status quo. This research has taken a step in elucidating the ways in which violence has become a pervasive element of political life, shaping statecraft, citizenship practices, political subjectivities, and state-citizenry relations. It has shown that in the context of a violent democracy like El Salvador's, a party shift—even one that ushered

---

[1] I refer here to the notion of 'critical events' coined by Das (1995) in her analysis of various traumatic events that occurred in India after this country's partition in 1947. By 'critical events', she refers to events that institute new modes of action and being, imbuing old concepts with new meaning (Das 1995: 3–4).

in an unprecedented leftwing government—is seen by ordinary people as incapable of undoing El Salvador's entanglement of violence and democracy, especially given the country's dependency on alternative circuits of accumulation and state's backstage domains of power as well as its relationship to neoliberalization and new economic opportunities.

CHAPTER 9

Epilogue

On 29 September 2016, Salvadoran anthropologist Juan José Martínez D'Aubuisson spoke about his book *Ver, oír y callar* (*See, hear and shut up*)—a phrase that encapsulates the gang code of conduct imposed on Salvadoran communities—at Madrid's bookshop Traficantes de Sueños.[1] A question-and-answer session followed his presentation about the origins of El Salvador's gangs. His eloquent reply to a question about how the FMLN has managed the country's gang problem began: 'The FMLN has, to a great extent, largely betrayed the Salvadoran population, those who placed their trust in them.' His remarks, which I only listened to a year after the event when I discovered a recording on the bookshop's website, called to mind matching assertions made since 2010 by acquaintances in Santiago and neighboring towns, as well as in other departments as I moved on to do research in other areas. As recounted earlier in the book, only a year and a half into the first FMLN administration, many left-leaning Salvadorans who had harbored hopes that this party's access to government might represent a meaningful shift were already deeply disappointed. They had hoped for the FMLN's incarnation of a different state as well as an improvement in the ongoing public and economic insecurity that plagued their daily lives. Seeing their hopes dashed soon after the 2009 FMLN victory was not surprising given the high expectations surrounding both the party shift and the FMLN's electoral pledge of

[1] A podcast of the event is available at https://soundcloud.com/traficantesdesue-os/un-ano-con-la-mara-salvatrucha-13-ver-oir-y-callar.

© The Author(s) 2018   249
A. Montoya, *The Violence of Democracy*, Studies of the Americas, https://doi.org/10.1007/978-3-319-76330-9_9

far-reaching change. Yet spiraling homicide figures from 2009 also explain left-leaning Salvadorans' discontent.

Figures have limitations. They often do not tell us much about a problem and can even obscure aspects of it. Figures can also make us numb to the harsh and appalling lived experiences of those being counted, whether they are victims of homicides, the disappeared, or refugees. Figures can vary depending on the source or the method of counting. Yet figures matter and have effects—just as the absence of figures and counting do. As I described in the book, homicides reported schematically as figures and collated as statistics can be bent to serve political purposes. Likewise, they can be symptomatic of the magnitude of a problem, of sudden changes, or persistent trends as well as of attempts to draw attention to them. For Salvadorans, the soaring figures reported daily by the media have served as the confirmation of their increasingly quotidian experience of violence, of its dreadful ordinariness. In postwar El Salvador, homicide figures and rates have reached unprecedented levels, way beyond those of wartime—regardless of whether they are police or Institute of Forensic Medicine collated. In 2009, homicides reached a peak relative to the previous postwar years, with an overall total of 4382. Homicide figures and rates dropped from 2012 with the government-brokered truce between El Salvador's main gangs but soared again as the truce fell apart around the end of 2013. In 2015, the deadliest year since the end of the country's war, and even compared to the average daily wartime death count,[2] the toll of yearly homicides was 6656, raising the homicide rate to 103 per 100,000 inhabitants and positioning El Salvador once again as the world's most violent country, or second to Syria if we include conflict-related deaths (Cantor 2016: 82–83). Sadly, these figures speak to the consolidation and growing severity of a problem; one that I have argued in this book cannot be understood by merely focusing on gangs.

THE FMLN TAKEOVER

While the FMLN's victory in 2009 augured an epochal shift, it is clear eight years later that this shift needs to be downplayed and qualified. Just as El Salvador joined other Latin American countries in a turn to the Left, it likewise pursued policies that, while seeking to alleviate poverty, did not achieve structural transformation. Most importantly, the political agendas

---

[2] 'Los salvadoreños cruzan fronteras de guerra a diario', *El Faro*, 4 January 2016.

of both Funes's and Sánchez Cerén's governments have largely maintained the economic and public security policies introduced by ARENA during the previous two decades; they have left neoliberal policies untouched while mitigating their impact on poor majorities via piecemeal welfare programs that have represented more of an assistance-based approach than an actual redistribution of the country's wealth. However, the FMLN's poverty relief programs could never come close to those in other progressive Latin American countries given that El Salvador's budget is one of the lowest in the region.[3] Nor have either of the two FMLN governments attempted to withdraw free-trade agreements, reverse dollarization, or renationalize or further regulate former public sector enterprises—all policies that have hindered these governments' ability to enact structural transformations.

In a context in which economic and public insecurity are tightly imbricated, the FMLN's continuation of ARENA's economic agenda has dramatically curtailed any possibility of turning away from ARENA's prioritization of increasing securitization. In other words, the lack of policies addressing the structural roots of violence has once again turned violence into a mere security issue. In addition, Funes's administration exhibited a distinct ambivalence toward public security policy (van der Borgh and Savenije 2014). While initially declaring an interest in implementing a more comprehensive approach to security that would have included prevention and rehabilitation components—and thereby addressed the structural roots of public insecurity—Funes's government soon began responding to escalating homicides and political pressure by expanding the militarization of public space and prisons and by appointing a former army general first as minister of defense and later of justice and public security after the initial appointment was declared unconstitutional. One year into its tenure, Funes's administration passed the 2010 Anti-Gang Law, which was essentially a continuation of the hardline and gang-centered policies introduced by ARENA that had exacerbated the gang problem and neglected other sources of violence, whether gang-related or not. By then, any prevention programs had already disappeared from the agenda. Even when Funes's administration led a dialogue with the country's main gangs in 2012, it maintained a repressive approach.

---

[3] While the FMLN has undertaken fiscal reforms of a progressive nature, these have not reported a significant revenue increase partly due to unfettered tax evasion and elusion (Menkos 2013).

The truce collapsed by the end of 2013, partly due to the government's inability to explain and legitimize its gang-related strategy to the Salvadoran population. In March 2012, the digital newspaper *El Faro* unveiled the motives behind the transfer of about 30 gang leaders from high-security prisons to centers with lower security standards and the abrupt drop of homicides during the days surrounding that month's municipal and legislative elections: a concealed FMLN government-led negotiation with the country's main gangs.[4] In exchange for benefits, the MS 13, Sureños, and Revolucionarios gangs had agreed to stop committing homicides and other felonies. In light of the scandal generated by this news, the government opted to deny it for months. Indeed, the transfer of the gang leadership to lower security prisons was initially explained by government officials as a preemptive measure to preclude a rumored plan to liberate them as well as a response to a humanitarian plea by the Catholic Church to address some of their deteriorating health conditions.[5] Although a gang truce was publicly declared by gang spokespersons soon after news of the prison transfers was made public, it was not until September of that year that the then-minister of Justice and Security General David Munguía Payés admitted that the truce had been a government-orchestrated strategy to bring down the country's homicide figures. President Funes, however, continued to deny this even after the end of his administration, all the more so given that those responsible for orchestrating the truce have been investigated by El Salvador's Public Prosecutor's Office for their alleged misuse of public funds to seal the deal with the gang leadership.[6]

Salvadorans' skepticism toward, or outright repudiation of, the truce persisted despite its contribution to homicide reduction while it lasted (see IUDOP 2012, 2014). In 2012 and 2013, thousands of lives were saved—a return to pre-*mano dura* homicide figures and rates that represented a roughly 40 percent reduction relative to 2011 (see FUNDAUNGO 2014). Arguably, Funes's government lacked the ability to sell to Salvadorans the negotiation with gangs as a legitimate means of curbing the country's homicide count. Yet the government's management of the gang problem, both during and after the truce, seems to have been largely

---

[4] 'Gobierno negoció con pandillas reducción de homicidios', *El Faro*, 14 March 2012.

[5] 'Munguía Payés justifica haber sacado de máxima seguridad a líderes pandilleros', *El Faro*, 16 March 2012.

[6] 'Versión de Funes contradice a la del resto de involucrados en la Tregua', *El Faro*, 20 October 2017.

geared toward the FMLN's electoral strategies rather than any genuine interest in finding a durable solution to the problem of public insecurity, an approach that resembled that of ARENA both during and after its administrations. The FMLN-facilitated truce, which was eventually justified as a means by which to thwart a presumed gang plan to boycott the March 2012 municipal and legislative elections, instead seemed more like a means of effecting a sharp reduction of the overall homicide count so as to benefit the party's stakes in those elections (Holland 2013). Meanwhile, as leaked by *El Faro*, in the months leading up to the 2014 presidential elections, high-ranking members of both the FMLN and ARENA met with gang leaders to strike deals by which to obtain their electoral support in exchange for concessions and even pecuniary gains.[7] Elections have thus continued to be tied to violence, albeit in different ways. If the 2009 electoral season amounted to a reenactment of wartime conflicts, the 2014 electoral competition continued the polarization and division between the FMLN and ARENA, albeit couched in both old and new rhetoric and imageries and involving alliances between political leaders and gang members (see Montoya 2018).

The 2014 speech by Norman Quijano, ARENA's presidential candidate, at the close of election day—when the vote tally was still ongoing, but it was already clear that the election would be a disputed one—epitomized this party's continued conjuring of wartime imageries. A solemn Quijano fired up a crowd of ARENA loyalists anxiously awaiting the final results by declaring: 'We're not going to let our victory be taken away! We're going to fight if necessary with our own lives, but we're going to make democracy prevail. From this very moment, more than a million and three hundred thousand compatriots who have granted us this victory are at war to defend this victory!' Then, on a menacing note that served as a vivid reminder of prewar decades, he added, 'Our armed forces, our armed forces are keeping an eye on this fraud that they're [referring to the FMLN] perpetrating. They can't play with the will of the people!'[8] The FMLN as danger, as a threat to democracy, reemerged in his speech, just as it had done in previous postwar elections. So did imageries reminiscent

---

[7] 'Arena prometió a las pandillas una nueva tregua si ganaba la presidencia', *El Faro*, 11 March 2016; 'El FMLN hizo alianza con las pandillas para la elección presidencial de 2014', *El Faro*, 6 May 2016; and 'Relato de un fraude electoral, narrado por un pandillero', *El Faro*, 11 August 2017.

[8] A portion of Norman Quijano's speech is available at https://www.youtube.com/watch?v=NT5lyDpuFLo.

of the war, as Quijano implicitly alluded to a potential confrontation between the armed forces and the FMLN should democracy need to be defended.

Even more troubling is the consolidation of the gray zone described throughout the book, especially as post-truce police-linked extermination structures and community cleansing groups have acted with state connivance and broad social tolerance. The increasingly repressive and extrajudicial use of the country's institutions of order has been met with a high number of homicides of police officers, presumably by gang members.[9] In a conversation in February 2017, a Salvadoran government official who requested anonymity acknowledged that members of the FMLN government had deliberated that having already fought a war, they were not going to accept defeat at the hands of gangs. Implicitly, he seemed to be admitting to the FMLN government's adoption of war-like responses to the country's escalating homicide problem. Indeed, ever since Sánchez Cerén declared in January 2015 that his government would not maintain a dialogue with the gangs, a covert policy of cracking down on gangs through increasingly ruthless and extrajudicial approaches has prevailed.[10] The PDDH has raised concerns about the police-linked extermination groups that have acted recursively since 2014, and research by this institution has subsequently presented evidence of extra-legal executions of ganglike youth.[11] Meanwhile, the media has reported raids on gang-controlled areas that have included torture of ganglike youth as well as the alteration of homicide scenes by, for instance, placing weapons on the dead bodies of alleged gang members so as to justify the killings.[12] The FMLN administrations have thus managed a problem partly rooted in structural inequality and United States policy toward the region with more violence—violence that has arisen largely from the state's backstage domains. In doing so, they have not distinguished themselves from previous ARENA-led administrations.

[9] See, for instance, 'En 2014–2015 se han asesinado la misma cantidad de policías que en 2009–2013', *El Faro*, 4 August 2015.

[10] See 'Casi que Guardia Nacional Civil', *El Faro*, 1 November 2017.

[11] See 'PDDH: Grupos de exterminio podrían estar operando en ESA', *La Prensa Gráfica*, 21 May 2014; 'PDDH concluye que Policía y militares cometieron ejecuciones extrajudiciales', *El Faro*, 25 April 2016.

[12] 'En la intimidad del escuadrón de la muerte de la policía', *Revista Factum*, 22 August 2017; 'Revelan comunicaciones internas y crímenes de grupo de exterminio en la PNC', *El Faro*, 23 August 2017.

The gang trope has therefore continued to garner both policy and media attention after 2009, while other aspects of the country's backstage circuits of power have continued to be neglected. Other violent actors and illicit activities, when acknowledged by government officials, have been linked to gangs—most notably El Salvador's drug trafficking, often attributed to alliances between gangs and Mexican cartels, and extortion. However, the actual control of drug transport through the country by long-operating Salvadoran organized crime structures, such as the already dismantled Los Perrones and the extant Cártel de Texis, and their links to politicians and public officials, have only made it secondarily or fleetingly to the news.[13] Silence has also reigned regarding the crucial role played by El Salvador—the only dollarized Central American economy in which to launder drugs revenues—as the region's 'drug trafficking bank', in the words of one of the country's Organized Crime Unit Chiefs at the Public Prosecutor's Office, and the corruption that inevitably accompanies money laundering.[14] Meanwhile, extortion, generally attributed only to gangs, has become consolidated and incorporated into businesses and families economic planning as a sort of tax—one that, as some have pointed out, amounts to a non-state welfare system. 'Extortion is allowing many poor families to survive. It works indirectly as a social investment to alleviate poverty, except that it is a social investment obtained at gunpoint', as a friend from San Salvador put it back in February 2017 (see also Zilberg 2011: 195).[15]

Of course, the gang problem is no fiction and has become increasingly more complex and multifarious, especially as repression remains the only government policy with which to address it. Yet, as I have argued throughout the book, El Salvador's problem of violence is not limited to gangs but has other germane ramifications that cannot be seen unless we shift our focus and zoom in on other aspects of political life. Indeed, in post-2009 El Salvador, the state's backstage circuits of power and the economies of violence thereof have become ever more convoluted, as police-linked extermination structures and community social cleansing groups have flourished, drug trafficking has continued to rely on corrupt state officials,

---

[13] See also 'El Cártel de Texis', *El Faro*, 16 May 2011; 'Maras y narcotráfico', *El Faro*, 19 March 2014.

[14] 'Maras y narcotráfico', *El Faro*, 19 March 2014.

[15] It is estimated that Salvadorans pay over US$390 million annually in extortion fees (Isacson et al. 2017: 6).

and security has remained as profitable a commodity as it was in the pre-2009 era discussed throughout the book. The grayness of El Salvador's political life thus continues to be reminiscent of that of the wartime era even as it has become populated by new actors and imbued with new meanings.

POST-2009 MEMORY WORK

Funes's government did distinguish itself from its ARENA predecessors in its rhetorical approach to the country's troubled wartime past. On 16 January 2010, at a celebration held to commemorate the eighteenth anniversary of the signing of Peace Accords, Funes publicly admitted the state's responsibility for wartime human rights violations and, on behalf of the state, begged the forgiveness of war victims. Such a public and official acknowledgment of the state's role in the egregious crimes of wartime was unparalleled. An important iteration of this event took place on the same date in 2012 at El Mozote. The site in and around which more than 1000 people were massacred by the Salvadoran military in 1981 was chosen by Funes's government to commemorate the twentieth anniversary of the Peace Accords. In addition to once again maintaining an apologetic attitude toward the victims on behalf of the Salvadoran state, Funes proclaimed that his administration would pursue a series of redress measures, from reparations for wartime victims and their relatives to the official recognition in educational curricula and military training materials of wartime human rights violations.

Since Funes made these declarations, reparation measures have progressed yet have been limited in practice. As explained earlier in the book, in 2013, three years after founding the National Commission for the Reparation of Victims of Human Rights Offenses, Funes's government enacted a program of reparations that was deemed insufficient—both in its financial endowment and its understanding of reparation—by victims' organizations and human rights NGOs alike. 'It doesn't embody the feeling of the people', a Father Cosme Spessotto leader explained when, as I interviewed him in April 2017, he reviewed FMLN's actions to offer redress to victims of wartime human rights offenses. At the 2017 anniversary of the signing of the Peace Accords, the second FMLN government publicly declared its intention of working toward a law for the integral reparation of wartime victims. Since the government had failed to offer any evidence of progress on it, in August 2017, Salvadoran human rights organizations involved in memory work as well as the country's main universities publicly presented their own proposal, which underscored the truth and justice components that had thus far been entirely neglected.[16]

Access to justice for victims of wartime human rights violations—clamored for by Salvadoran human rights NGOs and organizations of wartime victims alike, as well as a recommendation by the Truth Commission report—has been a rather controversial issue for the FMLN governments, one they have consistently relegated or even hindered. Concerned as they have been about the possibility of finding themselves prosecuted for their own crimes, FMLN members have eschewed supporting any efforts to attain retributive justice. Not only did Funes overtly reject the idea of repealing El Salvador's amnesty law during the 2009 electoral season, as described in Chap. 6, but he maintained the same position throughout his administration. So did other members of the FMLN party, notwithstanding the 1999 declaration by the IACHR that El Salvador's amnesty law was counter to international human rights law. Ruling on a lawsuit filed on 20 September 2013 by IDHUCA and FESPAD before El Salvador's Supreme Court of Justice, this court's Constitutional Bench on 13 July 2016, under Sánchez Cerén's administration, declared the amnesty law unconstitutional and deemed wartime human rights violations imprescriptible, thereby opening a window for their future judicialization and the prosecution of both direct perpetrators and intellectual authors.

Since then, however, human rights NGOs have complained that investigations and judicial proceedings have advanced only on the El Mozote case, even though more than a hundred lawsuits pertaining to uninvestigated wartime crimes have been filed since the end of the war.[17] On 5 September 2017, several of these NGOs, supported by the international organizations Center for Justice and International Law (CEJIL) and Due Process of Law Foundation (DPLF), presented before the IACHR a request for this institution to call out the Salvadoran state for not fulfilling its obligation, since the law was annulled, to facilitate the investigations, and subsequently to pursue the trial and punishment, of gross

[16] 'Proponen ley para dignificar a víctimas de guerra salvadoreña', *ContraPunto*, 23 August 2017.

[17] FMLN members' concerns about the possibility of being prosecuted themselves were not unfounded; lawsuits against some of them have been reopened or lodged since the annulment of the amnesty law and the first arrest warrants for wartime crimes since then have been issued against former FMLN combatants. See 'Órdenes de captura por derribo de helicóptero', *La Prensa Gráfica*, 20 July 2017.

wartime human rights violations.[18] The DPLF member who opened the presentation acknowledged some progress since the general amnesty had been overturned: the design of an about-to-be-created mechanism for the search of the disappeared, the organization of several commemorative public events that expressly recognized state responsibility for wartime massacres, and the opening up of forums for the debate of wartime narratives and victims' experiences. 'However, the prosecution and penal punishment for past crimes (...) has changed little or not at all', the DPLF member averred. During the same session, in responding to El Salvador's state representatives, Salvadoran human rights lawyer David Morales, another session petitioner, denounced the state Public Prosecutor's Office for its lack of enforcement of basic legal proceedings, such as obtaining relevant documentation of cases, such that defaulting in making any breakthroughs due to an alleged lack of resources is regarded as a mere pretext.

Overall, memory work has not been a driving force that has facilitated a deeper form of democracy, not even post-2009, when initially many foresaw the advent of a more friendly milieu for substantial transformations of the country's political life. This paucity of transformations does not lie in any lack of effort on the part of Salvadoran human rights NGOs or grassroots movements performing memory work in the postwar era, especially post-2009. Nor does it lie, I would suggest, in a lack of transformative potential on the part of memory work. Rather it lies in the lack of facilitation, first by the ARENA governments and later by the two consecutive FMLN governments, for memory work to overcome its marginality in the country's political life and thereby enjoy a greater impact. Both parties, haunted as they are by wartime ghosts, have not been keen to address the past through judicial avenues. Nor have they been sensitive enough to enable moral and material reparation through other means. While those involved in memory work accepted inaction from a party like ARENA, whose origins are probingly linked to death squads, the FMLN's lack of efforts has further disappointed left-wing sectors and human rights actors historically linked to that party and who have felt once again abandoned—counting and summoned only when they are electorally relevant. The ongoing limitations of El Salvador's memory work thus stem to a considerable extent from the FMLN's elusion not only of its promises but

---

[18] A video of the session has been made available by the IACHR at https://www.youtube.com/watch?v=rbsojsXCIoo.

also of its moral obligations—especially to the many Salvadorans who supported in one way or another the revolutionary process that eventually allowed the party to come into office.

FLEEING FROM VIOLENCE

The high figures of homicidal violence and the ever-present *possibility* of this kind of violence are the most unsettling manifestation of El Salvador's problem of postwar public insecurity but not the only one. Echoing parallel wartime outflows, beginning in 2009, Salvadorans of all ages, genders, sexual orientations, classes, and ideologies have fled the country by the thousands, just as has occurred in neighboring Guatemala and Honduras as well as in Mexico (see Cantor 2014, 2016).[19] As I noted throughout my fieldwork in 2009, and on subsequent visits, many Salvadorans without the means to leave El Salvador have internally relocated only to find that their new place of residence is no safer than the place they had fled. Increasingly, though, as I realized from the accounts of acquaintances and relatives of those who had fled, many have sold much of what they owned or incurred debt to finance their way out of the country, whether to other Central American countries, Mexico, or the United States, or even to Europe, so as to avoid the deadly trip north. Corroborating this trend are the increasing numbers of requests that are filling the mailboxes of Salvadoranists, including myself, from law firms and clinics seeking expert evidence in asylum appeals involving Salvadorans. Like other scholars, I have felt compelled to respond to requests to act as an expert witness, albeit not without concerns about the genres of writing I am asked to generate in the process[20] or concerns about my contribution in so doing to legitimizing policed regimes of citizenship.

The list of profile cases of forcibly displaced Salvadorans that I have come across is long. Police officers fleeing gang members' increasing attempts on their lives. Gang members wishing to leave the gang or persecuted by members of a rival gang, a community cleansing group, or police. Minors, whether male or female, from gang-controlled communities whose relatives seek to preclude their seemingly inescapable involvement

---

[19] In 2012, a total of 85 percent of all asylum applications lodged in the United States were from citizens from the Northern Triangle (UNHCR 2014).

[20] Moodie (2017) has included a poignant reflection about these concerns in the Epilogue of her Spanish-translated book.

with local gang members as they grow up.[21] Women running away from aggressive or controlling partners. Witnesses of police corruption and involvement in organized crime. People threatened by extortionists and thus unable to continue pursuing a livelihood in El Salvador and fearing for their families and their own lives. Men and women facing death threats by political opponents for their public political alignments with either the FMLN or ARENA. Activists threatened for their public defense of a natural resource or territory against the profit-led activity of a corporation, whether domestic or transnational. People with non-normative sexual orientations or gender identities who have been subject to harassment, physical violence, or death threats. Some of these cases speak about the ways in which violence has become the language with which to assert masculinity and heteronormative views; others speak about the intricacies of the country's political life and its gray zones. More often than not, these forms of violence are not unrelated (see for instance Hume 2009a).

Perhaps not surprisingly, the convoluted nature of El Salvador's problem of public insecurity defies the legibility and coherence that legal proceedings value. I have encountered asylum claims in the UK being refused by the Home Office because of an alleged lack of credibility, adding in the credibility assessment process a further layer of injury and violence.[22] For instance, a Salvadoran male who had fled his home after being subject to attempts on his life by local gang members returned briefly with some friends to recover some of his family's possessions before leaving El Salvador. The credibility of the threat was questioned. According to the immigration judge, the man could not possibly have been under a dire threat if he had dared set foot in his home again. This way of reasoning failed to recognize that recovering his possessions might have been this man's only chance to afford a way out of the country for him and his family—so inextricably linked are economic and public insecurity in El Salvador.

Many claims include gaps or inconsistencies or simply lack the documentary evidence that would lend credibility to unmaterialized threats or unsuccessful attempts on the claimants' lives—inconsistencies and gaps being carefully tracked by Home Office officials so as to justify refusals of claims (cf. Good 2004: 116). Not only have studies of trauma underlined

---

[21] From 2011 onward, the number of unaccompanied children from the Northern Triangle arriving in the United States experienced a dramatic surge (UNHCR 2014).

[22] On how credibility is assessed at British asylum courts, see Good (2011).

the often incoherent, illogical, and full-of-gaps narrations of violence by victims, but—as I myself have experienced when speaking to Salvadorans— the grayness of El Salvador's political life does not often lend itself to the clear-cut and logical accounts that courts look for. Nor have many waited for death threats to materialize so as to have the indisputable corroborative evidence that would serve as the basis on which to be granted refugee status or humanitarian protection. But how can we expect that of anyone living in a country with one of the world's highest homicide rates, where reporting can put one at further risk given the proven leakages of information through corrupt officers?

Refusals of asylum claims by Salvadorans tend to highlight the possibility that the claimant could in fact relocate in El Salvador with help from the existing official witness protection program. This kind of reasoning by immigration judges overlooks the country's geographies of violence and the state's backstage domains. Gangs and organized crime structures extend over large portions of El Salvador's territory; gangs specifically have even moved to new territories over time, and while *clicas* (cliques)[23] enjoy a great degree of autonomy, they also keep connections among them. More crucially, in a country of barely over 21,000 square kilometers, it is often not possible to escape death threats by simply relocating (UNHCR 2016: 45), and indeed, although official statistics do not exist, a UCA survey revealed that at least a third of those who were internally displaced in 2012 had felt compelled to relocate at least twice within that year alone (Cantor 2016: 88–89).

In a February 2017 interview with a PDDH member who had for years worked on cases of postwar forced displacement in El Salvador, she explained that even though a state witness protection program exists, this can be accessed only by those who are involved as actual witnesses in criminal trials. While in the program, they are separated from their family and sequestered in a house under the protection of police officers. Their protection ends with the conclusion of the trial. Funds are so meager that only critical witnesses are accepted and, even then, there is evidence that some witnesses have been murdered by gangs and organized crime structures who have uncovered the whereabouts of witnesses through corrupt police officers or public officials (see also UNHCR 2016: 24–25). Those judging asylum applications assume the existence of a state-maintained

---

[23] A *clica* is the term employed by gangs to designate the smallest gang subunit with control over a delimited territory and substantial autonomy from the gang leadership.

witness program that can guarantee the safety of victims, ignoring both its limited coverage and the hurdles and risks, both actual and perceived, involved in reporting through public institutions in El Salvador. Being deported to El Salvador, where structures with territorial control can easily identify deportees who previously fled the area and where corruption is deeply installed within the police, can thus amount to a death sentence (see, for instance, UNHCR 2016: 28). The lack of recognition of the deep entanglement between violence and democratic institutions, relations, and practices in El Salvador by immigration judges is thus neglecting the severity of the threats this entanglement poses for so many ordinary Salvadorans.

Reckoning with El Salvador's Violent Democracy

It is apparent that the 2009 party shift did not amount to a regime shift. As I discussed earlier in the book, especially in Chap. 5, ARENA and FMLN were born out of radically different aspirations and political projects. Although they both resorted to violence during the war to advance their goals, the motivations and rationales for their violence stood in stark opposition. While they both seemed to have acted as mirror images of each other in their war-like behavior during postwar elections until 2009, their ontological differences had not completely collapsed. However, the qualification of the 2009 shift as a mere party shift, on the grounds of the FMLN continuation of ARENA's policies and ordinary Salvadorans' assertions, begs a revisiting of the question of whether, through taking office, the FMLN has increasingly converged with ARENA. Perhaps we could even ask whether a certain degree of continuity and mimetic correspondence, despite the ongoing public reenactment of wartime conflicts, is what enabled the party shift to occur without any major confrontation on the part of the country's Right.

We could, of course, argue that the FMLN's apparent likeness to ARENA instead stems from the extent to which, through the peacebuilding process and being in government for four consecutive terms, ARENA managed to capture various state branches and institutions as well as state resources such that it inhibited postwar peacebuilding efforts and subsequent potential transformations by FMLN incumbents (cf. Wade 2016). Policies bent to the economic interests of the elite, unmet economic and political commitments reached during peace negotiations, bureaucracies overwhelmed with ARENA loyalists, the use of state resources for proselytism both during and outside electoral seasons, and the control of the judiciary are some of the ways in which ARENA elites 'captured peace' and indeed the state. This control over state institutions and resources, which has historical parallels, enabled ARENA to win elections through the maintenance of patronage relationships, which in turn facilitated continued state capture by this party to such an extent that a party shift amounted to little.

It is also the case that the Legislative Assembly has been controlled by the Right in the postwar era. Even when ARENA did not hold a majority, it received the support of the PCN and the PDC. Yet ever since the FMLN took office, a major fracture at the heart of ARENA precipitated a turning point in the balance of legislative power. Following ARENA's defeat, former President Elías Antonio Saca, who had been expelled from the party and had gone on to found the Great Alliance for National Unity (GANA), managed to attract a number of ARENA deputies and competed in elections from 2012. GANA won several parliament seats and municipality councils in 2012 and again in 2015. Defined as it has been in direct competition with ARENA, its deputies have frequently voted alongside those of the FMLN, thereby enabling this party to pass legislation and adopt annual national budgets that might have otherwise been blocked en masse by the predominantly rightwing Legislative Assembly. This window of opportunity to secure a legislative majority notwithstanding, the FMLN has not demonstrated a volition to transform El Salvador's violent political life—for example, by passing legislation or approving policies that would tackle the structural roots of postwar violence, or by facilitating Salvadoran society's reckoning with its wartime past. Most often, as discussed earlier, the party seems to have instead been motivated by electoral strategizing and self-interest. While the FMLN has at times discursively recovered a socialist discourse that considers its first two administrations only an intermediate step in the path toward socialism, this seems to have been a means to cater to its core constituency and to continue maintaining electoral support rooted in hopes for a different future.

In addition to the ARENA/FMLN convergence, disturbing parallels between the war and postwar gray zones have emerged under FMLN rule. These parallels have revealed a post-2009 hall of mirrors where the FMLN is regarded by many as no different from ARENA, policy-, corruption-, and electoral behavior-wise, and where, moreover, its incumbent government seems to have connived at ruthless police practices that are reminiscent of those by prewar police forces that were dismantled as per the Accords so as to eradicate those very practices—postwar mirrors that reflect wartime ghosts. Yet, unlike during the late 1970s and the 1980s, when popular-backed guerrillas rose against such repressive practices and human rights organizations actively denounced them, today's extrajudicial killings rely on broad social and electoral support—with human organizations who denounce the killings considered by public opinion to be defending criminals. In this vein, the peace that many yearn for risks being founded on a violence that mirrors that of previous eras. Exorbitantly high levels of homicidal violence and a consolidated gray zone of politics have cast an ominous shadow over El Salvador's future. Unless Salvadorans manage to weave together a different social fabric and political life, alternative political subjectivities and projects may be compromised for generations to come. A context in which wartime ghosts seem to have been resurrected calls among other things for enabling memory work, based on a collective ethos and rights-based aspirations as well as a peacebuilding orientation, to be recovered from the margins to which it has been relegated in contemporary political life.

GLOSSARY

Arenero	ARENA loyalist
Barrio	urban neighborhood
Cantón/Cantones	rural area/rural areas
Cateo	house search
Efemelenista	FMLN loyalist
Grupo de Tarea Conjunta	Joint Task Group
La renta	the rent
Mano dura	iron fist
Mara	gang
Marero	gang member
Matazón	blood-bath
Santiagueñas/Santiagueños	residents of Santiago
Sicario	hired assassin
Tribuna Abierta	Open Platform

REFERENCES

Abrahams, Ray. 1996. Vigilantism: Order and Disorder on the Frontiers of the State. In *Inside and Outside the Law: Anthropological Studies of Authority and Ambiguity*, ed. Olivia Harris, 41–55. London: Routledge.

Abrahamsen, Rita, and Michael C. Williams. 2009. Security Beyond the State: Global Security Assemblages in International Politics. *International Political Sociology* 3 (1): 1–17.

Acevedo, Carlos. 2008. Los costos económicos de la violencia en El Salvador. *América Latina Hoy* 50: 71–88.

Agamben, Giorgio. 1998. *Homo Sacer: Sovereign Power and Bare Life*. Stanford, CA: Stanford University Press.

Agosin, Manuel R., Roberto Machado, and Aaron Schneider. 2008. The Struggle for Tax Reform in Central America. In *The Political Economy of the Public Budget in the Americas*, ed. Diego Sánchez-Ancochea and Iwan Morgan, 147–162. London: Institute for the Study of the Americas, University of London.

Aguilar Villamariona, Jeannette. 2006. Los efectos contraproducentes de los Planes Mano Dura. *Quórum, Revista de pensamiento iberoamericano* 16: 81–94.

Ahmed, Sara. 2004. Affective Economies. *Social Text, 79* 22 (2): 117–139.

Alcántara Sáez, Manuel. 1994. Las "elecciones del siglo" salvadoreñas. *Revista de Estudios Políticos* 85: 323–337.

Almeida, Paul D. 2008. *Waves of Protest: Popular Struggle in El Salvador, 1925–2005*. Minneapolis and London: University of Minnesota Press.

Alvarenga, Patricia. 1996. *Cultura y ética de la violencia: El Salvador 1880–1932*. San Salvador: Concultura.

© The Author(s) 2018

A. Montoya, *The Violence of Democracy*, Studies of the Americas,
https://doi.org/10.1007/978-3-319-76330-9

Amaya, Luis Enrique, and Juan José Martínez. 2015. Escisión al interior de la pandilla Barrio 18 en El Salvador: Una mirada antropológica. *Policía y Seguridad Pública* 5 (1): 149–178.

Amaya, Rufina, Mark Danner, and Carlos Henríquez Consalvi. 1996. *Luciérnagas en El Mozote*. San Salvador: Ediciones Museo de la Palabra y la Imagen.

Americas Watch. 1991. *El Salvador's Decade of Terror: Human Rights Since the Assassination of Archbishop Romero*. London: Yale University Press.

Anderson, Thomas P. 1971. *Matanza: El Salvador's Communist Revolt of 1932*. Lincoln and London: University of Nebraska Press.

Andreas, Peter. 2004. The Clandestine Political Economy of War and Peace in Bosnia. *International Studies Quarterly* 48: 29–51.

Appadurai, Arjun. 2002. Deep Democracy: Urban Governmentality and the Horizon of Politics. *Public Culture* 14 (1): 21–47.

———. 2007. Hope and Democracy. *Public Culture* 19 (1): 29–34.

Aretxaga, Begoña. 2003. Maddening States. *Annual Review of Anthropology* 32: 393–410.

Arias, Patricia. 2009. *Seguridad privada en América Latina: El lucro y los dilemas de una regulación deficitaria*. Santiago, Chile: FLACSO.

Arias, Enrique Desmond. 2010. Conclusion: Understanding Violent Pluralism. In *Violent Democracies in Latin America*, ed. Enrique Desmond Arias and Daniel M. Goldstein, 242–264. Durham, NC: Duke University Press.

Arias, Enrique Desmond, and Daniel M. Goldstein, eds. 2010a. *Violent Democracies in Latin America*. Durham, NC: Duke University Press.

———. 2010b. Violent Pluralism: Understanding the New Democracies of Latin America. In *Violent Democracies in Latin America*, ed. Enrique Desmond Arias and Daniel M. Goldstein, 1–34. Durham, NC: Duke University Press.

Arnson, Cynthia. 1982. *El Salvador: A Revolution Confronts the United States*. Washington, DC: Institute for Policy Studies.

Arnson, Cynthia J., and Eric L. Olson, eds. 2011. *Organized Crime in Central America: The Northern Triangle*. Woodrow Wilson Center Reports on the Americas #29. Washington, DC: Woodrow Wilson International Center for Scholars.

Artiga-González, Álvaro. 2004. *Elitismo competitivo: Dos décadas de elecciones en El Salvador (1982–2003)*. San Salvador: UCA Editores.

———. 2009. Las elecciones 2009, en perspectiva. *ECA – Estudios Centroamericanos* 64 (719): 11–32.

Assmann, Jan. 1995. Collective Memory and Cultural Identity. *New German Critique* 65: 125–133.

Auyero, Javier. 2000. *Poor People's Politics: Peronist Survival Networks and the Legacy of Evita*. Durham and London: Duke University Press.

———. 2007. *Routine Politics and Violence in Argentina: The Gray Zone of State Power*. Cambridge: Cambridge University Press.

Bagley, Bruce. 2012. Tráfico de drogas y crimen organizado en las Américas: Tendencias principales en el siglo veintiuno. In *Anuario 2012 de la seguridad regional en América Latina y El Caribe*, ed. Hans Mathieu and Catalina Niño Guarnizo, 234–251. Bogotá, Colombia: Friedrich Ebert Stiftung.

Baires, Sonia. 2006. División social del espacio urbano y emergencia de los barrios cerrados en el Área Metropolitana de San Salvador. In *La segregación socio-espacial urbana: Una mirada sobre Puebla, Puerto España, San José y San Salvador*, ed. Anne-Marie Séguin, 47–84. San José, Costa Rica: FLACSO.

Ballinger, Pamela. 2004. Exhumed Histories: Trieste and the Politics of (Exclusive) Victimhood. *Journal of Balkan and Near Eastern Studies* 6 (2): 145–159.

Baloyra, Enrique A. 1982. *El Salvador in Transition*. Chapel Hill, NC: The University of North Carolina Press.

Banerjee, Mukulika. 2007. Sacred Elections. *Economic and Political Weekly* 42 (17): 1556–1562.

Barraza Ibarra, Jorge. 2001. *La gesta de Anastasio Aquino (Una aproximación histórica)*. San Salvador: Universidad Tecnológica de El Salvador.

Baud, Michiel. 2007. Indigenous Politics and the State: The Andean Highlands in the Nineteenth and Twentieth Centuries. *Social Analysis* 51 (2): 19–42.

Benjamin, Walter. 2007. Critique of Violence. In *Reflections*, ed. Peter Demetz, 277–300. New York: Schocken Books.

Berlant, Lauren. 2009. The Intimate Public Sphere. In *Emotions: A Cultural Studies Reader*, ed. Jennifer Harding and E. Deidre Pribram, 280–299. New York: Routledge.

Berryman, Phillip. 1986. El Salvador: From Evangelization to Insurrection. In *Religion and Political Conflict in Latin America*, ed. Daniel H. Levine, 58–78. Chapel Hill, NC: The University of North Carolina Press.

Bichkova de Hándal, Tatiana. 2009. *Recuerdos sin peinar: Mi vida con Schafik*. San Salvador: Ediciones El Independiente.

Binford, Leigh. 1996. *The El Mozote Massacre: Anthropology and Human Rights*. Tucson: The University of Arizona Press.

———. 2000. Empowered Speech: Social Fields and the Limits of Testimonio. Paper presented at the XXII LASA Congress. *LASA* website. Accessed May 15, 2008. http://lasa.international.pitt.edu/Lasa2000/Binford.PDF.

———. 2013. Migration, Tourism, and Post-Insurgent Individuality in Northern Morazán, El Salvador. In *Central America in the New Millennium: Living Transition and Reimagining Democracy*, ed. Jennifer L. Burrel and Ellen Moodie, 245–260. New York: Berghahn Books.

———. 2016. *The El Mozote Massacre: Human Rights and Global Implications*. Tucson: The University of Arizona Press.

Blakely, Edward J., and Mary G. Snyder. 1997. *Fortress America: Gated Communities in the United States*. Washington, DC: Brookings Institution Press.

Bonilla Alvarado, Raúl Antonio. 1995. *Estudio monográfico del Municipio de Santiago Nonualco*. Santiago Nonualco, El Salvador: Casa de la Cultura de Santiago Nonualco.

Borneman, John. 2002. Reconciliation After Ethnic Cleansing: Listening, Retribution, Affiliation. *Public Culture* 14 (2): 281–304.

Bourdieu, Pierre. 1999. Rethinking the State: Genesis and Structure of the Bureaucratic Field. In *State/Culture: State Formation After the Cultural Turn*, ed. George Steinmetz, 53–75. Ithaca, NY: Cornell University Press.

Bourgois, Philippe. 2001. The Power of Violence in War and Peace: Post-Cold War Lessons from El Salvador. *Ethnography* 2 (1): 5–34.

———. 2004. The Continuum of Violence in War and Peace: Post-Cold War Lessons from El Salvador. In *Violence in War and Peace: An Anthology*, ed. Nancy Scheper-Hughes and Philippe Bourgois, 425–434. Malden, MA: Blackwell Publishing.

Boutros-Ghali, Boutros. 1995. Report of the Secretary-General on the United Nations Observer Mission in El Salvador. *United Nations* website. Accessed May 18, 2011. http://daccess-dds-ny.un.org/doc/UNDOC/GEN/N95/085/29/IMG/N9508529.pdf?OpenElement.

Browning, David. 1971. *El Salvador: Landscape and Society*. Oxford: Clarendon Press.

Bruneau, Thomas C., Lucía Dammert, and Elizabeth Skinner, eds. 2011. *Maras: Gang Violence and Security in Central America*. Austin, TX: University of Texas Press.

Burawoy, Michael, and Katherine Verdery. 1999. Introduction. In *Uncertain Transition: Ethnographies of Change in the Postsocialist World*, ed. Michael Burawoy and Katherine Verdery, 1–17. Lanham, MD and Oxford: Rowman & Littlefield Publishers.

Burgerman, Susan D. 2000. Building the Peace by Mandating Reform: United Nations-Mediated Human Rights Agreements in El Salvador and Guatemala. *Latin American Perspectives* 27 (3): 63–87.

Burrell, Jennifer L., and Ellen Moodie. 2013. Introduction: Ethnographic Visions of Millennial Central America. In *Central America in the New Millennium: Living Transition and Reimagining Democracy*, ed. Jennifer L. Burrell and Ellen Moodie, 1–29. New York and Oxford: Berghahn Books.

Buur, Lars. 2002. The South African Truth and Reconciliation Commission: A Technique of Nation-State Formation. In *States of Imagination: Ethnographic Explorations of the Postcolonial State*, ed. Finn Stepputat and Thomas B. Hansen, 149–181. Durham, NC and London: Duke University Press.

Buzan, Barry, Ole Waever, and Jaap de Wilde. 1998. *Security: A New Framework for Analysis*. Boulder, Colorado: Lynne Rienner Publishers.

Byrne, Hugh. 1996. *El Salvador's Civil War: A Study of Revolution*. Boulder, Colorado: Lynne Rienner Publishers.

Cáceres Prendes, Jorge. 1989. Political Radicalization and Popular Pastoral Practices in El Salvador, 1969–1985. In *The Progressive Church in Latin America*, ed. Scott Mainwaring and Alexander Wilde, 103–148. Notre Dame, IN: University of Notre Dame Press.

Caldeira, Teresa P.R. 1996. Fortified Enclaves: The New Urban Segregation. *Public Culture* 8: 303–328.

———. 2000. *City of Walls: Crime, Segregation, and Citizenship in São Paulo.* Berkeley and London: University of California Press.

Call, Charles T. 2003. Democratisation, War and State-Building: Constructing the Rule of Law in El Salvador. *Journal of Latin American Studies* 35 (4): 827–862.

Cammack, Paul. 1997. *Capitalism and Democracy in the Third World: The Doctrine for Political Development.* London: Leicester University Press.

Cantor, David J. 2014. The New Wave: Forced Displacement Caused by Organized Crime in Central America and Mexico. *Refugee Survey Quarterly* 33 (3): 34–68.

———. 2016. As Deadly as Armed Conflict? Gang Violence and Forced Displacement in the Northern Triangle of Central America. *Agenda Internacional* XXIII (34): 77–97.

Carballido Gómez, Armando. 2008. *Seguridad pública y privada.* El Salvador and Washington, DC: OAS.

Carranza, Elías. 2012. Situación penitenciaria en América Latina y el Caribe: 'Qué hacer'. *Anuario de Derechos Humanos* website. Accessed March 22, 2013. http://www.anuariocdh.uchile.cl/index.php/ADH/article/viewFile/20551/21723.

Casáus Arzú, Marta E. 1992. *Guatemala: Linaje y racismo.* San José, Costa Rica: FLACSO.

Cazorla Sánchez, Antonio. 2010. *Fear and Progress: Ordinary Lives in Franco's Spain, 1939–1975.* Chichester: Wiley-Blackwell.

Ching, Erik. 2014. *Authoritarian El Salvador: Politics and the Origins of the Military Regimes, 1880–1940.* Notre Dame, IN: University of Notre Dame Press.

Clausewitz, Carl von. 1993. *On War.* London: David Campbell.

Coles, Kimberley A. 2004. Election Day: The Construction of Democracy Through Technique. *Cultural Anthropology* 19 (4): 551–580.

Collins, Cath. 2006. Grounding Global Justice: International Networks and Domestic Human Rights Accountability in Chile and El Salvador. *Journal of Latin American Studies* 38: 711–738.

———. 2010. *Post-Transitional Justice: Human Rights Trials in Chile and El Salvador.* University Park, PA: Pennsylvania State University Press.

Comaroff, Jean, and John L. Comaroff, eds. 2006. *Law and Disorder in the Postcolony.* Chicago and London: The University of Chicago Press.

Connerton, Paul. 1989. *How Societies Remember.* Cambridge: Cambridge University Press.

Cruz, José M. 1998. Por qué no votan los salvadoreños. *ECA – Estudios Centroamericanos* 595–596: 449–472.

———. 2001. *'Elecciones para qué' El impacto del ciclo electoral 1999–2000 en la cultura política salvadoreña.* San Salvador: FLACSO.

————. 2003. Violencia y democratización en Centroamérica: El impacto del crimen en la legitimidad de los regímenes de posguerra. *América Latina Hoy* 35: 19–59.

————. 2007a. Factors Associated with Juvenile Gangs in Central America. In *Street Gangs in Central America*, ed. José M. Cruz, 13–65. San Salvador: UCA Editores.

————., ed. 2007b. *Street Gangs in Central America*. San Salvador: UCA Editores.

————. 2012. The Political Workings of the Funes Administration's Gang Truce in El Salvador. *Wilson Center* website. Accessed July 25, 2017. https://www.wilsoncenter.org/sites/default/files/JOSE%20MIGUEL%20CRUZ.pdf.

Cruz, José M., Luis Armando González, Luis Ernesto Romano, and Elvio Sisti. 1998. *La violencia en El Salvador en los años noventa: Magnitud, costos y factores posibilitadores*. San Salvador: IUDOP.

Dahl, Robert A. 1971. *Polyarchy: Participation and Opposition*. New Haven and London: Yale University Press.

————. 2005. What Political Institutions Does Large-Scale Democracy Require? *Political Science Quarterly* 120 (2): 187–197.

Dalton, Roque. 1962. El turno del ofendido. Havana: Casa de las Américas.

Danner, Mark. 1994. *The Massacre at El Mozote: A Parable of the Cold War*. New York: Vintage Books.

Das, Veena. 1995. *Critical Events: An Anthropological Perspective on Contemporary India*. New Delhi: Oxford University Press.

De Zeeuw, Jeroen. 2010. 'Sons of War': Parties and Party Systems in Post-War El Salvador and Cambodia. *Democratization* 17 (6): 1176–1201.

DEES. 1989. Hacia una economía de mercado en El Salvador: Bases para una nueva Estrategia de Desarrollo Económico y Social. *FUSADES* website. Accessed January 5, 2013. http://www.fusades.org/index.php?option=com_jdownloads&Itemid=172&view=finish&cid=616&catid=54.

Derrida, Jacques. 2002. Force of Law. In *Acts of Religion*, ed. Gil Anidjar, 230–298. New York: Routledge.

Diamond, Larry. 1999. *Developing Democracy: Toward Consolidation*. Baltimore and London: The Johns Hopkins University Press.

Díaz, Nidia. 2006. *Nunca Estuve Sola*. San Salvador: UCA Editores.

DIGESTYC. 2007. *Censo de Población y Vivienda 2007*. San Salvador: Dirección General de Estadística y Censos.

Dimas, Leopoldo. 2007. 'El valor económico del agua en El Salvador' *Boletín 257*. San Salvador: FUSADES.

Domínguez Sosa, Julio Alberto. 2007. *Anastasio Aquino: Caudillo de las tribus nonualcas*. San Salvador: Ediciones Venado del Bosque.

Dudley, Steven. 2010. Drug Trafficking Organizations in Central America: Transportistas, Mexican Cartels and Maras. Working Paper Series on US-Mexico Security Collaboration. *Woodrow Wilson International Center for Scholars* website. Accessed August 18, 2017. https://www.wilsoncenter.org/sites/default/

files/Chapter%202-%20Drug%20Trafficking%20Organizations%20in%20
Central%20America%20Transportistas,%20Mexican%20Cartels%20and%20
Maras.pdf.

Duménil, Gérard, and Dominique Lévy. 2004. *Capital Resurgent: Roots of the Neoliberal Revolution*. Cambridge, MA and London: Harvard University Press.

Dunkerley, James. 1982. *The Long War: Dictatorship and Revolution in El Salvador*. London: Junction Books.

Dussel, Enrique. 1996. A Note on Liberation Theology. In *Ideas and Ideologies in Twentieth Century Latin America*, ed. Leslie Bethell, 275–283. Cambridge: Cambridge University Press.

Eastmond, Marita, and Anders H. Stefansson, eds. 2010. Beyond Reconciliation: Social Reconstruction After the Bosnian War. *Focaal – Journal of Global and Historical Anthropology* 57: 3–120.

Escobar, Galindo. 2002. *Tiempos de reconstruir, tiempos de recordar*. San Salvador: Mined.

Farah, Douglas. 2011. Organized Crime in El Salvador: Its Homegrown and Transnational Dimensions. In *Organized Crime in Central America: The Northern Triangle*, Woodrow Wilson Center Reports on the Americas #29, ed. Cynthia J. Arnson and Eric L. Olson, 104–138. Washington, DC: Woodrow Wilson International Center for Scholars.

Farmer, Paul. 2004. An Anthropology of Structural Violence. *Current Anthropology* 45 (3): 305–325.

Ferrándiz, Francisco. 2008. Cries and Whispers: Exhuming and Narrating Defeat in Spain Today. *Journal of Spanish Cultural Studies* 9 (2): 177–192.

———. 2010. The Intimacy of Defeat: Exhumations in Contemporary Spain. In *Unearthing Franco's Legacy: Mass Graves and the Recovery of Historical Memory in Spain*, ed. Carlos Jerez-Farrán and Samuel Amago. Notre Dame, IN: University of Notre Dame Press.

FESPAD, and CEPES. 2004a. *Estado de la seguridad pública y la justicia penal en El Salvador, Julio 2002–Diciembre 2003*. San Salvador: FESPAD.

FESPAD, and CEPES. 2004b. *Informe anual sobre justicia penal juvenil El Salvador 2004*. San Salvador: FESPAD.

FMLN. 2006. Estatuto del partido político FMLN. *Instituto de Iberoamérica, Universidad de Salamanca* website. Accessed May 8, 2009. http://americo. usal.es/oir/opal/Documentos/ElSalvador/FMLN/Estatutos%20FMLN%20 2006.pdf.

Font Fàbregas, Joan. 1998. Las derechas centroamericanas: Del anticomunismo al neoliberalismo. In *América Central, las democracias inciertas*, ed. Ana Sofía Cardenal and Salvador Martí i Puig, 109–150. Madrid: Editorial Tecnos.

FUNDAUNGO. 2014. *Evolución de los homicidios en El Salvador, 2009–2013*. San Salvador: FUNDAUNGO.

FUNDE. 2009. *Política de agua: Ampliación de la cobertura/Gestión descentralizada del agua/Institucionalización del pago de servicios ambientales*. San Salvador: FUNDE.

———. 2013. *Plan de competitividad municipal de Santiago Nonualco 2013–2017*. San Salvador: FUNDE.

Gaborit, Mauricio. 2006. Memoria histórica: Revertir la historia desde las víctimas. *ECA – Revista de Estudios Centroamericanos* 61 (693–694): 663–684.

Gaio, André M. 2006. O Estado delinqüente: Uma nova modalidade de crime? *Cadernos de Ciências Humanas – Especiaria* 9 (15): 137–157.

Galeas, Geovani. 2004. *Mayor Roberto D'Aubuisson: El rostro más allá del mito*. San Salvador: La Prensa Gráfica.

Galeas, Geovani, and Berne Ayala. 2008. *Informe de una matanza: Grandeza y miseria en una guerrilla*. San Salvador: Centroamérica 21.

Gambetta, Diego. 1993. *The Sicilian Mafia: The Business for Private Protection*. Cambridge, MA and London: Harvard University Press.

Gammage, Sarah. 2006. Exporting People and Recruiting Remittances: A Development Strategy for El Salvador? *Latin American Perspectives* 33 (6): 75–101.

García Dueñas, Lauri. 2006. La trascendencia de la campaña del "miedo" en las elecciones de 2004 y la propaganda del "peligro" en México en 2006. *Realidad* 109: 375–387.

Garibay, David. 2005. Del conflicto interno a la polarización electoral: Diez años de elecciones en El Salvador (1994–2004). *Trace – Travaux et Recherches dans les Amériques du Centre* 48: 30–45.

Ghosh, Anjan. 2008. The Role of Rumour in History Writing. *History Compass* 6 (5): 1235–1243.

Girard, René. 1977 [1972]. *Violence and the Sacred*. Baltimore and London: The Johns Hopkins University Press.

———. 1996. Mimesis and Violence. In *The Girard Reader*, ed. James G. Williams, 9–19. New York: The Crossroad Publishing Company.

Gledhill, John. 1999. Official Masks and Shadow Powers: Towards an Anthropology of the Dark Side of the State. *Urban Anthropology* 28 (3–4): 199–251.

———. 2004a. Corruption as the Mirror of the State in Latin America. In *Between Morality and the Law: Corruption, Anthropology and Comparative Society*, ed. Italo Pardo, 155–179. Aldershot and Burlington, VT: Ashgate.

———. 2004b. Neoliberalism. In *A Companion to the Anthropology of Politics*, ed. David Nugent and Joan Vincent, 332–348. Malden, MA and Oxford: Blackwell Publishing.

———. 2005. Citizenship and the Social Geography of Deep Neo-Liberalization. *Anthropologica* 47 (1): 81–100.

———. 2009. Securitization and the Security of Citizens in the Crisis of Neoliberal Capitalism. *The University of Manchester* website. Accessed April 8, 2010.

http://jg.socialsciences.manchester.ac.uk/Conferences/Securitization%20 and%20the%20security%20of%20citizens%20in%20the%20crisis%20of%20neo-liberal%20capitalism.pdf.

Gluckman, Max. 1963. Gossip and Scandal. *Current Anthropology* 4 (3): 307–316.

Godnick, William. 2010. Seguridad privada en América Latina y el Caribe: Marco de análisis en el contexto de la lucha contra el crimen organizado. In *Anuario 2010 de la seguridad regional en América Latina y el Caribe*, ed. Hans Mathieu and Catalina Niño Guarnizo, 456–468. Bogotá, Colombia: Friedrich Ebert Stiftung.

Godoy, Angelina Snodgrass. 2002. When "Justice" Is Criminal: Lynchings in Contemporary Latin America. *Theory and Society* 33 (6): 621–651.

Goldstein, Daniel M. 2004. *The Spectacular City: Violence and Performance in Urban Bolivia*. Durham, NC: Duke University Press.

———. 2010. Toward a Critical Anthropology of Security. *Current Anthropology* 51 (4): 487–517.

Gómez, Ileana. 2001. Rebuilding Community in the Wake of War: Churches and Civil Society in Morazán. In *Christianity, Social Change, and Globalization in the Americas*, ed. Anna L. Peterson, Manuel A. Vásquez, and Philip J. Williams, 123–144. New Brunswick, NJ: Rutgers University Press.

Gómez Hecht, Juan Ricardo. 2013. El crimen organizado en las cárceles: Las extorsiones desde los Centros Penales en El Salvador (2008–2009). *Policía y Seguridad Pública* 3 (1): 131–171.

Good, Anthony. 2004. 'Undoubtedly an Expert'? Anthropologists in British Asylum Courts. *Journal of the Royal Anthropological Institute* 10: 113–133.

———. 2011. Witness Statements and Credibility Assessments in the British Asylum Courts. In *Cultural Expertise and Litigation: Patterns, Conflicts, Narratives*, ed. Livia Holden, 94–122. London and New York: Routledge.

Gordon, Avery F. 1997. *Ghostly Matters: Haunting and the Sociological Imagination*. Minneapolis and London: University of Minnesota Press.

Gordon, Andrew, and Trevor Stack. 2007. Citizenship Beyond the State: Thinking with Early Modern Citizenship in the Contemporary World. *Citizenship Studies* 11 (2): 117–133.

Gould, Jeffrey L., and Aldo A. Lauria-Santiago. 2008. *To Rise in Darkness: Revolution, Repression, and Memory in El Salvador, 1920–1932*. Durham, NC and London: Duke University Press.

Grandin, Greg. 2004. *The Last Colonial Massacre: Latin America in the Cold War*. Chicago and London: The University of Chicago Press.

———. 2005. The Instruction of Great Catastrophe: Truth Commissions, National History, and State Formation in Argentina, Chile, and Guatemala. *The American Historical Review* 110 (1): 46–67.

Green, Linda. 1999. *Fear as a Way of Life: Mayan Widows in Rural Guatemala*. New York: Columbia University Press.

Grugel, Jean, and Pía Riggirozzi. 2012. Post-Neoliberalism in Latin America: Rebuilding and Reclaiming the State After Crisis. *Development and Change* 43 (1): 1–21.

Guilhot, Nicolas. 2005. *The Democracy Makers: Human Rights and the Politics of Global Order*. New York and Chichester: Columbia University Press.

Gupta, Akhil. 1995. Blurred Boundaries: The Discourse of Corruption, the Culture of Politics, and the Imagined State. *American Ethnologist* 22 (2): 375–402.

Gutierrez, Gustavo. 1999. The Task and Content of Liberation Theology. In *The Cambridge Companion to Liberation Theology*, ed. Christopher Rowland, 19–38. Cambridge: Cambridge University Press.

Halbwachs, Maurice. 1992. *On Collective Memory*. Chicago and London: The University of Chicago Press.

Hammill, Matthew. 2007. *Growth, Poverty and Inequality in Central America*. Mexico, DF: United Nations.

Hampson, Fen Osler. 1996. *Nurturing Peace: Why Peace Settlements Succeed or Fail*. Washington, DC: United States Institute of Peace.

Harvey, David. 2005. *A Brief History of Neoliberalism*. Oxford: Oxford University Press.

———. 2006. Neo-Liberalism as Creative Destruction. *Geografiska Annaler* 88B (2): 145–158.

Henríquez Consalvi, Carlos. 2005. *La terquedad del izote: La historia de Radio Venceremos*. San Salvador: Ediciones Museo de la Palabra y la Imagen.

Heyman, Josiah McC, ed. 1999. *States and Illegal Practices*. Oxford and New York: Berg.

Holland, Alisha C. 2013. Right on Crime? Conservative Party Politics and Mano Dura Policies in El Salvador. *Latin American Research Review* 48 (1): 44–67.

Holston, James. 2008. *Insurgent Citizenship: Disjunctions of Democracy and Modernity in Brazil*. Princeton and Oxford: Princeton University Press.

———. 2009. Dangerous Spaces of Citizenship: Gang Talk, Rights Talk and Rule of Law in Brazil. *Planning Theory* 8 (1): 12–31.

Hoppert-Flämig, Susan. 2013. A Salvadoran Turnaround? The FMLN's Response to Citizen Security Needs. In *Latin America's New Security Thinking: Towards Security as a Democratic Value*, ed. Alexandra Abello Colak and Pablo Emilio Angarita Cañas, 71–86. Medellín: CLACSO.

Hume, Mo. 2007a. Mano Dura: El Salvador Responds to Gangs. *Development in Practice* 17 (6): 725–738.

———. 2007b. '(Young) Men with Big Guns': Reflexive Encounters with Violence and Youth in El Salvador. *Bulletin of Latin American Research* 26 (4): 480–496.

———. 2009a. *The Politics of Violence: Gender, Conflict and Community in El Salvador*. Oxford: Wiley-Blackwell.

———. 2009b. Researching the Gendered Silences of Violence in El Salvador. *IDS Bulletin* 40 (3): 78–85.

Humphrey, Caroline. 2002a. Does the Category 'Postsocialist' Still Make Sense? In *Postsocialism: Ideals, Ideologies and Practices in Eurasia*, ed. Chris M. Hann, 12–15. London and New York: Routledge.

———. 2002b. *The Unmaking of Soviet Life: Everyday Economies After Socialism.* Ithaca and London: Cornell University Press.

IDHUCA. 2004. *Observatorio ciudadano de las elecciones presidenciales El Salvador 2004.* San Salvador: IDHUCA.

IML. 2009. *Epidemiología de los homicidios en El Salvador, periodo 2001–2008.* San Salvador: Instituto de Medicina Legal.

Isacson, Adam, Maureen Meyer, and Hannah Smith. 2017. Mexico's Southern Border: Security, Central American Migration, and U.S. Policy. *WOLA* website. Accessed November 8, 2017. https://www.wola.org/wp-content/uploads/2017/06/WOLA-Summary_Mexicos-Southern-Border-2017-1.pdf.

IUDOP. 2009a. *Encuesta de evaluación post-electoral de enero y sobre el proceso electoral de marzo. IUDOP* website. Accessed July 8, 2011. http://www.uca.edu.sv/publica/iudop/Web/2009/informe119.pdf.

———. 2009b. *Victimización y percepción de inseguridad en El Salvador. IUDOP* website. Accessed August 18, 2011. http://www.uca.edu.sv/publica/iudop/Web/2009/informe123.pdf.

———. 2011. *Encuesta de evaluación del año 2010. IUDOP* website. Accessed August 18, 2011. http://www.uca.edu.sv/publica/iudop/Web/2010/informeval126.pdf.

———. 2012. *Encuesta de evaluación del año 2012. IUDOP* website. Accessed June 8, 2017. http://www.uca.edu.sv/publica/iudop/archivos/informe131.pdf.

———. 2014. Encuesta de evaluación del Gobierno de Mauricio Funes, Asamblea Legislativa y Alcaldías y evaluación poselectoral. *IUDOP* website. Accessed June 8, 2017. http://www.uca.edu.sv/iudop/wp-content/uploads/INFORME-136.pdf.

Jeffery, Laura, and Matei Candea. 2006. The Politics of Victimhood. *History and Anthropology* 17 (4): 287–296.

Kalyvas, Stathis N. 2006. *The Logic of Violence in Civil War.* Cambridge: Cambridge University Press.

Karl, Terry L. 1992. El Salvador's Negotiated Revolution. *Foreign Affairs* 71 (2): 147–164.

———. 1995. The Hybrid Regimes of Central America. *Journal of Democracy* 6 (3): 72–86.

Kirk, J. Andrew. 1979. *Liberation Theology: An Evangelical View from the Third World.* London: Marshall, Morgan & Scott.

———. 1980. *Theology Encounters Revolution.* Leicester: Inter-Varsity Press.

Kirschke, Linda. 2000. Informal Repression, Zero-Sum Politics and Late Third Wave Transitions. *The Journal of Modern African Studies* 38 (3): 383–405.

Klein, Naomi. 2008. *The Shock Doctrine: The Rise of Disaster Capitalism*. London: Penguin.

Laplante, Lisa J., and Kimberley S. Theidon. 2007. Truth with Consequences: Justice and Reparations in Post-Truth Commission Peru. *Human Rights Quarterly* 29: 228–250.

Latinobarómetro. 2011. Centroamérica y sus democracias: Latinobarómetro 1995–2010. *Latinobarómetro* website. Accessed August 18, 2011. http://www.latinobarometro.org/latino/LATContenidos.jsp.

Lauria-Santiago, Aldo A. 1999. *An Agrarian Republic: Commercial Agriculture and the Politics of Peasant Communities in El Salvador, 1823–1914*. Pittsburgh, PA: University of Pittsburgh Press.

Lauria-Santiago, Aldo A., and Leigh Binford, eds. 2004. *Landscapes of Struggle: Politics, Society, and Community in El Salvador*. Pittsburgh, PA: University of Pittsburgh Press.

Lazar, Sian. 2004. Personalist Politics, Clientelism and Citizenship: Local Elections in El Alto, Bolivia. *Bulletin of Latin American Research* 23 (2): 228–243.

———. 2008. *El Alto, Rebel City: Self and Citizenship in Andean Bolivia*. Durham and London: Duke University Press.

Leftwich, Adrian. 1994. Governance, the State and the Politics of Development. *Development and Change* 25: 363–386.

Levine, Daniel H., ed. 1986. *Religion and Political Conflict in Latin America*. Chapel Hill, NC: The University of North Carolina Press.

Lievesley, Geraldine. 1999. *Democracy in Latin America: Mobilization, Power and the Search for a New Politics*. Manchester: Manchester University Press.

Lindo-Fuentes, Héctor. 1990. *Weak Foundations: The Economy of El Salvador in the Nineteenth Century*. Berkeley and Los Angeles: University of California Press.

López Bernal, Carlos Gregorio. 2007. Lecturas desde la derecha y la izquierda sobre el levantamiento de 1932: Implicaciones político-culturales. In *Las masas, la matanza y el martinato en El Salvador*, ed. Erik K. Ching, Carlos G. Bernal, and Virginia Tilley, 187–220. San Salvador: UCA Editores.

———. 2008. El levantamiento de los indios nonualcos en 1832: Hacia una nueva interpretación. *Hacer historia en El Salvador* 1 (1): 23–28.

López Pintor, Rafael. 1999. *Votos contra balas*. Barcelona: Editorial Planeta.

López Vigil, José Ignacio. 1991. *Las mil y una historias de Radio Venceremos*. San Salvador: UCA Editores.

Low, Setha. 2003. *Behind the Gates: Life, Security, and the Pursuit of Happiness in Fortress America*. New York and London: Routledge.

Lowenthal, David. 1985. *The Past Is a Foreign Country*. Cambridge: Cambridge University Press.

Mainwaring, Scott, and Alexander Wilde, eds. 1989. *The Progressive Church in Latin America*. Notre Dame, IN: University of Notre Dame Press.

Marshall, Thomas H. 1992 [1950]. Citizenship and Social Class. In *Citizenship and Social Class*, ed. Thomas H. Marshall and Tom Bottomore, 3–51. London and Concord, MA: Pluto Press.

Martí i Puig, Salvador. 2006. Nacimiento y mutación de la izquierda revolucionaria centroamericana. In *La izquierda revolucionaria en Centroamérica: De la lucha armada a la participación electoral*, ed. Salvador Martí i Puig and Carlos Figueroa Ibarra, 15–52. Madrid: Los Libros de la Catarata.

Martín Álvarez, Alberto. 2006. El Frente Farabundo Martí para la Liberación Nacional (FMLN): De movimiento de liberación a partido político. In *La izquierda revolucionaria en Centroamérica: De la lucha armada a la participación electoral*, ed. Salvador Martí i Puig and Carlos Figueroa Ibarra, 91–128. Madrid: Los Libros de la Catarata.

———. 2010. *From Revolutionary War to Democratic Revolution: The Farabundo Martí National Liberation Front (FMLN) in El Salvador*. Berlin: Berghof Conflict Research.

Martín-Baró, Ignacio. 1985. Oscar Romero: Voice of the Downtrodden. In *Voice of the Voiceless: The Four Pastoral Letters and Other Statements*, Oscar A. Romero, 1–21. Maryknoll, NY: Orbis Books.

———. 1991. The Appeal of The Far Right. In *Towards a Society That Serves Its People: The Intellectual Contribution of El Salvador's Murdered Jesuits*, ed. John Hassett and Hugh Lacey, 293–305. Washington, DC: Georgetown University Press.

Martínez D'Aubuisson, Juan José. 2015. *Ver, oír y callar. Un año con la Mara Salvatrucha 13*. Logroño: Pepitas de Calabaza.

McDonald, James H. 1997. A Fading Aztec Sun: The Mexican Opposition and the Politics of Everyday Fear in 1994. *Critique of Anthropology* 17 (3): 263–292.

McLeod, James R. 1999. The Sociodrama of Presidential Politics: Rhetoric, Ritual, and Power in the Era of Teledemocracy. *American Anthropologist* 101 (2): 359–373.

Melara, Michelle. 2003. *Desarrollo de los servicios privados de seguridad en El Salvador*. San José, Costa Rica: Fundación Arias para la Paz y el Progreso Humano.

Meléndez Reyes, Nohel Mario. 2016. La evolución histórica de la influencia del narcotráfico en las instituciones de El Salvador. *Realidad y Reflexión Año* 16 (43): 73–86.

Menkos, Jonathan. 2013. Reformas fiscales en América Latina. El caso de El Salvador (2009–2012). *CEPAL* website. Accessed November 18, 2017. https://www.cepal.org/ofilac/noticias/paginas/3/43813/Doc_16.1_El_Salvador.pdf.

Metzi, Francisco. 1988. *The People's Remedy: The Struggle for Health Care in El Salvador's War of Liberation*. New York: Monthly Review Press.

Misse, Michel, and Joana D. Vargas. 2010. Drug Use and Trafficking in Rio de Janeiro: Some Remarks on Harm Reduction Policies. *Vibrant* 7 (2): 88–108.

Mitchell, Timothy. 1991. The Limits of the State: Beyond Statist Approaches and Their Critics. *The American Political Science Review* 85 (1): 77–96.

Montgomery, Tommie Sue. 1982. *Revolution in El Salvador: Origins and Evolution.* Colorado: Westview Press.

———. 1995. Getting to Peace in El Salvador: The Roles of the United Nations Secretariat and ONUSAL. *Journal of Interamerican Studies and World Affairs* 37 (4): 139–172.

Montoya, Ainhoa. 2007. *Narratives on Civil War Violence in Santiago Nonualco: The War-Peace Continuum.* MPhil dissertation, University of Cambridge.

———. 2015. The Turn of the Offended: Clientelism in the Wake of El Salvador's 2009 Elections. *Social Analysis* 59 (4): 101–118.

———. 2018. La reedición del conflicto: La política electoral en El Salvador de la posguerra. *ECA – Revista de Estudios Centroamericanos* 73 (752): 45–63.

Moodie, Ellen. 2004. "El Capitán Cinchazo": Blood and Meaning in Post-War El Salvador. In *Landscapes of Struggle: Politics, Society, and Community in El Salvador,* ed. Aldo A. Lauria-Santiago and Leigh Binford, 226–244. Pittsburgh, PA: University of Pittsburgh Press.

———. 2006. Microbus Crashes and Coca-Cola Cash: The Value of Death in "Free-Market" El Salvador. *American Ethnologist* 33 (1): 63–80.

———. 2009. Seventeen Years, Seventeen Murders: Biospectacularity and the Production of Post-Cold War Knowledge in El Salvador. *Social Text* 27 (2): 77–103.

———. 2010. *El Salvador in the Aftermath of Peace: Crime, Uncertainty and the Transition to Democracy.* Philadelphia: University of Pennsylvania Press.

———. 2013. Democracy, Disenchantment, and the Future in El Salvador. In *Central America in the New Millennium: Living Transition and Reimagining Democracy,* ed. Jennifer L. Burrel and Ellen Moodie, 96–112. New York: Berghahn Books.

———. 2017. *Las secuelas de la paz: Criminalidad, incertidumbre y transición de la democracia en El Salvador.* Translated by Patricia Morales Tijerno. San Salvador: UCA Editores.

Moser, Caroline, and Ailsa Winton. 2002. Violence in the Central American Region: Towards an Integrated Framework for Violence Reduction. Working Paper 171. *Overseas Development Institute* website. Accessed December 8, 2009. http://www.odi.org.uk/resources/download/1199.pdf.

Murray, Kevin. 1997. *El Salvador: Peace on Trial.* Oxford: Oxfam UK and Ireland.

Navaro-Yashin, Yael. 2002. *Faces of the State: Secularism and Public Life in Turkey.* Princeton and Oxford: Princeton University Press.

Nordstrom, Carolyn. 2004. *Shadows of War: Violence, Power, and International Profiteering in the Twenty-First Century.* Berkeley: University of California Press.

Nugent, David. 2008. Democracy Otherwise: Struggles Over Popular Rule in the Northern Peruvian Andes. In *Democracy: Anthropological Approaches,* ed. Julia Paley, 21–62. Santa Fe: School for Advanced Research Press.

Nuijten, Monique. 2004. Between Fear and Fantasy: Governmentality and the Working of Power in Mexico. *Critique of Anthropology* 24 (2): 209–230.

O'Donnell, Guillermo. 1998. *Polyarchies and the (Un)Rule of Law in Latin America*. Paper presented at the XXI LASA Congress. *LASA* website. Accessed June 18, 2011. http://lasa.international.pitt.edu/LASA98/O%27Donnell.pdf.

O'Donnell, Guillermo, and Philippe C. Schmitter. 1986. *Transitions from Authoritarian Rule: Tentative Conclusions About Uncertain Democracies*. Baltimore and London: The Johns Hopkins University Press.

O'Donnell, Guillermo, Philippe C. Schmitter, and Laurence Whitehead. 1986. *Transitions from Authoritarian Rule: Prospects for Democracy*. Baltimore and London: The Johns Hopkins University Press.

OAS. 2012. Report on Citizen Security in the Americas. *OAS* website. Accessed March 18, 2013. http://www.oas.org/dsp/alertamerica/Report/Alertamerica2012.pdf.

OED. 2016. Violence, n. *Oxford English Dictionary Online* website. Accessed August 8, 2016. http://www.oed.com/view/Entry/223638.

Ong, Aihwa. 2006. *Neoliberalism as Exception: Mutations in Citizenship and Sovereignty*. Durham, NC: Duke University Press.

Orr, Robert C. 2001. Building Peace in El Salvador: From Exception to Rule. In *Peacebuilding as Politics: Cultivating Peace in Fragile Societies*, ed. Elizabeth M. Cousens and Chetan Kumar, 153–181. Boulder, CO: Lynne Reinner.

Paige, Jeffery M. 1993. Coffee and Power in El Salvador. *Latin American Research Review* 28 (3): 7–40.

———. 1997. *Coffee and Power: Revolution and the Rise of Democracy in Central America*. Cambridge, MA and London: Harvard University Press.

Paley, Julia. 2002. Toward an Anthropology of Democracy. *Annual Review of Anthropology* 31: 469–496.

———, ed. 2008a. *Democracy: Anthropological Approaches*. Santa Fe: School for Advanced Research Press.

———. 2008b. Introduction. In *Democracy: Anthropological Approaches*, ed. Julia Paley, 3–20. Santa Fe: School for Advanced Research Press.

Panamá Sandoval, David Ernesto. 2005. *Los guerreros de la libertad*. San Salvador: Versal Books.

Paniagua Serrano, Carlos R. 2002. El bloque empresarial hegemónico salvadoreño. *ECA – Revista de Estudios Centroamericanos* 645–646: 609–693.

Paris, Roland. 2004. *At War's End: Building Peace After Civil Conflict*. Cambridge: University of Cambridge Press.

Pearce, Jenny. 1986. *Promised Land: Peasant Rebellion in Chalatenango, El Salvador*. London: Latin American Bureau.

Peck, Jamie, and Adam Tickell. 2002. Neoliberalizing Space. *Antipode* 34 (3): 380–404.

Peck, Jamie, Nick Theodore, and Neil Brenner. 2009. Postneoliberalism and Its Malcontents. *Antipode* 41 (6): 1236–1258.

Peña, Lorena. 2009. *Retazos de mi vida: Testimonio de una revolucionaria salvadoreña*. México: Editorial Ocean Sur.

Perla, Héctor, Jr., and Héctor Cruz-Feliciano. 2013. The Twenty-First Century Left in El Salvador and Nicaragua. *Latin American Perspectives* 40 (3): 83–106.

Peterson, Anna L. 1997. *Martyrdom and the Politics of Religion: Progressive Catholicism in El Salvador's Civil War*. New York: State University of New York Press.

Peterson, Anna L., Manuel A. Vásquez, and Philip J. Williams. 2001. Introduction: Christianity and Social Change in the Shadow of Globalization. In *Christianity, Social Change, and Globalization in the Americas*, ed. Anna L. Peterson, Manuel A. Vásquez, and Philip J. Williams, 1–22. New Brunswick, NJ: Rutgers University Press.

Pine, Frances, and Sue Bridger. 1998. Introduction: Transitions to Post-Socialism and Cultures of Survival. In *Surviving Post-Socialism: Local Strategies and Regional Responses in Eastern Europe and the Former Soviet Union*, ed. Sue Bridger and Frances Pine, 1–15. London and New York: Routledge.

Planas, Ricardo. 1986. *Liberation Theology: The Political Expression of Religion*. Kansas City, MO: Sheed & Ward.

PNUD. 2003. *Informe sobre Desarrollo Humano El Salvador 2003*. San Salvador: PNUD.

———. 2005a. *Cuánto le cuesta la violencia a El Salvador*. San Salvador: PNUD.

———. 2005b. *Informe sobre Desarrollo Humano El Salvador 2005: Una mirada al nuevo nosotros. El impacto de las migraciones*. San Salvador: PNUD.

———. 2006. *El agua: Una valoración económica de los recursos hídricos en El Salvador. Cuadernos sobre Desarrollo Humano, No. 5*. San Salvador: PNUD.

———. 2009. *Informe sobre Desarrollo Humano para América Central 2009–2010: Abrir espacios para la seguridad ciudadana y el desarrollo humano*. Colombia: PNUD.

———. 2010. *Informe sobre Desarrollo Humano El Salvador 2010. De la pobreza y el consumismo al bienestar de la gente. Propuestas para un nuevo modelo de desarrollo*. San Salvador: PNUD.

———. 2013. *Informe sobre Desarrollo Humano El Salvador 2013. Imaginar un nuevo país. Hacerlo posible*. San Salvador: PNUD.

Popkin, Margaret. 2000. *Peace Without Justice: Obstacles to Building the Rule of Law in El Salvador*. University Park, PA: The Pennsylvania State University Press.

Pratten, David, and Atreyee Sen, eds. 2008. *Global Vigilantes*. New York: Columbia University Press.

Presswood, Timothy H. 1996. *Liberation Theology in Context: Drawing Hope from Reading El Salvador's 'Story'*. PhD thesis, University of Manchester, Manchester.

Przeworski, Adam. 1991. *Democracy and the Market: Political and Economic Reforms in Eastern Europe and Latin America*. Cambridge: Cambridge University Press.

Racine, Karen. 1997. Alberto Masferrer and the Vital Minimum: The Life and Thought of a Salvadoran Journalist, 1868–1932. *The Americas* 54 (2): 209–237.

Ramírez Fuentes, José Alfredo. 2017. Aglutinando a las derechas: Los primeros años del partido ARENA, 1979–1984. In *La Guerra Fría y el anticomunismo en Centroamérica*, ed. Roberto García Ferreira and Arturo Tarracena Arriola, 269–290. Ciudad de Guatemala: FLACSO.

Ramos, Carlos G. 1998. El Salvador: Transición y procesos electorales a fines de los noventa. *Nueva Sociedad* 158: 28–39.

———. 2000. Marginación, exclusión social y violencia. In *Violencia en una sociedad en transición: Ensayos*, ed. Carlos G. Ramos, 7–47. San Salvador: PNUD.

Reno, William. 1995. *Corruption and State Politics in Sierra Leone*. Cambridge: Cambridge University Press.

Réserve, Roody. 2016. El Salvador: Un año político y social convulso. *Revista de Ciencia Política* 36 (1): 177–194.

Robinson, William I. 2003. *Transnational Conflict: Central America, Social Change, and Globalization*. London and New York: Verso.

Rodgers, Dennis. 2006. The State as a Gang: Conceptualizing the Governmentality of Violence in Contemporary Nicaragua. *Critique of Anthropology* 26 (3): 315–330.

Romero, Oscar. 1987. Archbishop Oscar Romero: The Last Sermon (March 1980) [The Church and Human Liberation]. In *The Central American Crisis Reader*, ed. Robert S. Leiken and Barry Rubin, 377–380. New York: Summit Books.

Rowland, Christopher. 1999. *The Cambridge Companion to Liberation Theology*. Cambridge: Cambridge University Press.

Sánchez Cerén, Salvador. 2008. *Con sueños se escribe la vida: Autobiografía de un revolucionario salvadoreño*. México: Editorial Ocean Sur.

Sanford, Victoria. 2003. *Buried Secrets: Truth and Human Rights in Guatemala*. New York: Palgrave Macmillan.

Santacruz Giralt, María L., and Alberto Concha-Eastman. 2001. *Barrio adentro: La solidaridad violenta de las pandillas*. San Salvador: IUDOP.

Sassen, Saskia. 2003. The Repositioning of Citizenship: Emergent Subjects and Spaces for Politics. *CR: The New Centennial Review* 3 (2): 41–66.

Savenije, Wim. 2009. *Maras y barras: Pandillas y violencia juvenil en los barrios marginales de Centroamérica*. San Salvador: FLACSO Programa El Salvador.

Schirmer, Jennifer. 1998. *The Guatemalan Military Project: A Violence Called Democracy*. Philadelphia, PA: University of Pennsylvania Press.

Schneider, Jane C., and Peter T. Schneider. 2003. *Reversible Destiny: Mafia, Antimafia, and the Struggle for Palermo*. Berkeley and London: University of California Press.

Schumpeter, Joseph A. 2010 [1943]. *Capitalism, Socialism and Democracy*. London and New York: Routledge.

Segovia, Alexander. 2002. *Transformación estructural y reforma económica en El Salvador. El funcionamiento económico de los noventa y sus efectos sobre el crecimiento, la pobreza y la distribución del ingreso.* Guatemala: F&G Editores.

———. 2006. Integración real y grupos centroamericanos de poder económico. Implicaciones para la democracia y el desarrollo regional. *ECA – Revista de Estudios Centroamericanos* 61 (691–692): 517–582.

Sharpe, Jim. 1991. History from Below. In *New Perspectives on Historical Writing*, ed. Peter Burke, 24–41. Cambridge: Polity Press.

Sikkink, Kathryn, and Carrie Booth Walling. 2007. The Impact of Human Rights Trials in Latin America. *Journal of Peace Research* 44 (4): 427–445.

Silber, Irina C. 2011. *Everyday Revolutionaries: Gender, Violence, and Disillusionment in Postwar El Salvador.* New Brunswick, NJ and London: Rutgers University Press.

Silva Ávalos, Héctor. 2014. *Infiltrados: Crónicas de la corrupción de la PNC (1992–2013).* San Salvador: UCA Editores.

Smutt, Marcela, and Jenny Lissette E. Miranda. 1998. *El fenómeno de las pandillas de El Salvador.* San Salvador: FLACSO and UNICEF.

Sobrino, Jon. 1984. *The True Church and the Poor.* Maryknoll, NY: Orbis Books.

Sprenkels, Ralph. 2005. *The Price of Peace: The Human Rights Movement in Postwar El Salvador.* Amsterdam: CEDLA.

———. 2011. Roberto d'Aubuisson vs Schafik Handal: Militancy, Memory Work and Human Rights. *European Review of Latin American and Caribbean Studies* 91: 15–30.

———. 2012. La guerra como controversia: Una reflexión sobre las secuelas políticas del informe de la Comisión de la Verdad para El Salvador. *Identidades* 2 (4): 68–89.

———. 2014. *Revolution and Accommodation: Post-Insurgency in El Salvador.* PhD thesis, Utrecht University.

Stack, Trevor. 2003. Citizens of Towns, Citizens of Nations: The Knowing of History in Mexico. *Critique of Anthropology* 23 (2): 193–208.

Stahler-Sholk, Richard. 1994. El Salvador's Negotiated Transition: From Low-Intensity Conflict to Low-Intensity Democracy. *Journal of Interamerican Studies and World Affairs* 36 (4): 1–59.

Stanley, William D. 1996. *The Protection Racket State: Elite Politics, Military Extortion, and Civil War in El Salvador.* Philadelphia: Temple University Press.

Stephen, Lynn. 1995. *Este es mi testimonio. María Teresa Tula, luchadora pro-derechos humanos de El Salvador.* San Salvador: Editorial Sombrero Azul.

Taussig, Michael. 1993. *Mimesis and Alterity: A Particular History of the Senses.* New York and London: Routledge.

———. 2003. *Law in a Lawless Land: Diary of a Limpieza in Colombia.* Chicago and London: The University of Chicago Press.

Theidon, Kimberly S. 2008. Histories of Innocence: Post-War Stories in Peru. Working Paper 2008-0127. *Weatherhead Center for International Affairs, Harvard University* website. Accessed May 28, 2011. http://www.wcfia.harvard.edu/sites/default/files/theidon_innocence.pdf.

Tilly, Charles. 1985. War Making and State Making as Organised Crime. In *Bringing the State Back*, ed. Peter B. Evans, Dietrich Rueschemeyer, and Theda Skocpol, 169–191. Cambridge: Cambridge University Press.

Towers, Marcia, and Silvia Borzutzky. 2004. The Socioeconomic Implications of Dollarization in El Salvador. *Latin American Politics and Society* 46 (3): 29–54.

Tutela, Legal. 2006. *La Situación de los Derechos Humanos en El Salvador: Informe Anual de Tutela Legal del Arzobispado de San Salvador. Año 2005.* San Salvador: Tutela Legal del Arzobispado.

———. 2007. *La Violencia Homicida y Otros Patrones de Grave Afectación a los Derechos Humanos en El Salvador: Informe de las Investigaciones y Lucha Contra la Impunidad Realizadas por Tutela Legal del Arzobispado. Año 2006.* San Salvador: Tutela Legal del Arzobispado.

———. 2008. *La Violencia Homicida y Otros Patrones de Grave Afectación a los Derechos Humanos en El Salvador: Informe de las Investigaciones y Acciones de Lucha Contra la Impunidad Realizadas por Tutela Legal del Arzobispado. Año 2007.* San Salvador: Tutela Legal del Arzobispado.

Ungar, Mark. 2008. The Privatization of Citizen Security in Latin America: From Elite Guards to Neighborhood Vigilantes. *Social Justice* 34 (3/4): 20–37.

UNHCR. 2014. Children on the Run: Unaccompanied Children Leaving Central America and Mexico and the Need for International Protection. *UNHCR* website. Accessed November 1, 2017. http://www.unhcr.org/56fc266f4.html.

———. 2016. UNHCR Eligibility Guidelines for Assessing the International Protection Needs of Asylum-Seekers from El Salvador. *UNHCR* website. Accessed November 18, 2016. http://www.refworld.org/docid/56e706e94.html.

United Nations. 1992a. *Los Acuerdos de Paz.* San Salvador: Editorial Arcoiris.

———. 1992b. Peace Agreements: El Salvador. *United States Institute of Peace* website. Accessed January 8, 2011. https://www.usip.org/publications/2001/04/peace-agreements-el-salvador.

———. 1993. *Informe de la Comisión de la Verdad para El Salvador. De la Locura a la Esperanza: La Guerra de 12 años en El Salvador.* San Salvador: Editorial Arcoiris.

Valdivieso Oriani, Ricardo Orlando. 2008. *Cruzando el imposible: Una saga.* San Salvador: Imprenta Wilbot.

Van der Borgh, Chris, and Wim Savenije. 2014. De-Securitising and Re-Securitising Gang Policies: The Funes Government and Gangs in El Salvador. *Journal of Latin American Studies* 47 (1): 149–176.

Verdery, Katherine. 1999. *The Political Lives of Dead Bodies: Reburial and Postsocialist Change.* New York: Columbia University Press.

Vilas, Carlos M. 1998. La democratización en los escenarios posrevolucionarios de Centroamérica: Antecedentes y perspectivas. In *América Central, las democracias inciertas*, ed. Ana Sofía Cardenal and Salvador Martí i Puig, 281–329. Madrid: Tecnos.

Von Santos, Herard. 2016. El Servicio Territorial como parte del sistema de control social y territorial del Estado salvadoreño durante el conflicto armado (1979–1992). *Revista Policía y Seguridad Pública* 6 (1): 227–294.

Wacquant, Loïc. 2009a. *Prisons of Poverty*. Minneapolis and London: University of Minnesota Press.

———. 2009b. *Punishing the Poor: The Neoliberal Government of Social Insecurity*. Durham and London: Duke University Press.

Wade, Christine J. 2016. *Captured Peace: Elites and Peacebuilding in El Salvador*. Athens, OH: Ohio University Press.

Wagner, Sarah E. 2008. *To Know Where He Lies: DNA Technology and the Search for Srebrenica's Missing*. Berkeley and Los Angeles: University of California Press.

Wantchekon, Leonard. 1999. Strategic Voting in Conditions of Political Instability. *Comparative Political Studies* 32 (7): 810–834.

Ward, Thomas W. 2013. *Gangsters Without Borders: An Ethnography of a Salvadoran Street Gang*. Oxford and New York: Oxford University Press.

Webber, Jeffery R. 2017. *The Last Day of Oppression, and the First Day of the Same*. Chicago, IL: Haymarket Books.

Whitehead, Laurence. 1986. International Aspects of Democratization. In *Transitions from Authoritarian Rule: Comparative Perspectives*, ed. Guillermo O'Donnell, Philippe C. Schmitter, and Laurence Whitehead, 3–46. Baltimore and London: The Johns Hopkins University Press.

Williams, Philip J., and Knut Walter. 1997. *Militarization and Demilitarization in El Salvador's Transition to Democracy*. Pittsburgh, PA: University of Pittsburgh Press.

Wilson, Richard. 2001. *The Politics of Truth and Reconciliation in South Africa: Legitimizing the Post-Apartheid State*. Cambridge: Cambridge University Press.

Wimmer, Andreas, and Nina Glick Schiller. 2002. Methodological Nationalism and Beyond: Nation-State Building, Migration and the Social Sciences. *Global Networks* 2 (4): 301–334.

Wolf, Sonja. 2009. Subverting Democracy: Elite Rule and the Limits to Political Participation in Post-War El Salvador. *Journal of Latin American Studies* 41: 429–465.

———. 2010. Public Security Challenges for El Salvador's First Leftist Government. NACLA Report on the Americas. *NACLA* website. Accessed March 28, 2013. https://nacla.org/node/6650.

———. 2012a. Creating Folk Devils: Street Gang Representations in El Salvador's Print Media. *Journal of Human Security* 8 (2): 36–63.

———. 2012b. El Salvador: Debatiendo el papel de los militares en la seguridad pública. *Distintas Latitudes* website. Accessed March 8, 2013. http://www.distintaslatitudes.net/el-salvador-debatiendo-el-papel-de-los-militares-en-la-seguridad-publica.

———. 2012c. La crisis carcelaria de América Latina: Comayagua, Apodaca y otras tragedias anunciadas. *Distintas Latitudes* website. Accessed March 20, 2013. http://www.distintaslatitudes.net/la-crisis-carcelaria-de-america-latina-comayagua-apodaca-y-otras-tragedias-anunciadas.

———. 2012d. Mara Salvatrucha: The Most Dangerous Street Gang in the Americas. *Latin American Politics and Society* 54 (1): 65–99.

———. 2017. *Mano Dura: The Politics of Gang Control in El Salvador*. Austin, TX: University of Texas Press.

Wood, Elisabeth J. 2000. *Forging Democracy from Below: Insurgent Transitions in South Africa and El Salvador*. New York: Cambridge University Press.

———. 2003. *Insurgent Collective Action and Civil War in El Salvador*. Cambridge: Cambridge University Press.

Zilberg, Elana. 2004. Fools Banished from the Kingdom: Remapping Geographies of Gang Violence Between the Americas (Los Angeles and San Salvador). *American Quarterly* 56 (3): 759–779.

———. 2007. Gangster in Guerrilla Face: A Transnational Mirror of Production Between the USA and El Salvador. *Anthropological Theory* 7 (1): 37–57.

———. 2011. *Space of Detention: The Making of a Transnational Gang Crisis Between Los Angeles and San Salvador*. Durham, NC and London: Duke University Press.

Index[1]

---

[1] Note: Page numbers followed by 'n' refer to notes.

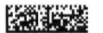